Materiality in Modernist Short Fiction

I0585627

Materiality in Modernist Short Fiction provides a fresh approach to reading material things in modern fiction, accounting for the interplay of the material and the cultural. This volume investigates how Djuna Barnes, Katherine Mansfield, and Jean Rhys use the short story form to evoke the material world as both living and lived, and how the spaces they create for challenging gendered social norms can also be nonanthropocentric spaces for encounters between the human and the nonhuman. Using the unique knowledge created by literary works to spark new conversations between phenomenology, cognitive studies, and new materialisms, complemented with a feminist perspective, this book explores how literature can touch the basic experience of being in, feeling and making sense of a material world that is itself alive and active. From a sensitive reading of how three women used the material world to make their readers see, feel, and question the norms shaping our experience, this volume draws a theory of reading affective materiality that illuminates modernism and the short story form but also reaches beyond them.

Laura Oulanne is a Postdoctoral Researcher at the University of Helsinki. She holds a PhD in Comparative Literature from the University of Helsinki and Justus Liebig University, Giessen. She has published on narrative form, materiality, affectivity, and the mind in Djuna Barnes, Jane Bowles, Jean Rhys, Gertrude Stein, and Virginia Woolf.

Among the Victorians and Modernists
Edited by Dennis Denisoff

This series publishes monographs and essay collections on literature, art, and culture in the context of the diverse esthetic, political, social, technological, and scientific innovations that arose among the Victorians and Modernists. Viable topics include, but are not limited to, artistic and cultural debates and movements; influential figures and communities; and agitations and developments regarding subjects such as animals, commodification, decadence, degeneracy, democracy, desire, ecology, gender, nationalism, the paranormal, performance, public art, sex, socialism, spiritualities, transnationalism, and the urban. Studies that address continuities between the Victorians and Modernists are welcome. Work on recent responses to the periods such as Neo-Victorian novels, graphic novels, and film will also be considered.

Catherine Crowe: Gender, Genre, and Radical Politics
Ruth Heholt

Peril and Protection in British Courtship Novels
A Study in Continuity and Change
Geri Giebel Chavis

The Intelligent Unconscious in Modernist Literature and Science
Thalia Trigoni

Music and Myth in Modern Literature
Josh Torabi

Materiality in Modernist Short Fiction
Lived Things
Laura Oulanne

For more information about this series, please visit: https://www.routledge.com/Among-the-Victorians-and-Modernists/book-series/ASHSER4035

Materiality in Modernist Short Fiction

Lived Things

Laura Oulanne

 Routledge
Taylor & Francis Group

NEW YORK AND LONDON

First published 2021
by Routledge
605 Third Avenue, New York, NY 10158

and by Routledge
2 Park Square, Milton Park, Abingdon, Oxon, OX14 4RN

Routledge is an imprint of the Taylor & Francis Group, an informa business

Library of Congress Cataloging-in-Publication Data
A catalog record has been requested for this book

ISBN: 978-0-367-74189-1 (hbk)
ISBN: 978-0-367-74190-7 (pbk)
ISBN: 978-1-003-15649-9 (ebk)

Typeset in Sabon
by MPS Limited, Dehradun

Contents

List of Figures   vii
Acknowledgments   viii
List of Abbreviations   x

1   Introduction   1
   Reading Things, Senses, and Meanings 3
   Intricate Things on the Page: the Modernist Short Fiction
     of Djuna Barnes, Katherine Mansfield, and Jean
     Rhys 10

2   Powerful Things   23
   Ironical Spirits and Living Mannequins: Jean Rhys,
     Magic, and Surrealism 26
   Dolls, Boots, and Madames: Djuna Barnes Rewrites
     Fetishism 37

3   Lively Things   49
   Djuna Barnes's Piled-up and Entangled Assemblages 50
   Katherine Mansfield Writing a Nonhuman Life 60

4   Touching Things   84
   Nice Things: Materiality and Positive affect in Katherine
     Mansfield's and Jean Rhys's Stories 86
   The Affective Journeys of Djuna Barnes's and Katherine
     Mansfield's Stories 100

5   Making Sense of Things   121
   Masses and Vividnesses: the Aesthetics and Ethics of
     The Left Bank *124*

*At the Indifferent Bay: Nonhuman Perspectives and
   Meaning in Katherine Mansfield's Stories 136*
*Djuna Barnes's Detail and the Materiality of the
   Symbolic 146*

6   **Conclusion: Reading Affective Materiality**   165

   Index   169

Figures

2.1   Man Ray: photograph of André Masson's
      "Mannequin." 1938. Gelatin silver print, 7 3/16 ×
      5 7/16 in. (18.3 × 13.8 cm.)   34
2.2   Atget, Eugène: Avenue des Gobelins. 1925. Gelatin
      silver printing-out-paper print, 8 11/16 × 6 9/16 in.
      (38.8 × 33 cm.)   35

Acknowledgments

In a study about things and materiality, it would be tempting to start with a litany of all the sustaining, nourishing, and enabling things and spaces that I have leant on while completing this book. However, as I suspect that the nonhuman elements do not care much for such lists, and in any case, the human and the nonhuman tend to be intermingled, I shall acknowledge that all these material things come with a community of human beings, to whom I wish to extend my deep gratitude here.

The work that this book is based on was started at the University of Helsinki, as a doctoral dissertation on lived things in Djuna Barnes's and Jean Rhys's short fiction. It benefited immensely from support and advice from my supervisor Heta Pyrhönen, as well as Hannu Riikonen, Klaus Brax, and Janna Kantola. I am very grateful for all the feedback I got especially from Merja Polvinen, Pirjo Lyytikäinen, Sanna Nyqvist, and Riikka Rossi, as well as everyone in the Comparative Literature research seminar, including Hannasofia Hardwick, Niina Into, Matti Kangaskoski, Vappu Kannas, Vesa Kyllönen, Arianna Marcon, Lauri Niskanen, Pekka Raittinen, and Tero Vanhanen. My work was supported by the Doctoral Programme in Philosophy, Arts, and Society, as well as Alfred Kordelin Foundation. I also want to extend my sincere gratitude to Maurizia Boscagli, who was a pre-examiner of my doctoral dissertation, and Suzanne Keen, who acted as a pre-examiner as well as the opponent in my doctoral defense, and whose encouragement and assistance have stayed with me ever since.

I worked on the topics of this book as part of The European PhdNet in Literary and Cultural Studies and as a visiting scholar at Justus Liebig University, Giessen. I would especially like to thank my supervisor Annette Simonis for her help and encouragement during and after my doctoral studies. I am grateful for all the generous comments I received in the seminars from Ingo Berensmeyer, Isabel Capeloa Gil, Angela Locatelli, Ansgar Nünning, and Elizabeth Wåghäll Nivre, among others, and for the administrative support of Nora Berning and Imke Polland. And of course I want to thank the wonderful colleagues and friends I had the joy to meet through this program: Ana do Carmo, Sara Eriksson, Eva Fauner, Ioanna

Kipourou, Stella Lange, Verena Lindemann, Sanja Nivesjö, Sabine Schönfellner, Emanuel Stelzer, Snezana Vuletic, and Anna Weigel.

This book was finished in Baltimore, during my period as a visiting scholar at Johns Hopkins University. I will always think about Jane Bennett and Bill Connolly with gratitude for their hospitality and kindness, and I thank Jane for the opportunity to be part of this community, as well as for all the extremely inspiring comments and conversations around my work and hers.

Throughout working on the material of this book, I have benefited from collaborations with scholars all over the world. I especially want to thank Marco Caracciolo, Marlene Karlsson Marcussen, Sarianna Kankkunen, Ágota Márton, Natalya Bekhta, Lieven Ameel, Caroline Kutsch, and Essi Varis for such encounters, which always left my work a little shifted, for the better.

I am very grateful to Michelle Salyga and Bryony Reece at Routledge for making this book possible and for their invaluable assistance in the final stages of its composition.

Some people deserve to be thanked both as colleagues, who provided ideas, inspiration, and a vibrant community to work with, and as friends. A million thanks to Sanna Tirkkonen, Pii Telakivi, Tuomas Vesterinen, Ferdinand Garoff, Saara Moisio, Elise Nykänen, Anna Tomi, Kaisa Kortekallio, Hanna Mäkelä, and Harri Mäcklin, for making this work both fun and meaningful. During my expatriate life and work, I have also been lucky to share the everyday struggles and joys of writing with virtual networks old and new, which have been vital especially during these distanced times: thank you Forest Workers, Enactivists, and Tinfoil Hats! My deepest gratitude goes to my dear friend Anna Ovaska, with whom I have been incredibly lucky to share the most meaningful moments of my academic journey, and whose comments, insights, and enthusiasm made first my dissertation, and then this book a reality.

I also want to thank my friends and families for being a continuing presence to lean on. Lauri Borén, always. Annika Lonkila, Marika Pulkkinen, and Caity Swanson, who know what it's like. Kyndl Walston, who welcomed me into her home and her community. Enna Mäki, Michael Jacobs, Tessa Siira, Liisa Tervo, Reeta Oksa, Hanna-Katariina Mononen, Eino Korkala, and others in Oulu, Helsinki, New York, Baltimore, and beyond, who I have learned will always be there, wherever I am.

Finally, no acknowledgements are big enough to house my gratitude for David Rodriguez, with whom I am so fortunate to be able to share thoughts, a library, and a life. This book would not be what it is without his generous reading and comments, not to mention his unwavering encouragement, support, and care.

Baltimore, November 2020

List of Abbreviations

BCS   Barnes, Djuna. 1996. *Collected* Stories. Los Angeles: Sun & Moon Press.

LB   Rhys, Jean. 1927/1984. *The Left Bank & Other Stories*. Salem, NH: Ayer Company.

MCS Mansfield, Katherine. 1973. *Collected Stories*. London: Book Club Associates.

1   Introduction

A man, dressed in an evening suit and a top hat, is crawling through the undergrowth around a country house.[1] Two children are sitting on a landing, looking down at preparations being made for a party, and thinking that they are observing plants and furniture moving on their own. A woman from Martinique stands in a shabby London flat, holding her best dress in her arms and crying. These scenes in short stories by Djuna Barnes (1892–1982), Katherine Mansfield (1888–1923), and Jean Rhys (1890–1979) are not necessarily their most important turning points or defining moments. Regardless, they convey a powerful sense of a meaningful experience that might stick with a reader as an image or a feeling, even after forgetting the names of characters or the general plotline of the story.

All these moments feature human characters interacting with things, that is, material, inanimate entities: clothes, natural debris, and furniture. The initial motivation behind this book is the insight that things have an important role to play in such affective moments in the short fiction of Barnes, Mansfield, and Rhys, so much so that to view them merely as background and props for the action of the stories is to overlook their possible importance. I will suggest that modernist fiction in general calls for a reading more aware of the presence of things and materiality, and further, that all narrative fiction might open up for such awareness. Material things help to shape characters' identities, provide indirect symbolic allusions, and convey information about historical time—all this is the familiar stuff of literary studies. However, this list of tasks does not completely account for their importance in fiction in general, or in these particular stories. First, material things can and need to be seen as agents in their own right, changing the course of the narratives, and affecting their characters as well as their readers; second, human beings interact and intermingle with the world of things through their lived bodies, and this fictional sense experience often translates into the most memorable instances of the stories for the reader. Sometimes even the idea that material things surround characters or fictional worlds might be a product of habitual human-centered thinking: it could equally well be said that characters surround or gather around things.

It has become an acknowledged necessity that even scholars in the humanities find new ways of recognizing the nonhuman players in this world. We are reminded of this by urgent ecological crises as well as posthumanist, new materialist, and ecocritical approaches to art and culture. Furthermore, emerging paradigms in cognitive sciences and philosophy of mind suggest that the interaction between our bodies and the material environments we inhabit is essential for the emergence of our experience, emotions, cognition, and even language. Importantly, this vein of thinking has also emerged within narrative studies. Human beings are bound not only to what phenomenologists call the "lived body" but also to the material world in which this subjectively felt, acting body is situated, among other, nonhuman bodies. Therefore, the title of this book suggests that the experience of being-in-the-world as a lived body in lived space is accompanied and partly defined by "lived" and lively things occupying this space and that this aspect of material things becomes highlighted in modernist short fiction.

While living with lived things, we remain cultural beings embedded in and shaped by our social environments, their norms, affordances, and restrictions that treat our lived bodies differently based on gendered categories, for instance. These cultural meanings unavoidably extend to the world of things as well—particularly the world of fictional things. Cultural and symbolic meanings, as noted above, also tend to dominate how these things are read. My book sets out to build a bridge between these ways of regarding the material world in narrative fiction. I propose an anti-anthropocentric approach to reading modern fiction that takes into account the materiality and affectivity of its fictional worlds and refrains from reducing them to human-centered categories of thinking, while asking how we *make sense* of fictional things, as human readers who engage with social and cultural meanings as well as experiences of the material world. More specifically, I suggest that Djuna Barnes, Katherine Mansfield, and Jean Rhys use the short story form to evoke the material world *as* material, that is, felt, lived, and sensed, and thereby to create potential spaces for challenging gendered social norms of, among other things, fetishism, family, life narratives, and empathy. By showing how the texts do this, I hope to demonstrate that this kind of reading not only changes how we can interpret specific modernist short stories but also opens up new pathways to see connections between the material, the formal, and the cultural in any narrative fiction.

The book is structured around the interconnected themes of power, agency, affectivity, and meaning. It asks how short stories by Barnes, Mansfield, and Rhys create a fictional "feel" for materialities and how this is conductive to the creation of experiential knowledge, meanings, and values. What kind of power and agency do material things have in the stories and how do they differ from human agents? What is their role in affective encounters and relations in the fictional worlds of the texts and how do they contribute to the potential evocation of readerly emotions? How do material things participate in the production of meaning and the processes of sense-making and interpretation involved in reading them? To provide the attention that the things in the fictional works seem to demand for themselves, I combine phenomenological and cognitive approaches to literature and reading with anti-anthropocentric thinking of the ways human culture and experience are entangled in different nonhuman materialities. These approaches are in line with the feminist understanding that informs this book, recognizing that the experience of materialities is always already a gendered phenomenon and that attention to such experience in fiction also reveals how the writers depict what it is like to be in the material world as a gendered subject, and most importantly, create spaces to reimagine both human-centered and gendered norms and categories. In the remainder of this introductory chapter, I will provide a brief overview of the starting points for my approach to lived things as material-cultural, affective agents in fiction and equally briefly chart and contextualize the texts and authors that will be read in the latter chapters.

Reading Things, Senses, and Meanings

"Things" might be the topic of the broadest study imaginable. This book is about something more specific than anything oreverything, as hinted at by the inclusion of "lived" as well as the word "materiality" in its title. The things in the scenes referred to at the beginning of this introduction all share certain qualities: they are material items usually conceived of as inanimate that can be used or interacted with by human beings. Their materiality is something readers can be assumed to be familiar with as a simple result of living in the world. We carry clothes about our person, and they can be so close that we may not always experience them as things, but rather as extensions of our lived bodies; we attach certain meanings and categories to natural and artificial things; we have learned to hold books and look at works of art in a specific way. The things evoked in the passages also have more or less recognizable borders, according to which readers engaging with them imaginatively will separate them from the environment, as they have learned to do with the things encountered in everyday life.

My choice to write about "things," not, for instance, "objects," reflects the aim to highlight both the very materiality and the potential agency of things, instead of their position in a binary logic of subjects and objects. The material things in the texts may be the grammatical objects of sentences, which also imply a grammatical subject. However, these linguistic relations do not completely define what the things do in the fictional world and what they do to the readers of fiction. Things exist and occupy space with their materiality, regardless of who is looking at them or doing something to them and regardless of the meanings that encircle them. In addition, not all materialities that are present in Barnes's, Mansfield's, and Rhys's fiction fit so easily under the definition of a "thing," which implies more or less clear borders separating them from the environment. These include the undergrowth through which the man in a top hat is crawling, or other environments that we are invited to imagine, however vaguely, to make up the spaces of the rented room or the children's house preparing for the party. Furthermore, the human bodies of the fictional characters are among the material existents in the stories, and as the analyses will show, the borderline between a human and a thing-body is not always clear-cut. Yet, for us humans, the world tends to be given as things, even if their boundaries sometimes overlap.

Things and materialities have taken center stage in some approaches to literature and culture that have emerged within the past 20 years. The initiator of "thing theory," Bill Brown, suggests that researchers should pay attention to the "thingness" of things and our relations to them as they appear in art and literature (Brown 2003, 2004, 2016). One point of departure for Brown's thinking is in Martin Heidegger's writings about the thing (*das Ding*) as a part of the lifeworld, whose being always remains unattainable for humans when they approach their world by way of objects and tools, yet is somehow graspable in moments when an object refuses to work (like a broken tool or a dirty window) (Heidegger 1984, 73; Heidegger 1971; Brown 2016, 28). Ultimately, Heidegger's thinking about "the thing" is much more complex and develops throughout his writings, while the tension between things as unattainable and obstinate or resisting, and the human attempt to understand something of their ways of being, is crucial for Brown's use of the concept. Brown also draws on "actor-network theory," Bruno Latour's seminal attempt to recognize the diversity of agencies (or "actants," a term borrowed from structuralist literary studies; see Greimas 1987) taking part in societies, including nonhuman ones (Latour 2005). Thing theory has led literary scholars to discuss, for instance, the narrative and political impact of 18th century stories narrated by things such as clothes, coins, and coaches (Lamb 2004) and the recalcitrance and obsolescence of things in American fiction (Tischleder 2014).

This book shares thing theory's sense of distinction between objects and things and the general project of paying attention to the world of things, yet I find that this is not a sufficient approach for studying the way humans and things are intermingled in modernist short stories. The notion of "thing" is useful because it reflects the human tendency to see the world as divided into individual things, as opposed to the crude physical level of general materiality. Yet I wish to focus on is materiality in general and look at things with the added denominator of "lived." Instead of only looking for the essence of things or thingness *an sich* as disclosed by the fictional work, the aim is to grasp more flexible, fluid, and potentially elusive relationships, in which the common denominator of materiality encompasses people, things, and environments alike. Instead of emphasizing the otherness of things, or their withdrawal into themselves (cf. also Harman 2002, 4), the literary texts at the heart of this research point toward a need to study how a human being-in-the-world is entangled in and defined by the presence of materiality and things. Material things may resist our actions when they cease to work for us as tools and objects, or as symbolic entities to guide the interpretation of a story. However, things also take active part in human lives, from the ways our bodies interact with and are permeated by chemical matter of the "environment" to the way appliances, means of transportation, and furniture direct our movements, postures, and relationships.

New materialisms, which are perhaps no longer so "new" but still developing, have emerged as part of a "material turn" in the humanities, a reaction to directions in postmodern thought resting on the primacy of language and social forms in constructing meanings, identities, and even bodies. This is also where the "new" materialisms differ from "old" materialism, whose origins can be attributed to Marx and which implies a focus on modes of production and economic systems, keeping the human at its center and the subject/object divide more or less intact, while new materialists work to challenge it. Such perspective, however, does not mean disregarding language and culture. Rather, the attention to nonhuman materialities, and the material makings of the human, can complement the study of culture, language, and human experience, and vice versa; new materialist thinking builds on the insight that "our material lives are always culturally mediated, but they are not only cultural" (Coole and Frost 2010, 27). The "material" of new materialism is not a lifeless lump of unattainable reality on which meanings are inscribed by linguistic and cultural practices: matter and bodies, too, produce meanings and actions (Coole and Frost 2010, 6; Bennett 2010, 1–4).

Fictional things need not be personified or magically animated to appear as lively and active, and to have an effect on us. Their seemingly mute and unattainable being is already permeated by life and agency of its own kind, which we often simply fail to notice or lack the words to describe. To find such words, this study looks at cultural, gendered meanings and materialities as intertwined. One central new materialist interest in the study is the view of agency as distributed between human and material things, in the fictional world as well as in reading and interpretation. In this vein, I follow the work of Jane Bennett (2010) and Karen Barad (2007), both of whom argue, through slightly different routes, that agency emerges when things and bodies come together: humans and nonhuman entities become agents only by way of each other. There is no bicycle rider without a bicycle and a ground on which it can be ridden; these are features we add, in our interpretive imagination, to even fictional evocations of the event of bicycling. Equally, there is no reader without the nonhuman agencies of the text and the book, other environmental contributors of the event of reading, or the influence of its cultural and linguistic context.

Another linked concern is the affective potential of things and materialities that is also linked to things' potential for agency. In the Spinozist-Deleuzean account of affectivity that overlaps with new materialisms, affectivity is conceptualized as something occurring *in-between* bodies—human and nonhuman (Seigworth and Gregg 2010, 2). In the fictional worlds of the texts discussed, emotions, feelings, and atmospheres are all created in encounters involving not only human characters but also nonhuman agents. For the narrative evocation of a feeling, a mood, or an ambience, it is not insignificant that the stories referred to at the beginning of this introduction show their characters holding a dress or crawling through a thicket. In concrete terms, the affectivity that can be ascribed to materialities relies on the senses, perhaps especially the sense of touch. Physically *feeling* the surfaces of things is used to evoke other forms of feeling and emotion that are not entirely attributable to the senses. The focus on things as sensed materials shows how they necessarily take on other meanings besides their potential symbolic associations and commodity values: the power of things to affect us is one facet of their potential agency (see Boscagli 2014, 4).

Such thinking beyond the human is helpful for analyses of things and materialities in this study because of the way it challenges the divide into human subjects and the "objective," inanimate material world. Much thinking rests on this divide, but it remains inadequate when trying to grasp the relations between human and nonhuman bodies and environments in modernist short stories. What I call anti-anthropocentric approaches, encompassing new materialisms as well as posthumanist thinking, are better suited than thing theory, for instance, to address the entangled, distributed, and networked being of humans, things, and cultural phenomena in the modernist texts I am about to read. Importantly, they are also significant for the feminist concerns of this book: pushing the human off the pedestal means also shifting ontologies of life, including tacit narratives about gendered structures; the otherness brought into focus instead includes what Rosi Braidotti calls "others of Man" (Braidotti 2017), those left outside the humanist norms that also tend to be patriarchal norms. Anti-anthropocentric reading asks us to profoundly shift our ontological categories of understanding the world and take on different, nonhuman perspectives. This kind of acknowledgement of otherness can be a politically significant and reparative process, as Braidotti, for instance, suggests (Braidotti 2011, 333).

All the following discussions deal with fictional encounters between people and things, human and nonhuman agents and bodies, in which sensed materiality always plays a role, and in which both the human and the thing act and are acted upon, affect and become affected. The event of reading, too, is here conceived of as such an encounter. Importantly, approaches to things as active and affective need to be combined with an analysis of literary devices, to show *how* it is that materialities are evoked in fiction, and how they participate in the experience of reading. Here, to analyze encounters that occur between reading minds and bodies, the fictional bodies of characters and things, and the body of the book, I turn to phenomenological and cognitive literary studies' insights into reading as an embodied activity.

What is especially important for my reading is the recognition of the reader of fiction as an embodied being. This is backed by a range of approaches in phenomenology, cognitive sciences, and philosophy of mind, grouped under the label "4E": they involve the theses of the mind as essentially embodied (Johnson 1987) and of the mind and the world as enacted, that is, co-created in the interaction between an organism and its surroundings (Varela, Thompson, and Rosch 1991), as well as influential explorations of the phenomenological implications of such mind (Gallagher and Zahavi 2012), and of the cognitive functions as extended into external instruments (Clark and Chalmers 1998). These approaches have some of their roots in 20th century phenomenology, especially in Maurice Merleau-Ponty's introduction of the lived body at the center of phenomenological investigation and the challenge his thinking poses to the Cartesian dualism of the subjective and the objective: "The world is not an object such that I have in my possession the law of its making [...] Truth does not 'inhabit' only the 'inner man,' 'inner man,' or more accurately, there is no inner man, man is in the world, and only in the world does he know himself" (Merleau-Ponty 2002, xii). As we can see, this is not a completely distinct theoretical sphere from anti-anthropocentric approaches: phenomenologists and cognitive scientists also note the "distributed" nature of thinking and other cognitive activities, even though they focus on human experience of being in the world (Colombetti 2016; Malafouris 2008). Furthermore, following the seminal "ecological psychology" of James J. Gibson, the environment offers affordances that invite certain kinds of action on the part of the organism living in it, and is therefore meaningful to it in a certain way, while the organism itself is also constituted by this environment and the actions it affords: according to Gibson, "[...] we were created by the world we live in" (1979, 130).

When focusing attention on lived experience in reading modernist fiction, we need to ask how fictional works manage to convey a sense of the livedness of a body, world, or a thing. According to the "natural narratology" initiated by Monika Fludernik (1996), all narratives imply a human experiencer, if not in their explicit content, then in the way they are received in the process of reading. The experientiality of fiction can be defined by the ability of a work to convey experiences in a dynamic where readers' experiences of engagement with the real world meet evocations of fictional experience in a fictional world (Fludernik 1996, 30, 35; Caracciolo 2014a). Stories, when they function experientially, are capable of giving their reader not only a sense of "what happened" but also "what it was like." The features of a narrative that contribute to experientiality include focalization, namely the use an internal or an external perspective or point of view of a character or a narrator (Genette 1972), yet they can involve description without an identifiable character focalizer and other devices such as rhythm and temporality (Caracciolo 2014b, 73–82). The "material" things we encounter in literary fiction are made of words, but these words can evoke the sense of various materialities in the fictional world. Fictional, nonhuman things, even when they display signs of independent agency and unruliness, always come to readers by way of an evocation of human experience, at least in the form of the reader's real-world memories of interacting with things, in light of which the fictional content can be felt and understood. Readers and readings are different, of course, which is why no single answer to this question can be given; yet it is not a case of complete subjectivism either. The focus here is on the text and the positions it invites its reader to take. I do not gather empirical data of real readers' actual experiences when reading the texts, except for my first-person experience as a reader. However, the analyses are supported by theoretical discussions of reading that are based on empirical evidence in cognitive psychology and linguistics, as well as narratological models of what occurs in the act of reading.

As suggested by cognitive research, readers respond to stories in embodied enactments by way of past experience that reading fiction calls forth. Our being-in-the-world is defined by a continuing process of sense-making, in which the world appears in a certain way, involving certain affordances, which are significant to us (Gibson 1979), and therefore always also evaluated, that is, affectively colored (Colombetti 2013). This kind of interaction and evaluation is necessarily also involved in our engagement with fictional texts and worlds, which always render a phenomenological quality of "what-it-is-like" that according to David Herman, for instance, is the most important defining quality of narrative (Herman 2009, 2). I follow Marco Caracciolo's (2014b, 55–71) suggestion that narratives tap into a reader's "experiential background," and readers, as embodied beings, engage with narratives by re-enacting these past experiences, involving basic sensorimotor perception as well as more complex results of sociocultural interaction. We recall what it is like to wear clothes or to feel the surface of marble, leather, or wood with our hands, and the text's suggestion of a character's encounter with material things invites us to re-enact these memories imaginatively, while enacting the new experience produced by our engagement with the story. We know, on a preconscious level, what it is like to catch a ball or grasp a door handle, and the presentation of such things in a story invites a cognitive enactment of the sensorimotor actions invited by the thing, even if our reading body remains still (ibid.; Gibbs 2017; Caracciolo 2016, 143). Instead of our minds becoming disembodied and transported into storyworlds, our embodiment enables our being immersed in and affected by stories. According to Karin Kukkonen (2014), the focus on the embodiment of the reader adds to the "implied reader" model by accounting for the ways making sense of fiction relies on how the body functions in the material world. This is the often ignored side of reading that I wish to take into account when looking at Barnes's, Mansfield's, and Rhys's material things and their effects within and beyond the storyworld, while also recognizing the gendered aspects of embodiment.

Importantly, this does not mean that my way of reading must remain on the level of basic embodied responses. There is an inescapable interaction and feedback loop between bodily experience and cultural practices, where both affect one another and can help make sense of a work of fiction, as well as the world (Kukkonen and Caracciolo 2014, 267; Caracciolo 2014b, 49–50). In my readings, the cultural meanings attached to things are seen as colored by the affective, bodily responses to things as material, experienced bodies-in-space, yet these experiences, too, are shaped partly by our embeddedness in sociocultural practices. Furthermore, as Merja Polvinen (2017, 143) points out, embodied and enactive engagement with fiction does not mean that our narrative experiences would be exactly like "natural" ones, or that we would unwittingly lose ourselves in the story. We may simultaneously go through paths of embodied affectivity, led by the textual design of a story, and be detached enough to understand this to be an experience of engaging with a work of fiction, and therefore able to use also other faculties of interpretation. These interactions and tensions between levels of experience and interpretation (the embodied and the cultural, the immersed and the detached) need to be taken into account when studying the ways fictional things contribute to experiential understandings of stories.

Conceptualized thus, the experientiality of stories is not a property of the text per se, nor is it completely dependent on the subjective experiences of an individual reader, but rather a sense of livedness that emerges between these two, requiring the material, formal constraints and affordances provided by the text (its language and the material form in which it is read, as well as the references to material entities in the fictional world), and the actual experience of the reader (see also Levine 2015, Cave 2016). Therefore, anti-anthropocentric views on agency, affectivity, and embodied approaches into the experientiality of fiction overlap, as they foreground the way life and meaning are not "interior" properties, but something constantly created between bodies in the world. While my method of reading affective materialities arises from a combination of these approaches, it also arises from the textual material of the stories by Djuna Barnes, Katherine Mansfield, and Jean Rhys. By this I mean that I want to take into account the unique ways literary texts have of creating knowledge, in what Louise Rosenblatt has called a "transactional" relationship with the reader (Rosenblatt 1995), which means that no two readings are alike. With the attention to the intermingledness of the material and the cultural, the embodied, and the social, I hope to address both the affective and the critical potential of these texts, and the intriguing, enchanted materialities that seem to haunt modernist literature in general, but also show how this kind of approach could benefit the ways we read and interpret fiction beyond modernism.

Intricate Things on the Page: the Modernist Short Fiction of Djuna Barnes, Katherine Mansfield, and Jean Rhys

Modernist fiction and short fiction in particular is an intriguing arena for studying material things and human engagement with them. In terms of cultural history, the first decades of the 20th century especially in the Western world mark the intensification of mass production of goods of all kinds, meaning an increase in both the number and variety of things owned, used, and desired by a growing number of people. The 1920s, the decade during which the majority of texts studied here were written and published, was a period of relative economic stability after the First World War and before the Great Depression, which meant an increase in the number of people identifiable as *consumers*. Consumerism brought with it a new kind of relation to things, highlighting many of them as purchasable and perishable commodities *en masse*, and created a difference between things of this kind and more singular art objects or things on display in a museum, for instance, which Walter Benjamin described as being in possession of an "aura" of authenticity (Benjamin 1936). Consumership was also a new mode of subjectivity available especially to women (see Wilson 2007, 77–79). Furthermore, Paris, the place of composition and recurring milieu of a great number of these stories was, especially during the 1920s, a dynamic locus considering the world of consumer goods and fashion. It was also, of course, a hub for international, especially Anglophone modernism.

This contemporary context of consumer culture influences especially Rhys's short stories of cosmopolitan women navigating urban spaces. Mansfield's stories set in New Zealand as well as in Europe often feature more timeless, domestic things and natural environments, while Barnes's work has its own particular way of presenting things as residues of an ambiguous past era, or as otherwise singular, "auratic" items like museum objects or theatre props. The modern tension between commodities and authentic objects can be seen as relevant to all three authors, but their employment of things, especially the *lived things* of interest in this book, is not reducible to the question of the commodity. Rather, things as material parts of the experienced, sensed, lived world are what all the writers are engaged in portraying.

In the context of the modern history of ideas, things as both commodities and experienced materialities were present especially in the directions of thought inspired by Karl Marx's materialist investigations of the production and consumption of commodities. A central Marxist worry is the commodification of human individuals for economic profit, and the "reification" or "thingification" of social relationships. Another vein of thinking arising from Freudian psychoanalysis introduced new ways of discussing material things as symbolic and affective objects of desire, especially as *fetishes;* this is a central notion to both Marx's critical theory and Freud's psychoanalysis. In general, there appears to be a "heightened sensitivity to sensation" as central to modern experience, brought about by developments in science and technology, in addition to a new understanding of the senses and new ways to interact with them (Armstrong 2005, 90). This phenomenon is parallel to the advent of commodity and consumer culture and the lived experience of rapid change and plentiful material stuff (Boscagli 2014, 270). It shows in modernist artists' interest in subjectivity and experience, and the fragmentation of them, as well as the material world as part of sense experience.

Writers and artists linked to modernist movements were involved in and inspired by the advent of things in consumer culture and the philosophical and psychoanalytical discussions of materiality and things. The surrealists displayed "found objects" and produced literary mystifications of banal detail for instance in Louis Aragon's *Le Paysan de Paris* (1926) and André Breton's *Nadja* (1928). Italian futurist and British vorticist pictorial art displayed a different fascination with human–thing relations powered by advances in technology. A special interest in things and materialities can already be seen in Gertrude Stein's work, especially her "cubist" prose poems in *Tender Buttons* (1914); further, in the American context in the work of such objectivist poets as Ezra Pound and William Carlos Williams, as well as in Wallace Stevens, there is a focus on things "as they are" (Stevens 1937). This is a phenomenological endeavor more than a Kantian attempt to grasp the thing before the perceiving subject: to see things not as necessarily symbolically loaded, but as they appear to individuals in experience. In prose fiction, formal experiments in the depiction of consciousness and experience also lead to special attention to the material world and its particular things, sometimes amounting to their animation or personification: a lemon-scented soap traveling in Leopold Bloom's pocket keeps reminding him of its very material existence throughout the day as depicted in James Joyce's *Ulysses* (1922), and finally, fantastically, begins to speak (Joyce 1990; Majumdar 2006); in a section of Virginia Woolf's *To the Lighthouse* (1927), the passage of time is represented, as it were, from the point of view of the furnishings of an empty summer house (Woolf 2004; Nishimura 2015). As David Herman among others has pointed out, beside the alleged inward turn of modernism, there is a turn toward the lived world to investigate the material reality as it is experienced, and as it participates in the construction of experience (Herman 2011). This is an important starting point for my book, and I wish to expand on it by investigating the role of material things and environments in the creation of modernist experiential worlds, as well as by recognizing the gendered aspects of those worlds.

Listing evocative materialities in modernist fiction leads to a question: why have I chosen to focus specifically on Djuna Barnes, Katherine Mansfield, and Jean Rhys? These singular authors and their texts are what gave rise to the questions that initially motivated the study. The short fiction by these three authors highlights the presence of material things in multiple ways, some of which are shared, while others are unique to the particular text. Barnes's interiors are filled with curious *bric-à-brac*, which at times seems to overrun the human characters, and the characters are conversely presented as thing-like; her narration favors a multisensory experience of the material world, bringing forth its things and textures as not only seen but also touched, heard, smelled, and tasted. Mansfield's stories experiment with point of view and narrative modes to render worlds-as-experienced. These worlds often feature apparently distorted perceptions of material things that seem to come to life, while the human beings of her stories, too, can appear as curiously thing-like. Rhys's humans also sometimes resemble things in how they are perceived by others in the fictional world, and some of her characters seem more capable of sympathizing with a thing than with a person. They dream of new, transformative dresses or just shoes with no holes in them, and sometimes experience fleeting moments of happiness and belonging that are mediated by such things. Degrees of dehumanization of humans and animation of things, a focus on multisensory experience, and the use of material things and environments in conveying affective tones and shifts that lend weight to critical points of view are characteristic of other modernist writers' texts as well, but by pointing to the unique qualities of Mansfield's, Barnes's, and Rhys's writing, importantly introducing several less-researched stories from Barnes and Rhys, I wish to bring them to the fore as significant modernist works and thereby do my part in shifting the modernist canon to include marginalized texts by women. This tightly framed corpus also enables a detailed discussion of textual features in the stories, but this discussion should prove enlightening in relation to the study of modernism, and materiality in literary fiction more broadly.

The cosmopolitan lives that all three writers led have some geographical overlaps. Djuna Barnes was born in upstate New York, and she had an early career as a student and writer in New York City, where she returned in the 1940s, after living in Europe, to stay until her death. Katherine Mansfield lived in her native New Zealand until 1903, when she moved to London to study and stayed in Europe until her early death of tuberculosis. Jean Rhys, on the other hand, had her origins in the British West Indies. After studying theater and working as an actress in Great Britain she lived and wrote in several European cities, to return to

Southwestern England for the final decades of her life. All writers lived and worked in Paris at some point during the 1910s through 1930s, which was the heyday of the modernist expatriate community. However, they were closer to the margins than the center of this male-dominated community, and do not seem to have interacted significantly with one another.

Barnes's varied oeuvre consists of early pieces of journalism and stories she wrote when living in New York, already a well-known figure in the bohemian center of Greenwich Village. She also wrote poetry, plays, and two novels: *Ryder* (1928), and her best known work, *Nightwood* (1936). Her work was mostly composed and published during the first three decades of the 20th century. The majority of her short stories were first published in magazines; later, some of them were compiled and revised into *A Book* (1923) and *A Night among the Horses* (1929) before the posthumous publication of her *Collected Stories* (1996). During her relatively short period of active writing while in Europe, Mansfield published stories and poems in magazines as well as the collections of short stories: *In a German Pension* (1911), *Bliss and Other Stories* (1920), and *The Garden Party* (1922). After her death, her husband and colleague John Middleton Murry took on publishing a significant number of her so far unpublished stories, including the collections *The Dove's Nest and Other Stories* (1923) and *Something Childish and Other Stories* (1924). Rhys's first publication was a collection of short fiction *The Left Bank and Other Stories* in 1927—which in fact does not contain a story titled "The Left Bank." In the following years between the two wars, she wrote four novels, to be followed by a silence of almost 30 years before her late breakthrough into wider popular and critical acclaim with the novel *Wide Sargasso Sea* (1966). During her later years, two collections of short fiction were also published: *Tigers Are Better-Looking* in 1968 and *Sleep It off Lady* in 1976, which remained her final work except for the posthumously published, unfinished autobiography, *Smile Please* (1979).

Barnes and Rhys are nowadays critically recognized and somewhat widely researched writers, although their work remains surprisingly little known outside the academia. Katherine Mansfield, on the other hand, is frequently listed as one of the most central Anglophone modernists (Kimber 2015, viii; Robinson 1994, 2; Mitchell 2011, 1). Her oeuvre consists mostly of short fiction, and her stories are among the most often cited and anthologized examples of the modernist short story (New 1999, xi). On the other hand, in the research on Rhys as well as Barnes, the short stories have generally received considerably less attention than their longer prose works. This book aims to bring a significant number of so far nearly ignored modernist short fiction to critical attention, while also offering new perspectives on some of the most canonized, studied, and read stories.

I use the term "short fiction" to do justice to the plurality of texts included among the shorter prose written by the three authors. While they mostly wrote what can conveniently be called stories, some of Barnes's works and the texts in Rhys's *Left Bank* are very short, impressionistic sketches or vignettes. This vein of modernist stories have been characterized as "spatial" or "anecdotal," focusing on the descriptive rendering of a situation rather than a temporal progression (Harrington 2007, 5). As a form, Ellen Burton Harrington calls short fiction an "outlaw" especially fit for experimentation and points out its importance for women writers (1), while Clare Hanson (1985, 89) sees feminist potential for challenging existing structures in the nonlinearity of many modernist short stories. Furthermore, the focus of modernist short fiction tends to be on a singular *experience,* a "blazing moment," in Mansfield's words,[2] and a visual effect, at the expense of a well-constructed plot (Hanson 1985, 5–6, 55; Harrington 2007, 4). This is a fitting description especially of Rhys's and Mansfield's fiction, while Barnes alternates between celebrating and parodying the tradition of well-plotted stories.

Modernist short stories or fictions themselves are often described as thing-like: as intricate items of artifice made by the skilled hands of the writer. Lorna Sage, in her introduction to Mansfield's *The Garden Party and Other Stories*, calls them "intensely crafted and evocative objects-on-the-page" (Sage 1997, vii). The short form may well invite special attention on the part of the reader to all material detail that is presented in it. Specific things may have importance as *leitmotifs,* devices used to maintain the cohesion of the text and assist in a critical moment which may lead to an "epiphany," a moment of revelation identified as typical of short stories (Harrington 2007, 6). Barnes's, Mansfield's, or Rhys's short fiction does not by any means always provide such moments, and as we are about to see, they often even go expressly against them, yet the highlighted presence of the material world is a characteristic they share.

Indeed, modernist short fiction is often characterized by ambiguity and openness instead of cohesion and a single moment of enlightenment of meaning, which are featured as the ideal characteristics of short fiction as famously suggested by Edgar Allan Poe's "single effect" doctrine (Poe 1984, 571; Head 1992, 2; Harrington 2007, 5). What remains typical for the stories I read here is the focus on specific moments conveying not only "intense and significant experience" (Hanson 1985, 55) but also an aesthetic vision and a descriptive attitude that draws attention to the material world. The following chapters will show the multiple ways in which things are used to convey such moments of experience and to construct aesthetic effect within multiple kinds of stories and vignettes. Thereby, I hope to provide insight on the variety of the means of expression in modernist short fiction, still a relatively under-researched topic. In previous research on things and materialities in modernist fiction, the thematic fields of commodity fetishism and psychoanalysis have generally been dominant. More recently, more research has emerged that takes an interest in the agency of things as well as their felt materiality in fiction, including modernist texts (Bernaerts et al. 2014; Majumdar 2006; Nishimura 2015).[3]

Several researchers have explored Barnes's interest in commodities and fashion (Oliver 2014), as well as the relationship of her work to the politics of space (Wilson 2011), and to nonhuman animals (Rohman 2009, 2007). Julie Taylor's (2012) work on affectivity in Barnes's work is in many ways in line with my approach to it, although it does not specifically focus on things, materialities or experientiality. As regards research on Mansfield's fiction, materiality has remained in the margins, while several researchers have focused on the embodied and affective characteristics of her stories (Besnault-Levita 2011; Hindricks 2018; Moran 1996), and the role of nonhuman animals (Harvey 2011); others have looked into materiality on a biographical level, as the often stringent economic conditions that may have led writers like Mansfield to focus on short stories in the first place (Bowler 2015). Studies on Jean Rhys have explored the ways her characters negotiate their identities and basic survival in the urban consumer jungle and the world of fashion (Joannou 2012, Oliver 2016), politics of space (Parsons 2000), and the culture of exhibitions (Britzolakis 2007). Some recent articles have also taken a materialist, ecocritical, or even posthumanist perspective on specific questions related especially to Rhys's use of postcolonial settings and motifs (Emery 2015; Savory 2015; Johnson 2015).

Importantly, these studies remain oriented more toward cultural questions than narrative structures, means and devices, or a theoretical interest in the readerly position, not to mention foregrounding things or matter as agents beyond their cultural or symbolic functions. Here I wish to build on their insights, while also devoting some more attention to the narrative, and specifically experiential means by which cultural dynamics, values, and effects are produced and conveyed to readers, and in particular how the material world plays a part in this creation of feeling and meaning. Thus, I will discuss how the cultural work that the stories of Barnes, Mansfield, and Rhys undoubtedly achieve as textual agents in the world is made into a felt, "lived" reader experience and how this affects the culturally sensitive interpretations. With the help of new materialist, anti-anthropocentric ways of thinking and embodied cognitive approaches to reading, the rest of this book takes to the task of reading the short stories of Barnes, Mansfield, and Rhys, closely but with attention to the surfaces of things and the spaces of encounter between them, to offer a new angle on questions of cultural and critical significance, too. It moves from discussions of animation and agency of things through affectivity to interpretation, aesthetics, and sense-making, while acknowledging the way these thematics overlap: the agency of fictional things is affective, and making sense of them relies on both their agential and affective qualities.

Chapter 2 differs from the subsequent ones in that it embraces the most commonly explored intersections of modernism and materiality, namely magical animism and fetishism. However, it also produces a new reading of them and thereby introduces my approach to reading modernist short fiction and materiality. I explore Jean Rhys's uses of material things and devices of focalization to complicate the tacit meanings attached to the animation of things in magical thinking and practices, fantastic and gothic motifs, and the surrealist employment of mannequin dolls. In the second section of the chapter, I study how Djuna Barnes turns Freudian fetishism around by descriptions that ask us to pay attention to the materiality and independent power of fetish objects and the women employing them. Through the encounter and contrast between a feminist, anti-anthropocentric reading of narrative devices such as description and focalization and a more traditional interpretation of magic and fetishism, I hope to provide a first example of how this way of reading can bring to light so far undervalued meanings of familiar modernist topoi.

Chapter 3 introduces more new materialist and posthumanist vocabulary to my analyses, to trace the ways the writers use the short story form to blur the boundaries between the human and the nonhuman. I explore the ways Djuna Barnes's stories create assemblages of affective bodies and embed them within their environments, to show how Barnes's descriptions of human and nonhuman bodies create alternative spaces where our habitual ways of seeing subjects and objects do not apply, and how this, too, expands our tacit knowledge of gendered bodies. In a similar vein, I read Katherine Mansfield's stories and in particular their experimentation with the modernist topos of the party and their use of children as focalizers, as expansions of the notion of "a life" beyond the normative boundaries of human life narratives, which I suggest serve both anti-anthropocentric and feminist ethical aims, thereby exemplifying how these aims in fact often intersect.

Chapter 4 focuses on the affectivity of fictional material things. I examine the way Mansfield and Rhys connect things with positive affect to again rewrite normative ideas attached to feelings such as being at home, being happy, and empathizing. This is a new perspective into stories whose readers often highlight gendered thematics of alienation, objectification, and victimization; I hope to provide a further reading of how these formulations of feminist concerns acquire affirmative tones that in fact enhance their critical potential when attention is paid to the materialities with the help of which they are rendered in the stories. Second, I look at the ways Barnes's and Mansfield's stories are structured around affective shifts and sequences that in turn are anchored in material things, as well as the way material things are "incorporated" in these affective structures. Hereby, I hope to find ways to show how paying attention to the affectivity of matter and its rendering in the narrative form can shift ideas of the extent and limits of sharing emotion, while further exploring how the boundaries between things and people are challenged in the modernist writers' works.

The fifth chapter asks how the sense experience of the texts and their evocations of materiality translates into making sense of the world at a basic, affective level as well as a critical, interpretive one. It is divided into three parts, one dedicated for each writer. The first subchapter looks closely at the form of a collection of short stories, namely Jean Rhys's *The Left Bank*, and discusses how its evocations of things and people as *masses*, another very modernist topos, invites the reader to engage with a blend of aesthetical, ethical, and affective sense-making. The second part discusses the beginnings of two of Mansfield's stories as an example of the way her work uses perception and perspective to challenge ontological categories, and how this, too, is conductive to ethical and critical interpretations of the stories as wholes. Finally, I read Djuna Barnes's short story "Cassation" with a focus on its abundant material detail and the way it evokes a variety of both cultural contexts and symbolic meanings, while acknowledging that these meanings, too, rest on the materiality of the things encountered by the reader.

My readings acknowledge that our understanding of texts is informed by our embodied being in the world, but they also highlight that this being is influenced both by gendered normativity and by the fact that we are in constant interaction and even permeated by "other," nonhuman agencies. Furthermore, they expose and explore how three modernist authors, writing 100 years ago from when I am writing this book, worked with and on the material world to create experiential understanding not only of our affective relations with it but also of complex, gendered sociocultural phenomena. In introducing a set of modernist stories by women as intricately crafted objects, or rather things, and as a form that does crucial work in creating understanding about the encounters between experience, materiality, and meaning, I hope this book will open up a potential space for an illuminating reading of fiction to address methodological and philosophical questions, while also proposing a new approach to reading materialities in fiction that is informed by modernist short stories but applicable beyond them.

Notes

1 This book is based on work that I did in my doctoral dissertation. *Lived Things: Materialities of Agency, Affect, and Meaning in the Short Fiction of Djuna Barnes and Jean Rhys* (Oulanne 2018).
2 From a review of Vita Sackville-West's novel *Heritage*. Quoted by Kimber and Smith 2014, 550.
3 Some, like Aaron Jaffe, have even celebrated a "material turn" in modernist studies, yet the works he cites in it are almost exclusively to do with specific topic of urbanity and the city space. See Jaffe 2009.

Works cited

Armstrong, Tim. 2005. *Modernism: A Cultural History*. Cambridge: Polity.

Barad, Karen. 2007. *Meeting the Universe Halfway: Quantum Physics and the Entanglement of Matter and Meaning*. Durham: Duke University Press. DOI: 10.1215/9780822388128.

Benjamin, Walter. 1936. "The Work of Art in the Age of Mechanical Reproduction." Accessed October3, 2017. https://www.marxists.org/reference/subject/philosophy/works/ge/benjamin.htm.

Bennett, Jane. 2010. *Vibrant Matter: A Political Ecology of Things*. Durham, NC: Duke University Press. DOI: 10.1515/9780822391623.

Bernaerts, Lars et al. 2014. "The Storied Lives of Non-Human Narrators." *Narrative* 22 (1): 68–93. DOI: 10.1353/nar.2014.0002.

Besnault-Levita, Anne. 2011. "'—Ah, what is it?—that I heard': Voice and Affect in Katherine Mansfield's Short Fictions." In *Katherine Mansfield and Literary Modernism*, edited by Janet Wilson, Gerri Kimber and Susan Reid, 89–100. Edinburgh: Edinburgh University Press.

Boscagli, Maurizia. 2014. *Stuff Theory: Everyday Objects, Radical Materialism*. New York: Bloomsbury.

Bowler, Rebecca. 2015. "Potboilers or 'Glimpses' of Reality? The Cultural and the Material in the *Modernist* Short Story." In *British Women Short Story Writers: The New Woman to Now*, edited by Emma Young and James Bailey, 50–65. Edinburgh: Edinburgh University Press.

Braidotti, Rosi. 2017. "Four Theses on Posthuman Feminism." In *Anthropocene Feminism*, edited by Richard Grusin, 21–48. Minneapolis, MN: University of Minnesota Press.

Braidotti, Rosi. 2011. *Nomadic Theory: The Portable Rosi Braidotti*. New York: Columbia University Press.

Britzolakis, Christina. 2007. "This Way to the Exhibition: Genealogies of Urban Spectacle in Jean Rhys's Interwar Fiction."*Textual Practice* 21 (3): 457–482.

Brown, Bill. 2016. *Other Things*. Chicago: University of Chicago Press. DOI: 10.7208/chicago/9780226283166.001.0001.

Brown, Bill. 2004. "Thing Theory." In *Things*, edited by Bill Brown, 1–22. Chicago: University of Chicago Press.

Brown, Bill. 2003. *A Sense of Things: The Object Matter of American Literature*. Chicago: The University of Chicago Press. DOI: 10.7208/chicago/9780226076317.001.0001.

Caracciolo, Marco. 2016. *Strange Narrators in Contemporary Fiction: Explorations in Readers' Engagement with Characters*. Lincoln, NE: University of Nebraska Press. DOI: 10.2307/j.ctt1gr7dkd.

Caracciolo, Marco. 2014a. "Experientiality." In *The Living Handbook of Narratology*, edited by Peter Hühn et al. Hamburg: Hamburg University. Accessed May 25, 2017. http://www.lhn.uni-hamburg.de/article/experientiality

Caracciolo, Marco. 2014b. *The Experientiality of Narrative: An Enactivist Approach*. Berlin: DeGruyter. DOI: 0.1515/9783110365658.

Cave, Terence. 2016. *Thinking with Literature: Towards a Cognitive Criticism*. Oxford: Oxford University Press. DOI: 10.1093/acprof:oso/9780198749417.001.0001.

Clark, Andy and David Chalmers. 1998. "The Extended Mind." *Analysis* 58 (1): 7–19. DOI: 10.1093/analys/58.1.7.

Colombetti, Giovanna. 2016. "Affective Incorporation." In *Phenomenology for the Twenty-First Century*, edited by. J. Aaron Simmons and J. Edward Hackett, 231–248. London: Palgrave Macmillan. DOI: 10.1057/978-1-137-55039-2.

Colombetti, Giovanna. 2013. *The Feeling Body. Affective Science Meets the Enactive Mind*. Cambridge, MA: MIT Press. DOI: 10.7551/mitpress/9780262019958.001.0001.

Coole, Diana and Samantha Frost. 2010. "Introducing the New Materialisms." In *New Materialisms: Ontology, Agency, and Politics*, edited by Diana Coole and Samantha Frost, 1–43. Durham: Duke University Press. DOI: 10.1215/9780822392996.

Emery, Mary Lou. 2015. "On the Veranda: Jean Rhys's Material Modernism." In *Jean Rhys: Twenty-First-Century Approaches*, edited by Erica L. Johnson and Patricia Moran, 59–81. Edinburgh: Edinburgh University Press. DOI: 10.3366/edinburgh/9781474402194.003.0004.

Fludernik, Monika. 1996. *Towards a 'Natural' Narratology*. London: Routledge. DOI: 10.1515/jlse.1996.25.2.97.

Gallagher, Shaun and Dan Zahavi. 2008/2012. *The Phenomenological Mind*. London: Routledge. 10.4324/9780203126752.

Genette, Gérard. 1972. "Discours du récit." In *Figures III*, 67–282. Paris: Seuil.

Gibbs, Raymond W. 2017. "Embodied Dynamics in Literary Experience." In *Cognitive Literary Science: Dialogues Between Literature and Cognition*, edited by Michael Burke and Emily T. Troscianko, 219–237. Oxford: Oxford University Press. DOI: 10.1093/acprof:oso/9780190496869.003.0012.

Gibson, James J. 1979. "The Theory of Affordances." In *Perceiving, Acting, and Knowing: Toward an Ecological Psychology*, edited by Robert Shaw and John Bransdord, 127–143. Hillsdale, NJ: Lawrence Erlbaum Associates.

Greimas, Algirdas J. 1987. *On Meaning: Selected Writings in Semiotic Theory*. Translated by Paul J. Perron and Frank H. Collins. Minneapolis: University of Minnesota Press.

Hanson, Clare. 1985. *Short Stories and Short Fictions, 1880–1980*. Basingstoke: Palgrave MacMillan.

Harman, Graham. 2002. *Tool Being: Heidegger and the Metaphysics of Objects*. Chicago: Open Court.

Harrington, Ellen Burton. 2007. "Introduction." In *Scribbling Women and the Short Story Form: Approaches by American and British Women Writers*, edited by Ellen Burton Harrington, 1–14. New York: Peter Lang Publishing,

Harvey, Melinda. 2011. "Katherine Mansfield's Menagerie." In *Katherine Mansfield and Literary Modernism*, edited by Janet Wilson, Gerri Kimber and Susan Reid, 202–210. Edinburgh: Edinburgh University Press.

Head, Dominic. 1992. *The Modernist Short Story: A Study in Theory and Practice*. Cambridge: Cambridge University Press. DOI: 10.1017/CBO9780511735356.

Heidegger, Martin. 1950/1971. "The Thing." In *Poetry, Language, Thought*. Translated by Albert Hofstadter, 163–186. New York: Harper & Row.

Heidegger, Martin. 1927/1984. *Sein und Zeit.* Tübingen: Max Niemeyer Verlag.

Herman, David. 2011. "1880–1945: Re-Minding Modernism." In *The Emergence of Mind. Consciousness in Narrative Discourse in English*, edited by David Herman, 243–272. Lincoln, NE: University of Nebraska Press. DOI: 10.2307/j.ctt1df4fwq.12.

Herman, David. 2009. *Basic Elements of Narrative.* Chichester: Wiley-Blackwell. DOI: 10.1002/9781444305920.

Hindricks, Cheryl. 2018. "The Fly and the Displaced Self: Affective Potential in the Epiphanic Moments of Mansfield, Woolf and Lawrence." In *Katherine Mansfield and Virginia Woolf*, edited by Christine Froula, Gerri Kimber, and Todd Martin, 102—116. Edinburgh: Edinburgh University Press. DOI: 10.3366/edinburgh/9781474439657.003.0008.

Jaffe, Aaron. 2009. "Modern Literature: General." *The Year's Work in English Studies* 88, 866.

Joannou, Maroula. 2012. "'All right, I'll do anything for good clothes': Jean Rhys and Fashion." *Women: A Cultural Review* 23 (4): 463–489. DOI: 10.1080/09574042.2012.739849.

Johnson, Erica L. 2015. "'Upholstered Ghosts': Jean Rhys's Posthuman Imaginary." In *Jean Rhys: Twenty-First-Century Approaches*, edited by Erica L. Johnson and Patricia Moran, 209–227. Edinburgh: Edinburgh University Press. DOI: 10.3366/edinburgh/9781474402194.003.0011.

Johnson, Mark. 1987. *The Body in the Mind: The Bodily Basis of Meaning, Imagination, and Reason.* Chicago: University of Chicago Press. DOI: 10.3366/edinburgh/9781474402194.003.0011.

Joyce, James. 1922/1990. *Ulysses.* New York: Vintage Books.

Kimber, Gerri. 2015. *Katherine Mansfield and the Art of the Short Story.* Basingstoke: Palgrave Macmillan. DOI: 10.1057/9781137483881.

Kimber, Gerri and Angela Smith, eds. 2014. *The Poetry and Critical Writings of Katherine Mansfield.* Edinburgh: Edinburgh University Press.

Kukkonen, Karin. 2014. "Presence and Prediction: The Embodied Reader's Cascades of Cognition." *Style* 48 (3): 367–384.

Kukkonen, Karin and Marco Caracciolo. 2014. "Introduction. What is the 'Second Generation'?" *Style* 48 (3): 261–274.

Lamb, Jonathan. 2004. "Modern Metamorphoses and Disgraceful Tales." In *Things*, edited by Bill Brown, 193–226. Chicago: University of Chicago Press.

Latour, Bruno. 2005. *Reassembling the Social: An Introduction to Actor-Network-Theory.* Oxford: Oxford University Press.

Levine, Caroline. 2015. *Forms: Whole, Rhythm, Hierarchy, Network.* Princeton, NJ: Princeton University Press. 10.23943/princeton/9780691160627.001.0001.

Majumdar, Saikat. 2006. "A Pebblehard Soap: Objecthood, Banality and Refusal in Ulysses." *James Joyce Quarterly* 42 (¼): 219–238.

Malafouris, Lambros. 2008. "At the Potter's Wheel: An Argument for Material Agency." In *Material Agency: Toward a Non-Anthropocentric Approach*, edited by Carl Knappett and Lambros Malafouris, 19–36. Dordrecht: Springer. DOI: 10.1007/978-0-387-74711-8_2.

Merleau-Ponty, Maurice. 1945/2002. *The Phenomenology of Perception.* Translated by Colin Smith. London: Routledge. DOI: 10.4324/9780203994610.

Mitchell, J. Lawrence. 2011. "Introduction." In *Katherine Mansfield and Literary Modernism*, edited by Janet Wilson, Gerri Kimber, and Susan Reid, 1–10. London: Continuum.

Moran, Patricia. 1996. *Word of Mouth: Body Language in Katherine Mansfield and Virginia Woolf*. Charlottesville: University Press of Virginia.

Nishimura, Satoshi. 2015. "Personification and Narrative. The Blurred Boundaries of the Inanimate in Hardy and Woolf." *Narrative* 23 (1): 27–39. DOI: 10.1353/nar.2015.0003.

Oliver, Sophie. 2016. "Fashion in Jean Rhys/Jean Rhys in Fashion." *Modernist Cultures* 11 (3), 312–330. DOI: 10.3366/mod.2016.0143.

Oliver, Sophie. 2014. "Djuna Barnes in a Material World: Fashion and Transatlantic Modernity in the 1910's." *Literature Compass* 11 (6): 347–366. DOI: 10.1111/lic3.12141.

Oulanne, Laura. 2018. "Lived Things: Materialities of Agency, Affect, and Meaning in the Short Fiction of Djuna Barnes and Jean Rhys." Dissertation, University of Helsinki.

Parsons, Deborah. 2000. *Streetwalking the Metropolis: Women, The City, and Modernity*. Oxford: Oxford University Press.

Poe, Edgar Allan. 1842/1984. "Review of Twice-Told Tales." In *Essays and Reviews*, 569–577. New York: Library of America.

Polvinen, Merja. 2017. "Cognitive Science and the Double Vision of Fiction." In *Cognitive Literary Science: Dialogues Between Literature and Cognition*, edited by Michael Burke and Emily T. Troscianko, 136–150. Oxford: Oxford University Press. DOI: 10.1093/acprof:oso/9780190496869.003.0008.

Robinson, Roger. 1994. "Introduction." In *Katherine Mansfield: In from the Margin*, edited by Roger Robinson, 1–8. Baton Rouge: *Louisiana* State University Press.

Rohman, Carrie. 2009. *Stalking the Subject: Modernism and the Animal*. New York: Columbia University Press. DOI: 10.7312/rohm14506.

Rohman, Carrie. 2007. "Revising the Human: Silence, Being, and the Question of the Animal in *Nightwood*." *American Literature* 1: 57–84. DOI: 10.1215/00029831-2006-071.

Rosenblatt, Louise. 1938/1995. *Literature as Exploration*. New York: MLA.

Sage, Lorna. 1997. "Introduction." In Katherine Mansfield: *The Garden Party and Other Stories*, vii–xxi. London: Penguin Books.

Savory, Elaine. 2015. "Jean Rhys's Environmental Language: Oppositions, Dialogues and Silences." In *Jean Rhys: Twenty- First-Century Approaches*, edited by Erica L. Johnson and Patricia Moran, 85–106. Edinburgh: Edinburgh University Press. DOI: 10.3366/edinburgh/9781474402194.003.0005.

Seigworth, Gregory and Melissa, Gregg. 2010. "An Inventory of Shimmers." In *The Affect Theory Reader*, edited by Gregg, Melissa and Seigworth, Gregory, 1–25. Durham: Duke University Press.

Stevens, Wallace. 1937. "The Man with the Blue Guitar." *Poetry: A Magazine of Verse*, May 1937, 50 (2): 64–69.

Taylor, Julie. 2012. *Djuna Barnes and Affective Modernism*. Edinburgh: Edinburgh University Press.

Tischleder, Babette Bärbel. 2014. *The Literary Life of Things: Case Studies in American Fiction*. Frankfurt: Campus Verlag.

Varela, Francisco J., Evan Thompson, and Eleanor Rosch. 1991. *The Embodied Mind: Cognitive Science and Human Experience*. Cambridge, MA: MIT Press. DOI: 10.7551/mitpress/6730.001.0001.

Wilson, Elizabeth. 2007. *Adorned in Dreams: Fashion and Modernity*. London: I.B. Tauris. DOI: 10.5040/9780755699506.

Wilson, Mary. 2011. "No Place Like Home: *Nightwood's* Unhoused Fictions." *Studies in the Novel* 43 (4): 428–448. DOI: 10.1353/sdn.2011.0053.

Woolf, Virginia. 1927/2004. *To the Lighthouse*. London: Vintage.

2   Powerful Things

Things are more powerful than people.
Jean Rhys: "The Sound of the River"[1]

Magical thinking and practices, animistic beliefs, and fetishism haunt the literature and culture of the early 20th century, which is otherwise often labeled as a time of rationality. In many ways, this means also a heightened experience of the world of things as animated and powerful. Occult magic and forms of paganism intrigued writers and artists, as did the practice and doctrine of spiritualism, which involved experiences of the spirits of the dead manifesting as shifts in the material world, such as the appearance of messages on an Ouija board or "table-turning," in which a table seems to move on its own. The popularity of magic and animism has been attributed to both the revival (and invention) of spiritual and occult practices and the metaphorical and ironical adaptation of magical thinking in art. The animated world of things fascinated surrealist and symbolist writers, who found magical meaning in uncanny fusions of the animate and the inanimate, and unexpected places and encounters with people and things. (During 2002; Landy and Saler 2009.)

On the other hand, things came alive for modernity as fetishes, a notion that is housed by different contexts from paganism and primitivist art to economical philosophy to sexology and finally psychoanalysis. Intriguingly, the concept is central for both Karl Marx and Sigmund Freud, the quintessential thinkers of the budding century. In the Marxist idea of commodity fetishism, the mysterious production of value for an object arises not only from its material qualities and the work put into it but also from the magical commodity character of the thing. In an oft-cited passage, Marx evokes the context of spiritualism: he uses an image of a table that as a commodity becomes a "transcendent" thing full of "metaphysical subtleties" that "evolves out of its wooden brain grotesque ideas, far more wonderful than 'table-turning' ever was" (Marx and Engels 2001, 75). For Marx, things as fetishes are agents as far as they form relations among themselves and come to define human social relations; they also exercise a persuasive power in the way they lure humans to consume. In Freud's account, on the other hand, the fetish is a product of castration anxiety, "a substitute for the woman's (the mother's) penis that the little boy once believed in," a sign of the simultaneous disavowal and acceptance of this (imaginary) lack (Freud 1974, 352). The eroticized fetish object becomes animated in a process of metonymy comparable to magical thinking.

Consequently, animism and fetishism are probably the most obvious ways of approaching the lively world of nonhuman things that come to mind in the modernist context, and certainly the ones most often explored in research. By beginning this book with them, I want to take into account the undeniable presence of these cultural phenomena in modernist literature. However, I also want to offer a new way of reading them that builds on but also adds to earlier studies, such as work on the cultural meanings of modern magical thinking and feminist analyses of fetishism, thereby beginning to conceive of a new way of reading materiality in modernity. What tends to be missing in accounts of literary animism and fetishism is, first, a recognition of the "lived" materiality of the animated or fetishized objects in the fictional world and second, an analysis of the actual textual and narrative means of conveying these relations: a study of how animated and fetish objects are experienced *in their materiality* in the fictional world and imaginatively by the embodied reader, and how this, perhaps, gives them their unique power.

The Marxist and Freudian accounts of fetishism share a vision of the unique power of material things. However, they trace the origins of this power confidently back to human power relations and repressed desires. In the anti-anthropocentric vein that this book is following, we could see the power of things from a different point of view, as something intrinsic to them, in constant interaction with the human but not reducible to human origins. From Bruno Latour's actor network theory to Timothy Morton's hyperobjects to Deleuzean affect theory, different branches of criticism have highlighted the necessity to view material things as agents in their own right. I am borrowing the concept of "thing-power" from Jane Bennett, who draws on Spinoza's idea of the "conatus," namely the "striving" inherent to every human and nonhuman body, and Thoreau's "wildness." Bennett defines thing-power as "the curious ability of inanimate things to animate, to act, to produce effects dramatic and subtle" (Bennett 2010, 6). We feel the effect of nonhuman things in our human being: the material scaffoldings of our everyday actions, randomly encountered assemblages of things that become highlighted by the power of their unique combination, the nonhuman materials that form part of our bodies—and, crucially for this study, even fictional things and assemblages on the pages of books.

Thing-power exemplifies something "other" that resides outside of our anthropocentric worldview, yet also affects it by its presence, even if covertly, and even in works of fiction. Addressing the possibilities of a posthumanist reading, Karoliina Lummaa (2019) borrows the metaphor of "haunting" from Stefan Herbrechter (2013, 86, 90) to express the agential presence of nonhuman otherness such as the sonoric qualities of birdsong, the logic of a computer, or animal movements in literary texts. Similarly, I suggest that it is not just repressed desires, gendered dynamics, or structures of commodification that haunt modernist stories about fetishized and magical things. These can serve as a point of entry to a more broadly understood thing-power, whose ghostly presence can in fact be felt in a variety of texts that may not even be overtly presenting or satirizing animistic or fetishistic thinking. On the other hand, I suggest that while it is an expression of "otherness," this nonhuman presence is in fact also central to our everyday experiences of being human, which lends it part of its power.

In the following readings of magic and fetishism in Jean Rhys's and Djuna Barnes's short fiction, as in the analyses throughout this book, I will follow the post-anthropocentric call to pay attention to this force in things and their haunting presence without being too quick to attribute either the power or the presence to human cultural and emotional structures. Rather, I suggest that the acceptance of non-human, material haunting may change the understanding of the presence of those structures in fiction. My method of reading, which I develop throughout this book, traces the means the texts use to evoke the lived, felt "weight" of the material things presented, and connects this experiential meaning-making with the critical, cultural work that their rethinking of magic and fetishism does in the world. This chapter will begin to show how this way of reading affective materialities and cultural contexts supports and is supported by a feminist interest in rethinking cultural categories, which here means reshuffling the dynamics of fetishism and the intermingled dyad of animism/objectification. A careful reading of the devices with which the texts construct meaning out of materiality can serve both feminist and anti-anthropocentric interests.

Jean Rhys crafts characters who are drawn to commodity fetishes and animistic thinking and writes stories in which dresses have the power to change lives and speak, magical appearances of things evoke gothic topoi, and mannequins blend the categories of human and thing. A typical reading of her stories would highlight how, being charmed by the material world, the female characters and their bodies risk being objectified themselves (cf. Karagouni 2010; Britzolakis 2007; Zimring 2000). However, contrary to this tradition in Rhys studies, my reading suggests that the texts in fact complicate the idea that women are made passive or victimized by their reliance on and parallelization with things:

rather, via choices of focalization and narratorial presence, their agency seems to be enhanced by and extended into the things.

Djuna Barnes, on the other hand, plays with the psychoanalytical notion of the fetish but repeatedly turns the Oedipal schema that it rests on around in service of other forms of extended, material agency. A psychoanalytically oriented reading might identify a fetish with lack or absence that is filled by the fetish object, while Barnes's descriptive stories evoke a sense of abundance beyond the economy of lack. While the contemporary phenomena that Rhys and Barnes engage with constitute the starting point of this chapter, its focus is on their narrative techniques of evoking materiality, and their implications for the ontological and ethical questions of agency. A reading of lived things takes crucial steps toward grasping how Rhys and Barnes experiment with the form of the short story to rewrite contemporary economical, psychological, and sexological discourses and how the weight of their critical endeavors rests on their texts' capacity to tap into our shared, bodily understanding of the lively world of things.

Ironical Spirits and Living Mannequins: Jean Rhys, Magic, and Surrealism

A few of Jean Rhys's short stories have overt references to the magical practice of spiritualism, which was popular in the early 20th century and intrigued writers such as H.D., James Joyce and Virginia Woolf (Armstrong 2005, 123).[2] In "At the Villa d'Or" (1927), a story published in Rhys's first collection *The Left Bank*, philanthropists Mrs. and Mr. Valentine host promising artists in their home on the French Riviera. Mrs. Valentine bores Sara, one of the guests and the focalizer of the story, with her talk of how spiritualism has changed her life. She also transfers her belief in the presence spirits to new, technological gadgets, whereby her quoted speech gains an animistic tone:

> "Sometimes", said Mrs. Valentine to Sara, "I play the Victrola[3] for hours all by myself when Bobbie is in the billiard-room, and I think how strange it is that lovely music—and voices of people who are dead—like Caruso—coming out of a black box. Their voices—Themselves in fact—And I just get frightened to death—terrified. I shut it up and run up the stairs and ring like mad for Marie."
>
> (Rhys 1927 = LB, 163–164)

In Mrs. Valentine's mind, modern audio technology becomes infested with magic and the uncanny. The reader, however, is expected to keep her guard up, not share the bias toward the magical, but rather maintain an ironical distance. This is achieved by the focalization of Sara, for whom the stay at the house appears as a transitory, curious episode, the length of an impressionistic short story that does not dwell on the charting of the motives and psychology of each character. Mrs. Valentine is cast as a comical character at whom readers are invited to marvel as a spectacle of privilege and ignorance, in the spirit of satire. This is contrasted with the superior clarity of mind but inferior socioeconomic position of Sara, whose point of view readers *are* invited to share.

At the same time, Mrs. Valentine's quoted speech exposes her as a feeling, living character who has a peculiar relationship with a powerful thing, the "black box" of the phonograph. In this way, she is not that different from most of Rhys's characters, who are affected by things in one way or another. "Haunting," in addition to its posthumanist use, has also been suggested as a recurring device with which Rhys's fiction destabilizes gendered spaces by non-normative presences (Johnson and Moran 2015, 6, 8). It appears justified to claim that is not only characters but also the nonhuman things that haunt Rhys's fictional spaces. Even with its satirical and ironically distant narration and focalization, "Villa d'Or" as both a fictional and a textual space is haunted by the animated machine that demands characters' and readers' attention. Seen this way, the story, in its treatment of powerful things, in fact aligns with both Mrs. Valentine's and Sara's perspectives: the acutely, "naïvely" felt one and the ironical one. Furthermore, Sara appears equally enthralled by the material world, even alongside her critical attitude—I will return to this topic in Chapter 4. In a gesture that we will see repeating in Rhys's stories, a narratorial dynamic that at a first glance seems like a clear-cut critical irony becomes more complex and refuses to completely objectify even the most apparently caricature-like female character.

In "A Spiritualist" (1927), which explicitly refers to the popular contemporary practice, the dynamic of readerly alignment with focalization plays out a little differently. This story introduces another privileged character faced with the spirits of the dead meddling in the material world. It begins with a framing story, in which the unnamed narrator listens to a man referred to simply as "Commandant." He relates a story of his visit to the apartment of his lover, Madeleine, after her sudden and untimely death, to gather some of her things to give to her mother. The visit turns unexpectedly supernatural:

> "Well, suddenly, there came from the closed sitting-room a very loud, a terrible crash. The floor shook." [...]
> "You must understand that it was a flat on the fourth floor; all the windows of the sitting-room were tightly shut, naturally, and the blinds were drawn as I had left them on the day of the funeral. The door into the hall was locked, the other led into the bedroom where I was."
> "And, there, lying right in the middle of the floor was a block of white marble, perhaps fifty centimeters square." (LB, 40)

The crash and the appearance of the block of marble are persuasively framed by detailed descriptions of the circumstances and even the estimated measurements of the block. This framing, combined with the "you must understand" aimed at the narratee, serves rhetorically to underline the supernatural potential of the block of marble: it cannot have been placed there by someone with human strength, someone who would have been held back by closed doors and windows. The loud, unexpected, and unexplainable materialization of a block of marble recalls an early gothic motif in Horace Walpole's *The Castle of Otranto* (1764). The events of this novel are set forth when a gigantic steel helmet falls from out of nowhere and crushes the young prince of the castle on his wedding day. This intertextual link is illustrative of the theme, and partly the tone, of Rhys's story, but also adds a dose of irony: in "A Spiritualist," nobody is crushed, the tragedy has met the "princess," and the "prince" who is left to tell the story is presented in a rather unflattering and unreliable light.

The gothic mode continues in the Commandant's report of the reactions of the two characters in Madeleine's apartment. He himself freezes, looking at "the thing"; Gertrude, the housekeeper, crosses herself, "pale as death," and leaves, saying: "[t]here is something strange about this flat" (41). The Commandant portrays his staying in the flat as courageous, and reproduces a gothic trope in which the point of view of an educated, upper-class focalizer is contrasted with that of a superstitious, unreliable, lower-class domestic.[4] The ironical distance of the narration of the framing short story, however, reverses these roles. The Commandant explains his bravery by knowledge of the reasons of the occurrence, which do not, however, "naturalize" it:

> I had promised her a beautiful, white marble tombstone, and I had not yet ordered it. Not because I had not thought of it. Oh, no—but because I was too sad, too tired. But the little one doubtless thought that I had forgotten. It was her way of reminding me. (Ibid.)

His interlocutor, the first-person narrator of the frame story, reacts incredulously to this explanation: "I looked hard at the Commandant. His eyes were clear and as naïve as a child's" (ibid.). Narrated like this, the short story itself is not a straightforward leap into fantasy that the reader is invited to join in a willing suspension of disbelief. The magical event appears in it only as related by a character, one who is clearly unreliable. The Commandant would like to present himself as the bright and fearless hero of a gothic tale, but the frame story presents him as naïve and childish. The ghost of Madeleine, on the other hand, is cast as the resourceful heroine.

No "natural" explanation is given for the appearance of the block, except for the unreliability of the Commandant, yet the whole story revolves around its materiality. The framing structure doubtlessly makes it easier for readers to distance themselves from the magical, fantastic elements of the story, but for its materialized irony to work fully, readers must to some extent be immersed in the story of the girl spirit's material revenge through a block of marble. This is entirely plausible: as Merja Polvinen suggests, while engaging enactively with the events and characters in the fictional world, readers are likely to engage with these experiences *as ones produced by fiction.* We can play along with the suggestions and conventions of the story, while also remaining rooted in the real world—and as I would like to emphasize, the material world. Similarly, engaging in critical reflection need not mean being aloof from the story (Polvinen 2016, 20). Readers may be able to tolerate the ontological ambiguity of the block of marble in the fictional world, as its rules are different from the real one, while also drawing on their real experience to imaginatively live through the events of the story (Caracciolo 2014). We use our experience of the real world of heavy, material things to engage with all kinds of fictional things, but this does not mean that they need to obey all the laws of our world to make sense to us as part of the fictional world. The possibilities for ontological experimentation give fiction leverage to experiment with new arrangements of normative cultural attitudes, like the gendered gothic stereotypes that Rhys is rewriting. On the other hand, the way stories root this experimentation in the lived material world gives them the experiential depth that can also introduce new critical potential, as I wish to show in the analyses throughout this book.

Compared to many material elements in Rhys's fiction, a marble tombstone is a heavy thing in several senses. An unused tombstone is heavy with meaning, with its white, smooth surface evoking youth, purity, and death, all highlighted by the out-of-placeness of the thing in the storyworld. A falling block of "fifty centimeters square" will make a loud noise and cause a floor to shake. Its concrete weight gives more sense of weight to the imagined, symbolic act of Madeleine, "the little one," hurling it from the realm of the spirits. In this blend of metaphor and stony materiality, the block of marble, as narrated by someone who believes in it as real (the Commandant) *through* someone who does not (the frame story narrator), becomes real to the extent that it can be used as a fictional tool for evoking imaginary materiality, while maintaining a critical distance from the fantasy it implies. It is a conceptual metaphor that not only presents an image but also appeals to a variety of senses, relying on the embodied cognitive association of heaviness with a somber mood or difficulty, in addition to the culturally defined meanings readers will be able to attach to a tombstone. The reader is invited to feel the material reality—the thing-power—and the sound made by the tombstone and to connect them to the subsequent interpretation as the basis of its cultural, symbolic functions.

"A Spiritualist" satirizes both modern magical thinking and gothic characterization, but does so in a reparative way that finds new affordances in appropriated tropes. Like "Villa D'Or," it uses the haunting presence of nonhuman things to point out and challenge normative structures of privilege. Rhetorically, the focalization of Sara as well as the presence of the unnamed narrator of "A Spiritualist" work to summon a community of implicitly like-minded subjects set against the ontologically stable (male) humanness of the likes of the Commandant. What feminist posthumanists call the "others of Man" (Braidotti 2017), here in the form of less fortunate women whose perspective the reader is invited to take, come to haunt the normative stories of privileged superstition and gothic fantasy, to cast an ironic light on them. The ontological instability of the fantastic, which readers can engage with without getting sucked in, creates a potential space for this ironical reimagining, while the material presence and thing-power of the gadgets and tombstones grounds these ideas affectively in the lived body of the reader and the world of lived things, which lend experiential weight to them.

This recalls Wolfgang Iser's exploration of the ways fiction presents the "repertoire" of the world[5]:

> The manner in which conventions, norms, and traditions take their place in the literary repertoire varies considerably, but they are always in some way reduced or modified, as they have been removed from their original context and function. In the literary text they thus become capable of new connections, but at the same time the old connections are still present, at least to a certain degree (and may themselves appear in a new light); indeed, their original context must remain sufficiently implicit to act as a background to offset their new significance. Thus the repertoire incorporates both the origin and the transformation of its elements, and the individuality of the text will largely depend on the extent to which their identity is changed.
>
> (Iser 1978, 70)

Readers are faced with things and structures that are familiar on a very basic, bodily level, but these are presented in a new connection, which encourages readers to shift their experience of it ever so slightly. This is the unique way literature creates understanding of the world, and that Rhys's stories certainly harness in their evocation of haunting material things to rewrite gendered norms.

"Illusion" (1927), for instance, is a story about the temperate expatriate artist Miss Bruce, whose secret habit of collecting exquisite dresses and luxurious cosmetics is revealed to the first-person narrator who enters her room in Paris to retrieve some of her things after she has been hospitalized—a pattern similar to "A Spiritualist," yet with different character positions. The narrator imagines a dress talking: "'Wear me, give me life', it would seem to say to her, 'and I will do my damnedest for you!'" (LB, 34–35). The dress needs a human being to come alive, as it were, but then it promises to act as a talisman: protect its wearer, work against threats, and provide potential success. Talking things can be read simply as a manifestation of prosopopoeia and personification, rhetorical devices that lend voice to and humanize the nonhuman, which is a common enough tendency. As Satoshi Nishimura notes, "it is difficult to speak about inanimate objects without giving them any human properties" (Nishimura 2015, 34). However, the frequency and emphasis of these devices in Rhys's writing invites further scrutiny.

In "Illusion," the voices of the things are imagined by the narrator of the story and they arise out of an empathic relation toward *both* the clothes and their owner, the outwardly tidy and unnoticeable collector of flamboyant dresses (for a discussion of empathy in the story, see Chapter 4). In this light, it makes sense to conceive of things as agents rather than as parts of the background of the story. Researchers have demonstrated how narratives with nonhuman narrators such as animals or things point to a tendency to highlight the other as an object to maintain the image of oneself as a subject (Bernaerts et al. 2014, 70). I would argue that in Rhys's, as in many other modernist (women) writers' fiction, talking things in fact work to de-center the human ideal subject. These curious objects are textual-rhetorical devices that make use of poetic license to imagine, occasionally for the purpose of criticizing human cruelty and alienation, while remaining strictly rooted in the "real" as material agents that affect the reader's sensory imagination. As we will see in Chapter 4, they are capable of evoking empathy both as things and as stand-ins for people, and as anthropomorphic but decidedly nonhuman they offer a way to recontextualize the categories of human and nonhuman beyond the usual positions of subject and object. At the same time, the stories are a manifestation of a view of literature itself as magical, by which I do not mean a way of re-presenting something existing but absent (in the economy of lack) but a way of creating worlds and things and giving them life and power to affect readers' lives and worlds: it is an "illusion" but it also does real things in the world.

In addition to overt references to magical thinking and devices of personification, Rhys's stories, like "Illusion," give fetishist, "lucky," and "unlucky" powers to things. Judith Kegan Gardiner writes of the narrator of a later story, "On Not Shooting Sitting Birds" (1976), a typical Rhysian character whose well-prepared date goes awry because of class differences and prejudices: "[she is] in a sexual transaction, agreeing to a tryst whose conclusion seems foreknown and complicitly making herself a commodity or fetish for the affair by packaging herself in new silk underwear" (Gardiner 1989, 10). The notions of trading, lack, and loss, and masking them by "packaging," seem inseparable from the modern conception of fetishism. As a protection from a threat that originates in negation (the alleged "nothing" that the theory substitutes the female genitals with) *and* a surplus, a material "representation" of nothingness whose very materiality is used and enjoyed, fetishism thus conceived implies a fantasy of having it both ways: eating the cake and having it too (Freud 1974, 154, 156). I suggest that Rhys's stories actually provide readers with a more nuanced, experientially fortified picture of *what it is like* to be a fetishized body, and that they use lived materialities to do this. Reading Rhys's reconfigurations of modernist fetishes, especially in relation to the surrealist employment of the mannequin motif, we will see how even items such as "new silk underwear" and the experiences of women whose lives intersect with these things contribute to a sense of distributed agency beyond the subject-object dichotomy. This is an ethical perspective inclusive of the "others of Man," including both things and thingified women.

Intertextually, mannequins come alive evoke E.T.A. Hoffmann's Olimpia doll in *Der Sandmann* (1816). In Freud's analysis of the story in his essay on *das Unheimliche* (1919), he links the horror caused by animated dolls with a transgression of the boundary of animate and inanimate to draft the theory of the uncanny as a covert recognition of a repressed desire. However, as Jukka Sarjala (2015, 125) points out, Hoffman's doll may also be terrifying because it shakes the foundational belief in the superior agency of a (rational) human subject, and instead suggests that there may be forms of agency and power in the nonhuman world—another instance of the nonhuman haunting the normative anthropocentric order. Again, this kind of anti-anthropocentric, posthumanist reading is in line with the critical, feminist cultural work that Rhys's stories are more obviously engaged in, as the anthropomorphism of dolls and the uncanny prospect of their animation both complicates the dynamics of objectification of the female body and exposes a thin line between the human and the nonhuman.

Even though the word "mannequin," in French as well as in English, refers primarily to an anthropomorphic dummy used for presenting clothes, the subjects of Rhys's story "The Mannequin" (1927) are live women working as models in a store on the Place Vendôme, the most prestigious shopping area in Paris. The models the main character Anna works with are defined as different types, and the women seem to retain their roles even when not on display for customers, for example when they share the lunch table. Their positioning in the shabby dressing-room referred to as a "conservatory" (LB, 61) and their luncheon in an austere underground room parallel them with mechanically produced types of mannequin dummies in a storehouse. When Anna exits the shop after a busy day, she seems to be a mannequin dummy come alive, still pretty and an object of gazes, relying on the pretty things she is wearing, yet also a feeling subject:

> At six o'clock Anna was out in the rue de la Paix; her fatigue forgotten, the feeling that now she really belonged to the great, maddening city possessed her and she was happy in her beautifully cut tailor made and a beret. (69)

The very use of the term "mannequin" in the title of the story questions the ontological distinction between human and nonhuman bodies. Fashion dummies transcend human imperfections and mortality, but at the same time bind the human form to the world of objects. They display a sexualized, commodified version of an ideal, female body as an object of desire, yet Anna, the "Mannequin" of the story is also a lived, living body that readers are invited to feel with. This makes the use of the motif stand out in the context of modernist mannequins.

Mannequins and their body parts frequent surrealist and dada photographs and installations (Figure 2.1) as well as paintings by "metaphysical" artists such as Giorgio de Chirico and Salvador Dali. What makes the mannequin a perfect modern but transcendent thing is its origin in the world of fashion and consumption and its place in the public spaces of the city, enhanced by more journalistic documents such as Eugène Atget's street photography of Paris (Figure 2.2). The mannequin is simultaneously familiar and strange, banal and potentially magical, human and nonhuman.

The encaged mannequin by André Masson was part of The Surrealist Exhibition of 1938 in Paris, which featured a specific corridor called "*Rue des Mannequins*," through which the viewers passed to reach the rest of the exhibition. All the mannequins-as-sculptures are gendered female[6] and presented with innuendoes of prostitution, violence, restriction, and objectification. The event, according to Lewis Kachur, confirms "the long-standing surrealist fetishization of the female body" (Kachur 2001, 38). The installation perpetuates and celebrates this logic of objectification by transforming the artificial bodies from commercial to surrealist fetishes, transcendental symbols of the movement. The *Rue des Mannequins* reproduces normative parallels of woman and interiority (André Breton's chest of drawers with legs, Masson's birdcage) and the image of woman as silent (mannequins with their mouths covered by flowers and cockroaches), and celebrates the public display of the female body as subversive. The *Rue des Mannequins* may have been shocking to the contemporary audience but it did not shake normative ideas about the materiality of the female body or its agency.

Jean Rhys was staying in Paris at the time of the exhibition and set her last interwar novel, *Good Morning, Midnight* (1939), there in the year 1937. This year housed one of the last Great Exhibitions in Paris, which

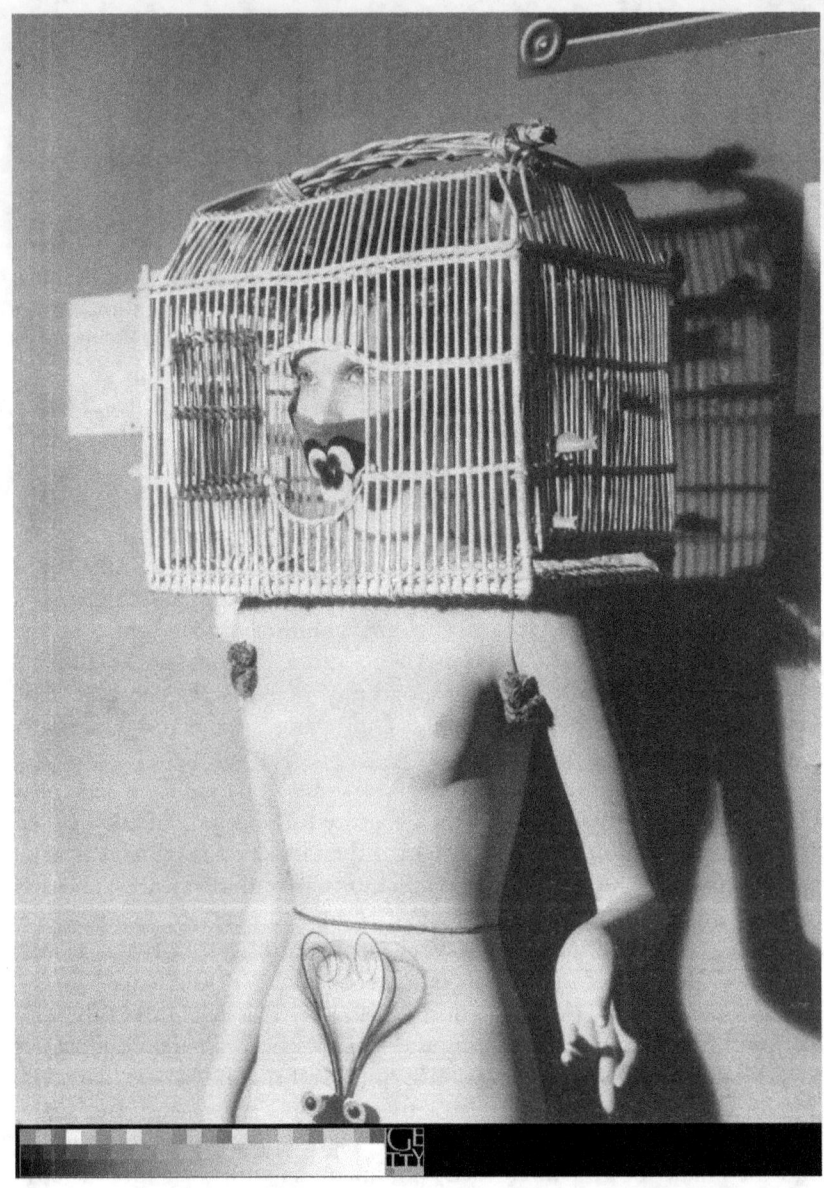

Figure 2.1 Man Ray: photograph of André Masson's "Mannequin." 1938.
André Masson © 2020 Artists Rights Society (ARS), New York/
ADAGP, Paris. Man Ray © Man Ray 2015 Trust/Artists Rights
Society (ARS), NY/ADAGP, Paris 2020.

Figure 2.2 Atget, Eugène: Avenue des Gobelins. 1925. Digital Image © The Museum of Modern Art/Licensed by SCALA/Art Resource, NY.

the novel explicitly features, as well as the "Degenerate Art Exhibition" organized by the Nazi party in Munich. The novel, which presents the motif of exhibitions mostly as haunting and oppressive, evokes a sur-realist connection by featuring striking motifs of mannequins and a nightmare scene with inanimate fingers pointing and street signs reading: "This way to the Exhibition"[7] (Rhys 1985, 350; Britzolakis 2007, 472–474). Sasha Jansen, the narrator and focalizer, experiences both an abstract sense and concrete occurrences of the threat of violence and different forms of sexual trading, which evoke the darker associations of the mannequin motif. However, Rhys uses the parallel between woman and mannequin to a different end than the works in the Surrealist Exhibition. Sasha is shown dreaming of dresses, trying on hats, and having her hair dyed in ways that emphasize her role as a consumer and a potential "mannequin" exhibiting the things she has purchased, but her hopes and disappointments and moments of happiness related to the things she experiences in fact make her perspective lived and embodied in a way that differs starkly from the surrealist presentations of manne-quins.

Similarly, in "Mannequin," we follow Anna throughout her first day in the shop. It is clear that her body is objectified by the gaze of others, but her perspective is maintained as a focalizing subject. Anna is cast as a "type" and her job is to be used more or less as an inanimate dummy might be. However, in the passage quoted earlier, we have her feeling happy and at home. Are we to read the passage as wholly ironical, as a critical comment on a brief moment of bliss in the life of an underdog? Is the feeling itself produced by adhering to normative notions of femi-ninity and consumership, or simply by the fetishist magic that has brought the dummy to life? Anna's lived perspective implies that like her, the other models, however typified and objectified they are even by the narrating voice of the story, have their own "subjective" lives and in-terests beyond the type. "Mannequin" offers textual cues for the en-actment of embodied experience especially in its depiction of the relationship between Anna's body, the spaces of the shop, and the clothes that she is wearing, enough to lend her character a sense of subjectivity and agency that counterbalances her presentation as an object of gaze comparable to a fashion dummy. Many of Rhys's char-acters are themselves presented as fetishes, but in her texts, this means animate, powerful things, *as well as* parties in a system of lack and objectification. Rhys gives voice, a lived body, and a first-person per-spective to an emblem of the reification and objectification of woman, while criticizing these practices; the surrealist focus on the mannequin and woman as a transcendent symbol and a sexualized fetish neither achieves nor pursues this goal.

Jean Rhys rewrites the modern topoi of spiritualist magic and fe-tishism by mixing up the categories of subject and object, human and nonhuman. Her characters engage with magical things and talismans that display thing-power, and the excursions toward fantasy taken in her stories ask the reader to stretch the boundaries of received onto-logical structures. Women are cast as things, but things have power. Reading with an attention to the production of lived experience through focalization structures and thing motifs we can see how these texts, by recontextualizing such notions as subjects and objects, do both feminist and anti-anthropocentric cultural work. This they do not as precociously new materialist enterprises but as sensitive observa-tions and experiential explorations of a world populated by lively things that the theoretical approach also gains its power from. Following Lummaa's inspired formulation, reading like this could be compared to a kind of sorcery:

> We are the ones to question the exclusive tradition of humanism, and we are the ones to initiate any alternative epistemologies, ethics, and ontologies. With regard to art, literature, and poetics, ours is the challenge to summon nonhuman powers. We are the sorcerers.
>
> (Lummaa 2019, 54)

The combined power of texts and their engaged readers can produce magic. All subsequent chapters, including the following exploration of fetishism and haunting things in Djuna Barnes's fiction, follow the conviction that an investigation of *how* the nonhuman haunts these texts leads to an understanding of how the texts create possibilities of imagining alternative world-views and ethics.

Dolls, Boots, and Madames: Djuna Barnes Rewrites Fetishism

Djuna Barnes's stories from the first decades of the 20th century are populated with staple fetish objects. Like Rhys, she summons dolls, but pairs them with a repertoire of boots and whips, corsets, velvet, and lace. In part, these things function as intertextual references toward decadent and naturalist fiction of the end of the 19th century, as well as to the discourses of psychoanalysis and sexology. However, the way these motifs recur constitutes repetition with a difference. Barnes's fictional women might well be said to refuse their castrated condition, as per the Freudian doctrine, but in this refusal they challenge the whole discourse of fetishism. Like Rhys's stories, Barnes's writing makes use of the lived materiality of powerful, fetishized things to present them to the reader as something that can enhance female bodies, instead of filling out a lack inherent to them. While Rhys uses "haunted" narration and focalization techniques to recontextualize anthropocentric and gendered norms and to render her fetishized mannequin characters lively and powerful,

Barnes's rewriting of fetishism resorts especially to description, which thins the line between lived bodies of characters and lived things further.

For this purpose, it is useful to recall the multiple meanings of the notion of fetish. Emily Apter suggests that the fetish seen *as a talisman* rather than as an expression of lack could be a reparative way of recognizing the power the fetishized body gains power over its fetishizer (Apter 1991, 43). To be effective, a talisman should be touched and worn close to the body; such material and sensory factors tend to be forgotten in modern discourses of fetishism (cf. Pietz 1993, 144). In her new materialist account of fetishism, Maurizia Boscagli suggests that we could reclaim embodied pleasure in relation to fetishism "by looking at the object as a visual-tactile phenomenon, to be approached synaesthetically through all the senses rather than through the mind or the eye" (Boscagli 2014, 47). I would add that fetish objects have the power to affect our bodies simply because of their basic properties as material things in the world that we interact with. This is the ontology on top of which cultural ideas of talismanic fetishism as well thing-power can be built.

In Barnes's novel *Nightwood* (1936), Robin Vote gives her lover, Nora, a doll as a present, and dubs its significance as "the life they cannot have, [...] their child" (Barnes 2007, 128). In a fit of rage, Robin is seen holding the doll (as she has earlier held her own baby) above her head as if to smash it, and evidently, she does destroy it. Nora, the main focalizer, also finds a similar doll in the house of Robin's new lover, Jenny. The doll is converted into a subject of theory by Doctor Matthew O'Connor, the parodic psychoanalyst/sexologist of the novel:

> The doll and the immature have something right about them, the doll because it resembles but does not contain life, and the third sex because it contains life but resembles the doll. The blessed face! It should be seen only in profile, otherwise it is observed to be the conjunction of the identical cleaved halves of sexless misgiving! (133–134)[8]

Ambiguity surrounds the doll as a fetish object. It is a metonymical reference to a human child beyond the bipolar gender system and the Oedipal family, yet it also embodies normative notions of motherhood and femininity. As an object of desire, the doll points toward incest; as a plaything made of inanimate matter that is given life and agency in the imagination, it embodies life and death. But the doll is also a material thing with its own talismanic power, or rather its thing-power. According to Clare Taylor (2003, 155–158), the novel parodies the discourses of sexual inversion and pathology but remains built on its own fetishist logic of absence and disavowal, dismemberment and idealized wholeness (150; see also Allen 1996, 19). Accordingly, in my interpretation, what is lacking from the text and its characters as desiring fetishists is the *whole* body in which the idea or a feeling of a self might reside; the female body, as it is, does not suffer from any lack, yet its limbs are picked apart by the narrative, as we will see in Chapter 3. The multifaceted motif of the doll contributes to this discourse, appearing as not only an anthropomorphic image and signifier but also a material, concrete thing.

The short story "Dusie" (1927), whose titular character can be seen as a precursor of Robin, exemplifies a similar dynamic. The comparison shows one example of Barnes's technique of recycling motifs and characters in different contexts. "Dusie" is one of the stories narrated by a young, cosmopolitan woman, who is named Katya in most of them, to an older, silent listener occasionally referred to as "Madame."[9] "Dusie" is situated in Paris, and in it Katya relates an obscure drama of love and jealousy taking place in a "splendid" house belonging to Madame K—, an older lady hosting young women in the house converted to a salon.[10] Dusie at the center of the drama is a "very young" girl, "tall, very big and beautiful, absent and so pale" (Barnes 1996 = BCS, 404). We are told that she wears big shoes, has large ankles and wrists and long legs, and is adored by everyone:

> All people gave her their attention, stroking her, and calling her pet or beast, according to their feelings. They touched her as if she were an idol, and she stood tall, or sat to drink, unheeding, absent. You felt that you must talk to Dusie, tell her everything, because all her beauty was there but uninhabited, like a church, *n'est-ce pas, madame?* Only she was not holy, she was very mortal, and sometimes vulgar, a ferocious and oblivious vulgarity. (406)

Even though Dusie is "absent," "oblivious," and "uninhabited," the description provides a multifaceted image of her proportions and appeal *as a body*. In that she is not that different from the other things described in the story, which I will also return to in the following chapter. The description of the size of her limbs links her to the psychoanalytical fetishist schema of dismemberment, beside which Barnes evokes the language of *religious* fetishism of worshipped idols. As an "uninhabited church" and pet or beast, depending on the mood of others, Dusie is cast as an empty locus that can take on any meaning and serve the purposes of others. Katya's narration, or rather description, as this is the predominant attitude of the story to both people and material environments, grants Dusie agency only in an animistic sense, comparable to a magically animated idol or doll. Like Rhys's mannequins, she is thing-like, but this does not mean the opposite of an agent in the storyworld or in her capacity to affect readers with fictional thing-power. The narrator selects details to persuade the reader, via the silent madame as narratee, to accept and feel the contextual shifts evoked by these ambiguities and unconventional metaphors of materiality and fetishism with her "*n'est-ce pas?*"

A quadrangle drama leads to violence and Dusie lying in bed with a "crushed," bleeding foot. The story draws attention to parts of Dusie's body, which can be seen as a fetishist act. On the other hand, it exposes the fetishized members as capable of sensing: even in its descriptive attitude, it invites readers to enact imagined experiences of bodily pain and thereby complicates the attribution of simple objecthood to the fetishized body. What has happened remains unclear, and Katya merely presents the crushed foot and even the cry of pain as elements of the scene, yet their presentation is nonetheless likely to have at least a minimal embodied effect on the reader. Naomi Schor has shown how the fetishization of wounds in the work of George Sand enables readings of fetishism as a strategy available for women to slip out of a binary gender order, and to be seen as fetishist instead of fetishized (Schor 1995, 93, 95). Something similar could be seen happening in in Barnes's story by virtue of the bleeding foot. Furthermore, as a bleeding idol, Dusie points toward Roman Catholic imagery such as bleeding statues of Christ and the saints, a visual tradition also recurrently evoked in Barnes's fiction (see Chapter 5). Like Rhys, Barnes thus complements and complicates the Marxist-Freudian tradition with other forms of fetishism, rewriting habitual bodily metaphors and combining religious, talismanic fetishism with simply abundant descriptions of the material qualities of bodies. In this way, the fetish as a magical (even if profane, vulgar, and bleeding) idol does not fall neatly into the dynamic of lack and representation. The agency and power of the idol rather point toward abundance and enhancement.

Shoes, more specifically large and heavy boots, are another repeating thing motif in Barnes's work. In "The Grande Malade" (1962), another story with Katya as narrator and "madame" as narratee, one of the leitmotifs is a pair of boots, albeit absent ones. Katya remembers her father and his "tall shining boots" and resolves: "Some day, when I have money, my shoes will be higher and come under my knee" (BCS, 394–395). Monsieur x (always in the lower case), the lover of her sister Moydia, promises Katya "a pair of great boots" (399) but falls ill and dies; the sisters are eventually given his cape but no boots. The boots remain a dream image, one that is incorporated in the lived, fictional body of the character of Katya, and invites a lived relation in the reader as well. The absence of boots is paired with the absence of the abstracted masculine figures of the story, the father and Monsieur x, which locates the fetishist schema of lack in the paternal instead of the maternal sphere. Here, too, Barnes has turned the Freudian discourse of fetishism at least partly upside down: it is the young woman, Katya, who fetishizes the boots as a token connected to her father. For her, the boots would be a talisman of power and an enhancement of her body, and her behavior expresses an already powerful, not customarily feminine position; she "rambl[es] on about father and his cap and boots" and "rages" that her own boots are too short when performing a drunken "Tartar dance" to her sister and Monsieur x (399). The fetishist of this story is not a boy afraid and in denial of imaginary castration in the female body, but a girl wishing to appropriate a powerful material thing belonging to her absent father, which would afford her more actions in the world. Furthermore, the thematic of lack seems to be challenged by how "full" the girls' life already is: Moydia forgets Monsieur x quite easily but keeps the "*tragique*" air that the death of the lover has lent her, along with the lover's cape, another powerful thing. Katya briefly laments that her boots are forgotten in the debacle, but the sisters already have other things in mind: they are going to America.

Thus the fetish-like things of the story evoke abundance instead of lack. While they still fit within a fetishist framework that Barnes clearly is toying with, the story expands the concept by creating space for new tacit, experientially enforced meanings attached to it. Reminding readers of the original meaning of the term "fetish" related to religious, animistic practices, and complicating the Oedipal schema in a manner similar to feminist, post-Freudian accounts of fetishism and, most importantly, the power of materiality and its appeal to the readerly senses and sense-making, Barnes's stories reconfigure potential meanings of fetishism. As animated magical talismans, the things have "performative power" to do things in the world and to the human subject (Boscagli 2014, 50); what is more, their power is not reducible to the systems of economic and sexual exchanges they are part of. It is evoked in the material ways they affect and support the body, available for any reader to re-enact experientially drawing on the basic experiences we all have of wearing and being supported by clothes. The sexual content of the fetish is not erased in this process, but it becomes more complex and incorporates elements of the nonhuman into its human core—once again, a normative notion is haunted by otherness and recontextualized by the literary power to bring this presence to the fore.

The dynamic between fetishism and the senses is strongly present in "A Night among the Horses," (1918, revised version 1962), another story with characters that come across as both fetishists and fetishized things. The focal character, an ostler called John, describes Freda, the "lady of the house": "[...] that small fiery woman, with a battery for a heart and the body of a toy, who ran everything, who purred, saturated with impudence, with a mechanical buzz that ticked away her humanity" (BCS, 249). Freda is like Dusie in her resemblance to a nonhuman anthropomorphic fetish object, like a mechanical doll with a will (if not a mind) of its own: "She darted and bobbled about too much, and always with the mindless intensity of a mechanical toy kicking and raking about the floor" (252). However, she is "small and fiery" instead of large and absent-minded; from the start, she is clearly the active agent of the story, even though it is focalized by John whose narration objectifies her.

Freda has decided to "make a gentleman" out of John (249), who attempts to resist, but submits to a game of cat and mouse with sexual innuendoes. The game is played out through things such as Freda's "aggravating yellow veil," and "objects of culture" like miniatures and ancient books with which she "torments" him (251). She also tempts him with imaginary tokens of phallic power:

> "You will rise to governor-general—well, to inspector"
>
> "Inspector!"
>
> "As you like, say master of the regiment—say cavalry officer. Horses, too, leather, whips—" (250)

Their interaction is referred to as "a game without any pleasure" in which both parties are "on the wings of vertigo" (250). The whip is one of the things in the story that embodies simultaneous suffering and pleasure: the couple ride together, and John, angry at Freda's provocations, lashes at her boot with his whip. In this encounter between the materials of two fetish objects, Freda also appears as a thing, like an animated puppet: "the foot flew up in its stirrup, as though she were dancing." (249–250).

The vertigo-inducing mixture of torment and delight goes together with the two characters' ontological wavering between thing and human, object and subject. Freda's reported speech casts her pursuit as a humanizing one: "I'll step you up from being a 'thing.' You will see, you will enjoy it" (249). John, using the same word, is more doubtful:

> He wouldn't fit in anywhere after Freda, he'd be neither what he was nor what he had been; he'd be a *thing*, half standing, half crouching, like those figures under the roofs of historic buildings, the halt position of the damned.
>
> (251, emphasis in the original)

An ostler is a "thing," but so is an ex-ostler, not fit to his new role as a gentleman and perhaps abandoned by his gentlewoman. The liminal area between the two subject positions, in which John is caught, does not seem any better. Freda holds a masked ball, in which she would like to have John take part as a human fetish object with his whips and boots: "Come [...] just as you are, and be our whipper-in," she suggests, which is taken by John as an "unpardonable insult" (253). Instead, John dresses in the conventional evening clothes of a gentleman, which makes him stand out even more: "he was the only person present therefore who was not 'in dress'" (253). There is no way out: he would be thingified equally by his old clothes and the new costume.

At the same time, very unthing-like feelings and sensory experiences are attributed to John as a character. The story begins and ends on the night of the masked ball. John has just escaped the interior, using his crudely phallic gentleman's cane as a magical item of protection: "He stepped free, and with the knob end of his cane, he drew a circle in the rosin clear around her, then backward went through the French windows" (254). The beginning of the story, which the rest of the events follow as analepsis, narrates the result of his escape in an inverse, parodic parade of symbols of masculine, upper-class power: "Toward dusk, in the summer of the year, a man in evening dress, carrying a top hat and a cane, crept on hands and knees through the underbrush bordering the pastures of the Buckler estate" (247). Here the narrator describes John from the outside, but it seems impossible for the description not to also become an invitation to imagine an experiencing, embodied subject, who feels pain in his wrists and whose confused feelings of the shaking ground, his beating heart, and the surrounding odors and lights the story evokes simply by describing the environment. As in Rhys's "Mannequin," readers are first given the character as solidified into an image and spatiotemporal coordinates ("Twelve o'clock. Déjeuner chez Jeanne Veron, Place Vendôme," LB, 59; "Toward dusk …"). These are then endowed with a sense of life embedded in its environment, by virtue of cues for embodied experience. The vividly depicted, intermingled textures of the underbrush and John's evening dress cannot help but contribute to the reader's ability to imagine John as an experiencing subject as well as a thing.

The end of the story discourse finds him, now focalizing, in the same situation, undecided between a desire to go back to his horses and the ambition to try and succeed as a gentleman. The horses, however, fail to recognize John as he tries to wave at them, and the story implies that they trample him under their hooves. The tragic ending is made more powerful by the embodied experientiality evoked by the image of John in his formal attire crawling in the underbrush. Thus, the fictional materiality of this body, combined with its material surroundings, makes him simultaneously a thing and an experiencing subject. While in "The Grande Malade" the motif of boots contributes to a version of female fetishism where lack is replaced by abundance, in "A Night among the Horses" both main characters are simultaneously too much and not enough. Things have power over people, who see themselves in danger of becoming a thing, yet the way their merging with things is described in the stories constructs them as lived bodies—that is, "subjects"—in the reader's imagination.

While some of the masculinized items of clothing in Barnes's work are worn by explicitly small women, the detailed description of feminine dress often accompanies a larger, older lady—a Madame, as she is frequently called in the stories.[11] Both types of characters are endowed with an unmistakable aura of strength and power. Madame K—of "Dusie," for instance, is described as "large, very full and blond," with an gnomic addition that "[s]he went with the furniture as only a childless Frenchwoman can" (405). We do not learn much about her dress, but her "going with the furniture" hints at something elaborate and abundant, these being the properties of the furniture in her house. In her salon, she embodies power, wit, and reason, having kept from her days as a physician a capability to "remove" an argument "within the exact bounds of its sickness" (406). In "The Hatmaker" (1996),[12] on the other hand, the protagonist, named simply Madame, is also an independent professional living in a splendid house ("a sort of *Schönbrunn*," 468). She runs not a salon but a hat maker's workshop with younger women as apprentices. Like Madame K—, she is linked to excess and plenty, which manifest in descriptive passages and lists; her house is "filled" with "Louis Quinze chairs, Empire sofas, dolls, crazy jades, heavy Buddhas, and Roman busts" (ibid.). As if explicitly playing with the connotations of woman and negativity, the narrator explains that "[...] she could not write a letter that was understandable, being incapable of employing a negative in any sentence" (469).

Both women are made thing-like by their parallelization with the abundantly described things with which they are surrounded, but at the same time they are shown to gain a talismanic power from these surroundings, *in addition* to seemingly being "filled" with power in several ways, thanks to a large or refined body (although we know of Madame in "The Hatmaker" only that she has been told "she resembled Récamier,[13] was a little like the Gioconda and had Early Italian bones," 470), and an independent social status or even exact monetary worth, as in "The Hatmaker": "In the year nineteen hundred and thirty-two Madame was worth half a million dollars" (469).

In "Aller et Retour" (1924), a story that will be discussed in more detail in Chapter 4, the main character, Madame von Bartmann, is also "a woman of great strength" (362). She is large and heavily jeweled, and her "bosom was tightly cross-laced, the busk bending with every breath" (ibid.). Her husband has just died, and she describes him as a "queer, mad fellow" (367). In fact, the stories "queer" both male and female characters. The tight corseting of large, strong women as a repeating motif evokes femininity in several of its normative, material senses (parts of body and dress) but omits everything fragile and submissive as well as the idea of negativity and lack; these qualities are replaced with power and fullness, in comparison with the male characters who come to embody the opposite. Barnes's Madames certainly eat the cake and have it too. Madame von Bartmann's character actually blends the support of feminine undergarments and the phallic motif of boots: she also wears "tan boots laced high on shapely legs" (362). These stories and characters again point to- ward fetish objects more as talismans of power than as a signifiers of lack. There is still absence and lack in the stories but once again the *whole* woman is missing and has been replaced. The Madames may well be thing- like, but thanks to the combination of bodily, sensory experience described for readers to engage with imaginatively, they emerge both as a material thing obstinately occupying space and an affective indicator of a lived body—never a signifier of a lack lurking behind the wholeness.

The repeated tropes of excess and abundance transform the topos of fetishism in Barnes's stories from a fantasy and disavowal of lack to a fantasy of plenty, power, and wholeness, or even bulging excess. The ne- gation of negativity is at the heart of Freudian fetishism, but in Barnes's hands this double negative becomes positive, and this happens through the texts' attention to material things. The fetishized things—corsets and boots, whips and dolls—are removed from the sphere of symbolic re- presentation of the absent signified and entered into the realm of talismanic fetishism and thing-power, as things with affective and agential potential in their own right. Barnes's descriptions bring things and people close to one another and evoke thing-like bodies but also intense feeling, thus doing similar work as Rhys's mannequin motifs in blurring the line between human and nonhuman bodies at the service of fictional experientiality. As I will argue throughout this book, the ways the stories tap into our everyday experience with descriptions of material things and environments, reveals something of the intermingledness of this experience in the material world.

The reading of these stories through their affective materialities has exposed the way Rhys's and Barnes's modernist texts that are "haunted" by the nonhuman presence of things become potential spaces for new ontologies of humans and things, subjects and objects, and thereby also feminist breeding grounds for new ways of imagining normative socio- cultural meanings attached to male and female bodies. In both authors' rewritings of the modernist topos of fetishism, human and nonhuman bodies are exposed in their materiality that is made available to the senses of the reader, constructing awholeness defining both fictional things and people in place of dismemberment. The following chapter moves further into the direction of postanthropocentric thinking to ex- plore the extent to which things and people as narrative elements in fact become mixed, even in stories that do not open up for readings in light of the cultural phenomena of fetishism or animism.

Notes

1 Rhys 1972, 130.
2 Interestingly, Zadel Turner Barnes, Djuna Barnes's grandmother, was one of the pioneers of spiritualism (Armstrong 2005, 122).

3 A brand name for a phonograph produced from the beginning of the 20th century until the 1960s by the American company named, appropriately hauntingly, Victor Talking Machine Company.

4 This contrast is found in addition to *Otranto* in Ann Radcliffe's *The Mysteries of Udolpho* (1794), for instance.

5 I thank David Rodriguez for pointing out this connection.

6 Sonia Mossé was the only female artist in this installation.

7 The *Rue des Mannequins* in the surrealist exhibition also featured street signs pointing to real and imaginary places.

8 This is one clear example of *Nightwood's* highly problematic use of the concepts 'the third sex', inversion and mirroring, as well as the notions of sexlessness and immaturity, and ultimately the "equation of lesbian desire with the death drive" that Clare Taylor has shown the text to present, but not completely support (Taylor 2003, 182).

9 The cycle also contains the stories "Cassation" and "The Grande Malade," originally published as "A Little Girl Tells a Story to a Lady" and "The Little Girl Continues" respectively, and "Beyond the Heart."

10 The salon is doubtless inspired by the one Natalie Barney held in Paris, which Barnes also frequented. In his introduction to Barnes's *Collected Stories*, Philip Herring is bolder in charting the biographical referentiality of the story: "'Dusie' [...] is less a story than a descriptive narrative centered on the Left Bank lesbian scene which Barnes knew so well. [...] it is unmistakably about Barnes's lover Thelma Wood; the setting is Natalie Clifford Barney's house at 20 rue Jacob [...]" (Herring 1995, 20). Regardless of the compelling evidence Herring has for this claim, I think it is still justified and necessary to read "Dusie," like the rest of Barnes's fiction, more as a story than as a biographical account.

11 One of the stories that are left outside of this analysis is "Madame Grows Older" (1924); Barnes also wrote a play manuscript titled "Madame Collects Herself," in which Madame Zolbo is, in an overtly fetishist manner, constructed of the body parts of her former lovers (Taylor 2003, 183).

12 The first publication of the story is in the *Collected Stories*.

13 Probably a reference to Juliette Récamier (1777–1849), who held literary salons in Paris at the beginning of the 19th century, yet it also evokes a piece of furniture, a *chaise longue*, "the *Recamier*," that was named after her.

Works Cited

Allen, Carolyn. 1996. *Following Djuna: Women Lovers and the Erotics of Loss.* Bloomington: Indiana University Press.

Apter, Emily. 1991. *Feminizing the Fetish: Psychoanalysis and Narrative Obsession in Turn-of-the-Century France.* Ithaca: Cornell University Press. DOI: 10.7591/9781501722691.

Armstrong, Tim. 2005. *Modernism: A Cultural History.* Cambridge: Polity.

Barnes, Djuna. 1936/2007. *Nightwood.* London: Faber & Faber.

Barnes, Djuna. 1996. *Collected Stories.* Los Angeles: Sun & Moon Press.

Bernaerts, Lars et al. 2014. "The Storied Lives of Non-Human Narrators." *Narrative* 22 (1): 68–93. DOI: 10.1353/nar.2014.0002.

Braidotti. Rosi. 2017. "Four Theses on Posthuman Feminism." In *Anthropocene Feminism*, edited by Richard Grusin, 21–48. Minneapolis, MN: University of Minnesota Press.

Bennett, Jane. 2010. *Vibrant Matter: A Political Ecology of Things*. Durham: Duke University Press. DOI: 10.1515/9780822391623.

Boscagli, Maurizia. 2014. *Stuff Theory: Everyday Objects, Radical Materialism*. New York: Bloomsbury.

Britzolakis, Christina. 2007. "This Way to the Exhibition: Genealogies of Urban Spectacle in Jean Rhys's Interwar Fiction." *Textual Practice* 21 (3): 457–482.

Caracciolo, Marco. 2014. *The Experientiality of Narrative: An Enactivist Approach*. Berlin: DeGruyter. DOI: 0.1515/9783110365658.

During, Simon. 2002. *Modern Enchantments: The Cultural Power of Secular Magic*. Cambridge, MA: Harvard University Press.

Freud, Sigmund. 1974. "Fetishism." In *The Complete Psychological Works, Vol. XXI*. Translated by James Strachey, 147–157. London: Hogarth and the Institute of Psychoanalysis.

Gardiner, Judith Kegan. 1989. *Rhys, Stead, Lessing, and the Politics of Empathy*. Bloomington: Indiana University Press.

Herbrechter, Stefan. 2013. *Posthumanism: A Critical Analysis*. London: Bloomsbury.

Herring, Philip. 1995. *Djuna: The Life and Work of Djuna Barnes*. New York: Viking.

Iser, Wolfgang. 1978. *The Act of Reading: A Theory of Aesthetic Response*. Baltimore: Johns Hopkins University Press.

Johnson, Erica L. and Patricia Moran. 2015. "Introduction: The Haunting of Jean Rhys." In *Jean Rhys: Twenty-First-Century Approaches*, edited by Erica L. Johnson and Patricia Moran, 1–17. Edinburgh: Edinburgh University Press.

Kachur, Lewis. 2001. *Displaying the Marvelous: Marcel Duchamp, Salvador Dali, and Surrealist Exhibition Installations*. Cambridge, MA: MIT Press.

Karagouni, Villu. 2010. "Implicitly Political: The Aesthetics of Jean Rhys's *Voyage in the Dark*." eSharp 16 (Winter).

Landy, Joshua and Michael Saler, eds. 2009. *The Re-Enchantment of the World: Secular Magic in a Rational Age*. Stanford, CA: Stanford University Press. DOI: 10.11126/stanford/9780804752992.001.0001

Lummaa, Karoliina. 2019. "Posthumanist Reading: Witnessing Ghosts, Summoning Nonhuman Powers." In *Reconfiguring Human, Nonhuman and Posthuman in Literature and Culture*, edited by Sanna Karkulehto et al., 41–56. London: Routledge. DOI: 10.4324/9780429243042-3.

Marx, Karl. 2001. *Marx's Capital: A Student Edition. Volume I, Book One: The Process of Production of Capital*. Translated by Samuel Moore and Edward Aveling, edited by Frederick Engels. London: The Electric Book Company.

Nishimura, Satoshi. 2015. "Personification and Narrative: The Blurred Boundaries of the Inanimate in Hardy and Woolf." *Narrative* 23 (1): 27–39. DOI: 10.1353/nar.2015.0003.

Pietz, William. 1993. "Fetishims and Materialism: the Limits of Theory in Marx." In *Fetishism as a Cultural Discourse*, edited by William Pietz and Emily Apter, 119–151. Ithaca, NY: Cornell University Press.

Polvinen, Merja. 2016. "Enactive Perception and Fictional Worlds." In *The Cognitive Humanities: Embodied Mind in Literature and Culture*, edited by Peter Garratt, 19–34. London: Palgrave MacMillan. DOI:10.1057/978-1-137-59329-0_2.

Rhys, Jean. 1985. *The Complete Novels*. New York: W.W. Norton.

Rhys, Jean. 1927/1984. *The Left Bank & Other Stories*. Salem, NH: Ayer Company.

Rhys, Jean. 1969/1972. *Tigers are Better-Looking*. London: Penguin Books.

Sarjala, Jukka. 2015. "Maailmaan uppoava subjekti: Riippuvuuden teema E.T.A. Hoffmannin Nukuttajassa." In *Posthumanismi*, edited by Karoliina Lummaa and Lea Rojola, 109–127. Turku: Eetos.

Schor, Naomi. 1995. "Female Fetishism: The Case of George Sand." In *Bad Objects*, 93–100. Durham: Duke University Press. DOI: 10.2307/1772136.

Taylor, Clare L. 2003. *Women, Writing, and Fetishism 1890–1950: Female Cross-Gendering*. Oxford: Oxford University Press.

Zimring, Rishona. 2000. "The Make-up of Jean Rhys's Fiction." *Novel* 33 (2): 212–234. DOI: 10.2307/1346080.

3 Lively Things

The scene is set but seems the actor gone.

Djuna Barnes: *Antiphon*[1]

The previous chapter explored some specific topoi and motifs in the modernist context that foreground the powers of the nonhuman, material world, and the ways writers such as Jean Rhys and Djuna Barnes tapped into this cultural material to create engaging short stories as well as social and political commentary. I suggested that this call for readerly engagement gains its effectivity not only from the rendering of the sociocultural meanings attached to the material things, but from the experiential, sensory, and affective properties of the material world familiar to readers. In this chapter, I will stay with the topic of the life and agency of things in modernist short fiction, but instead of the most apparently animist realms of spiritualism and fetishism, I will focus on stories in which the power of things is less obvious, yet undeniably present. The realm of enchantment is, however, still present in the stories discussed here, especially in the form of another very modernist topos, the party, as it appears and reappears in Katherine Mansfield's stories.

To keep thinking about agency, power, and liveliness, I employ ideas and concepts especially from contemporary posthumanist and new materialist thinkers. I will use notions such as intra-action, affective assemblages, trans-corporeality and different re-writings of the concept of "life" to discuss the ontological questions of a world divided into subjects and objects as well as to keep exploring the ethical and political implications of the way modernist stories employ materiality. Furthermore, I maintain that it is necessary to combine these concepts to a close reading of narrative techniques and the understanding of the reader's mind as embodied and enactive. Obviously, these are not concepts or readings that modernist writers would have thought with, and I want to be wary about forcing their writing into a newly discovered theoretical pigeonhole. To show that the lively world of things extends beyond the most obvious contexts for it is not to suggest that writers such as Djuna Barnes and Katherine Mansfield were precociously anticipating the current postanthropocentric shifts in theory, but that they were simply in tune with experiences of a lively, lived, and entangled world of things that are part of our human being in the world.

To begin, we will remain in the company of Djuna Barnes, looking more closely at the plentiful world of things housed by her experimental stories and the equally unconventional interiors in their fictional worlds. I will explore how these worlds open up for discussions of how agency and affect are distributed among the bodies of humans and things, and ask whether "the thing" even is the right unit to discuss Barnes's worlds of intermingled agencies. The second part of this chapter introduces the short fiction of Katherine Mansfield into the discussion of agency. Drawing on the concepts introduced in the first part, yet focusing especially on that of a nonhuman life, I will look at how Mansfield, in a way not dissimilar from Jean Rhys, creates a lively world of things and constant reshuffling of ontological categories to produce critical points of the gender and class norms of society. She does so especially in stories that harness the enchanted spheres of parties and childhood to animate the inanimate, and parallels children as focalizers with readers who are drawn to engage with the enchanted realm of fiction, with its own animating powers. The analysis of how nonhuman influences creep into her stories supports but also expands on the ideas of impersonality and fragmentariness of the human self exemplified by the stories that previous critics have pointed out. Both discussions will suggest the need to go further than most critical readings of Barnes and Mansfield in recognizing the affirmative potential of a shift of perspective away from human exclusivity and the way this shift also contributes to ethical and political aims to do with our human life.

Djuna Barnes's Piled-up and Entangled Assemblages

We left the previous chapter with a grasp of assemblages of things that wield power as fetish objects in Barnes's stories. However, we also gained an understanding that this power is due to them acting not only as proxies or symbols for human bodies and meanings, but also as powerful in virtue of their materiality, in the fictional world, and evocative for the reader because of the capacities of such materiality to affect the reader physically and emotionally. Barnes's stories are unique in their disregard for the human interest factor in the form of the psychology of characters, paired with the plentifulness of things that the characters seem to be gathered around instead of the things being there to support the formation and development of characters. I wish to study the interaction of human and nonhuman bodies in Barnes's stories, moving from the recognition of agentive assemblages and "intra-active" phenomena to reading the human and nonhuman bodies as profoundly intermingled with and permeated by one another, and to pair these observations with a study of Barnes's thing-like characters. I will start by rereading "Dusie," one of the "madame" stories introduced in the previous chapter, in which fetishism is not the only means for things to gain and hold power.[2]

In "Dusie," characters are presented primarily as aesthetic bodies surrounded by elaborately described things. In fact, the mode of the story, like most of Barnes's stories, is descriptive. The excerpts below are only approximately half of the descriptive passage dedicated to Madame K—'s house, in a story that is less than eight pages long, which makes them excellent examples of Barnes's use of detail and list-like forms:

> The house was very French. All gold and blue, and, in the boudoirs, pink. There were three, but the part of the house I saw most often was blue and white, with much lace and gold. The walls were blue satin, and hanging from tasselled cords were many golden framed women hung. [...]
> There were many chrysanthemums, and a long white harp in the embrasure of the window, and in the dust lying upon it many women had written "Dusie." And above all, in an enamelled cage, two canaries, the one who sang, and the one who listened.
> But in the boudoirs there was much pink, and everything was brittle and glazed and intricate. Ribbons dangled from everything and bonbons were everywhere, and statuettes of little boys in satin breeches, offering tiny ladies in bouffant skirts, fans and finches and flowers, and all about in the grass were stuck shiny slinking foxes.
>
> (BCS, 404–405)

A list-like description such as this conveys both the importance of detail and a sense of the whole, which according to Julie Taylor, for instance, is what makes Barnes's writing enjoyable: "Not to pay attention to the particular things is to miss out on most of the pleasure, but the nature of abundance conveyed by the list as a whole is equally important" (Taylor 2012, 156, emphasis in the original). The repetition of certain quantifying and qualifying words in the list extends to a spectacle of abundance almost ad absurdum: "many chrysanthemums," "many women," "much pink," "long harp"; "everything," "everywhere," and "all about." The description of the house bulges with luxurious materiality, which becomes more "stuff" than things: a mass of matter in the unstable state of becoming, as Maurizia Boscagli describes "stuff" (2014, 14). There is pain, too, in the love drama that results in the crushed foot, later in the story, but all this is presented rather as part of the excess than as its balancing other.

The choices of words according to which there is so much of everything cause the contents of the house to swell beyond its limits. Katya, the narrator, also describes Dusie and Madame K— along with other women present in the house. However, the most extensive and vivid descriptions are devoted to the things surrounding them. This is not quite the conventional (realist) procedure of building up characters with the help of their surroundings, because the abundance of the preceding descriptions of the environment and things all but swallow up the character, and create a hybrid constellation of human and nonhuman elements akin to the "golden framed women" hanging on the walls of the fictional space. As a result, in "Dusie," agency appears as a constellation of human and nonhuman elements, in a way that most obviously out of the three writers opens up for an anti-anthropocentric reading, for which I am turning above all to the theoretical initiatives of Karen Barad and Jane Bennett.

According to Barad, the habitual way of conceiving of agency as the property of individuals is inadequate. Instead, she suggests that agency emerges in constellations involving more than one party, out of which any number can also be nonhuman and even ones that can be considered inanimate. Agents not only interact in these constellations, what she calls "phenomena"; they themselves are also constituted in and through them in what she calls "intra-action": "agencies are only distinct in relation to their mutual entanglement; they don't exist as individual elements" (Barad 2007, 33, emphasis in the original).[3] Following this kind of a relational account calls for a question: does Barnes's work celebrate *things* or a complex materiality whose "intra-action" precedes the individual agencies of its parts? First, we can observe that while living in a world of such entangled agencies, humans still tend to experience the world as divided into things, even if from a purely physiological point of view they were made of innumerable micro-agencies. A table, a book, and a building appear as separate things with their specific affordances as do more abstract entities such as the society or the family, or even other people, as bodies occupying space. However, it is also useful look at the literary "phenomena" in Barnes's stories as entanglements of action, in which the elements constitute one another, and see how such non-habitual elements and perspectives can enter our experience via the form of fiction. Barnes's texts are largely constructed in and for a world made of discernible things, human and nonhuman. It is possible to simultaneously take the cognitive-phenomenological perspective to things as they are experienced and be aware of the possibility to think differently, remain open to instances where even experience supports a more intra-active, entangled interpretation instead of a neat division into things as separate agents.

Considering the experiential participation of the reader in these phenomena gives reason to foreground the role of affectivity, in the manner of Jane Bennett's analysis of distributed agency (2010). Following the thinking of Deleuze and Guattari (2013), among others, Bennett's influential notion of "vibrant matter" conceives of agency in assemblages, "confederation[s] of human and nonhuman elements," in which the force of the confederation is more than the sum of its parts, although the parts need not be completely constituted by one another:

> Assemblages are not governed by any central head: no one materiality or type of material has sufficient competence to determine consistently the trajectory or impact of the group. The effects generated by an assemblage are, rather, emergent properties, emergent in that their ability to make something happen [...] is distinct from the sum of the vital force of each materiality considered alone.
>
> (Bennett 2010, 24)

An assemblage such as the combination of things and human characters in the descriptive sections of "Dusie" gains its potential to affect—in this case, the reader—through the grouping of different material agents. The force of this argument lies, first, on the deconstruction of the boundary between matter and life. It enables looking at humans as well as non-humans and things as simultaneously material and potentially animate bodies. To address the agential potential of nonhuman existents in a text, we thus need not limit our scope to instances of animism or fetishization. Even more importantly, the notion of the affective body as a party in the emergence of agency is a fruitful one for the reading of fictional texts, as it addresses the embodiment of readers and thereby enters into dialogue with what an embodied cognitive approach, combined with a cultural sensitivity, has to offer to my readings.

Most of the things in the passage from "Dusie" are human-made and infused with human culture. We recognize a rococo style in the color scheme and in the anthropomorphic statuettes of boys in breeches and tiny ladies. There are paintings described as "golden women," and even the intrusion of a character, Dusie, whose name is written in the dust on the surface of the harp. The whole is observed through the human eyes of Katya. The house encompasses all these things, the boudoirs afford dreams and encounters, the dust makes up the words, the statuettes seem to be engaged in a completely independent activity, while adding their ambiguous gestures to the "phenomenon" of the house. On the level of reader–text interaction, the materialities of language participate in the action: the form of the list of items linked with commas and conjunctions creates a sense of abundance, while the synesthetic potential of words such as "bon-bons," "glazed," and "brittle," as well as the sense of accumulation evoked by the repetition of "many," invites an embodied, schematic understanding of the plentiful presence of things. The words on the page give the impression of having gathered[4] there to make up the plenitude of fictional things gathered in the fictional house; the culture is inscribed onto the material, but it is also the material that gives rise to the cultural.

The things are presented as though it was they who made up the action of the story, and they interrupt the flow of readerly interest in the direction of characters and events: what are Madame K—and Dusie like? What is going to happen to them? We can imagine these questions more vividly because of the inclusion of the other "madame" as the narratee. Instead, however, Katya's narrating voice provides a flood of decorative objects small and large, along with pets, dust, furniture, and fabrics, which continues long enough to leave a multisensory impression on the reading mind. The description constitutes a fictional assemblage of tassels, pictures, statuettes, ribbons, and women, with the power to affect a reader, in addition to the more ambiguous power the things seem to have in the fictional world, engaged in a gathering all their own, where characters are invited only as quick references—like Dusie's name written in dust.

How does such an effect of things act as a constellation created in readers? Bennett writes of an experience of being "struck" by a random arrangement of debris she encounters on a Baltimore street:

> [...] stuff exhibited its thing-power: it issued a call, even if I did not quite understand what it was saying. At the very least, it provoked affects in me: I was repelled by the dead (or was it merely sleeping?) rat and dismayed by the litter, but I also felt something else: a nameless awareness of the impossible singularity of that rat, that configuration of pollen, that otherwise utterly banal, mass-produced plastic water bottle-cap.
>
> (Bennett 2010, 4)

We could argue that the fictional assemblages of objects, such as the ones described in "Dusie," are capable of setting the stage for "enchantment" and fictional encounters phenomenologically resembling the one described by Bennett. Such passages consist of deictic gestures offering the reader a specific array of things: "that" cage, those canaries, tassels, chrysanthemums, and statuettes. In providing a thing as a fictionalized focus of attention, they have the capability to defamiliarize and thereby make the things tangible and, paradoxically, more real, as in Viktor Shklovsky's classic definition of the stoniness of literary stones (Shklovsky 2004). In Bennett's description, the things are not animated or personified, but the enchantment of the observer of the assemblage implies the capacity of humans to be affected as well as the capacity of things to affect (Bennett 2010, xii).

As she is the human narrator of in Barnes's story, Katya's body can be said to yield itself as a proxy for the reader to align their bodily experience with (see Caracciolo 2014). However, in Barnes's case, a human body in the fictional world does not seem utterly necessary for the production of experiences. This is a classic question of narratology:

instances that can be called "figuralization," an "empty deictic center" in a passage without a character experiencer is filled by readerly immersion (Banfield 1987, 273; Fludernik 1996, 192–207). Therefore, it can be argued that a text implies a human subject and thereby a lived body even if one is not explicitly mentioned. If we see affectivity as a property of human–nonhuman assemblages and agency as distributed, even more opportunities open up for readerly engagement beyond human focalizers. As another example, let us look at "Finale" (1918), a two-page story narrated extradiegetically and focalized by an empty deictic center.

The focus of "Finale" roams around a room at the center of which lies a dead man in a coffin, surrounded by candles and a mourning family. Clearly, this is not a "lived" body immediately inviting the attribution of mind or experience: "Everything else in the room seemed willing to go on changing—being. He alone remained cold and unwilling, like a stoppage in the atmosphere" (BCS, 232). The narration contributes to the ambiguity of the story in relation to the bodies presented: the categories of animate/lived and inanimate, passive, and active do not coincide neatly with those of the human and the nonhuman. The dead body seems "cold and unwilling," but physically speaking it certainly is "changing" and "being" in its way: the biological processes of its decomposition must already be in action.[5] Around the dead man, the human and nonhuman elements in the room, all included under the scope of "everything," are still living. There are the kneeling bodies of his wife, mother, and children, explicitly lived; we learn of the mother's weeping, the girl's damp palms, the boy's private, pleasurable memory of rubbing his head against a nurse's arm. There are also burning candles, and in the corner, "the dead man's dearest possession: a bright blue scarf embroidered with spots of gold" (233). The scarf has been acquired during a possible romantic encounter in Italy and has a history of sensory contact with the man's once-lived body: "It was a lovely thing, but much treasuring had lined it; and the marks of his thumbs as they passed over it in pleasant satisfaction had left their tarnish on the little spots of gold" (ibid.).

After this description of the room, the narration marks the passing of time by introducing growing shadows. The end of the brief story moves from stagnation to action, but positions a nonhuman agent at its center:

> A large rat put his head out of a hole, long dusty, and peered into the room.
> The children were going to rise and go to bed soon. The bodies of the mourners had that half-sorrowful, half-bored look of people who do something that hurts too long.
> Presently the rat took hold of the scarf and trotted away with it into the darkness of the beyond.

One thing only had the undertaker forgotten to do; he had failed to remove the cotton from the ears of the dead man, who had suffered from earache. (Ibid.)

In "Finale," the form of the human body is not clearly present in a focalizer's fictional body, but the room is full of more or less thing-like bodies that still invite experiential engagement. The characters are emphasized as lived bodies in postures. They arguably invite readers to resonate with their briefly narrated experiences, and the general reference at the end to what it is like to "do something that hurts too long." In the description of the scarf, a clear opening for a reader's bodily experience comes in the reference to the man's thumbs having touched it. Traces of human agency and experience become entangled with nonhuman elements: the rat is the most vivid, fast-moving agent in the story, while the scarf is described in the liveliest manner. The human bodies are thing-like except for their briefly narrated experiences of pain, while the corpse keeps changing its own, invisible way. The last sentence returns from the entrance and exit of the rat to the slow rhythm of description, the changing and being of bodies. It foregrounds the contrast between a live and a dead body by pointing out the pointlessness of the cotton in the ears of a dead man, which are no longer capable of hearing nor hurting; paradoxically, the mention of earache may be enough for the activation of some readers' bodily memory of such an experience.

No character in the fictional world of "Finale" is expressly shown to experience these goings-on between the human and the nonhuman. The scarf has been held dear and caressed, but is now forgotten; the once helpful, now out-of-place cotton is ignored, making a part of the body-turned-nonhuman of the dead man. I suggest that these encounters, revealed by the narrator of the story as though behind the backs of the kneeling mourners, are crucial for the story's potential to strike and enchant the reader. The rat, unlike the one in Bennett's description, is a very lively one, but also the scarf has some vividness of its own, relying on both its history and its material properties. Most importantly, the scarf is described so vividly as to leave a mark on the reader as well. Solicitations of sensory experience are not reducible to the human fictional bodies, but arise between them and the nonhuman ones. Furthermore, even if there were no descriptions of or hints toward experience, readers would still be able to associate them with the description of the scarf, for instance: an introduction of a scarf in a story can't avoid evoking at least a brief sense of how it feels to wear one.

This story and the experiences it creates, like other stories by Barnes, could also be read in the light of the notion of trans-corporeality that Stacy Alaimo develops. In her new materialist thinking, Alaimo wants to foreground the relational and intermingled aspects of human and nonhuman bodies, especially the connection between bodies and their environments. She suggests that the two are "ultimately inseparable": "the human is always the very stuff of the messy, contingent, emergent mix of the material world" (Alaimo 2010: 2, 11). The man is dead but his body is still the arena for a multitude of biological processes, as well as the carrier of a reminder of medical procedures in the form of the cotton in his ear; the scarf is permeated by human use, memories, and even dirt, has been part of the man's life but after its end becomes enmeshed in rodent life instead. As I have suggested at length elsewhere in an analysis of Barnes's writing (Oulanne 2020), literary fiction, with its flexible perspectives and experiental intensity, can awaken us to observe such entanglements, which according to Alaimo can mostly only be accessed with the help of scientific instruments (Alaimo 2010, 11, 28).

The readerly capacity to be affected by a story reaches beyond representations of human bodies and experience. On the basis of my reading, I suggest that readers respond to fictional things, bodies, and entanglements of matter because they have their own experience of sensing, using, and even being permeated by actual things, being-in-the-world as three-dimensional bodies themselves. We do not read descriptions of material detail passively, waiting for the human agent to come along. The experience of agency in the stories emerges in the affective assemblage of fictional elements, both human and nonhuman, in their materiality, grasped in the materialities of language by material readers with lived bodies, all molded by the very experience of the phenomenon of reading. The stories experiment with techniques where the representation of human experience is delayed or removed, but they still invite readers to draw on their reservoir of experience of life shared with things like those presented in the stories, what Caracciolo (2014, 55–71) calls the "experiential background." This does not mean they need to have the actual experience of completely "similar" things: the stories give cues for basic, bodily experience in the ways they point out the materials, textures, and colors of the items.

None of this requires the characters to gain a human-like psychological interiority; Barnes's stories show how very thing-like characters can contribute to affective experientiality, just like material things can. Her impenetrable characters have puzzled interpreters, and they have been likened to animals (Taylor 2003; Rohman 2009, 2007). According to Carrie Rohman (2007, 131), Robin, the elusive and deceptive lover in the novel *Nightwood*, "figures nonidentity as a form of subjectivity, where the nonlinguistic, the undecidable, and the animal serve to revise what counts as human." Clare Taylor sees Robin, who as a character is remarkably similar to Dusie, as the manifestation of a fantasy of wholeness that *Nightwood* ultimately shows to be destructive (Taylor 2003, 168–169). Robin is introduced in the novel when she is seen by her future husband Felix Volkbein and doctor Matthew O'Connor, lying unconscious in a luxurious hotel room. The narrator of the story takes its time before reaching Robin's body, passing first by way of a carpet, two windows and several furnishings and decorations:

> On a bed, surrounded by a confusion of potted plants, exotic palms and cut flowers, faintly oversung by the notes of unseen birds, which seemed to have been forgotten—left without the usual silencing cover, which, like cloaks on funeral urns, are cast over their cages at night by good housewives—half flung off the support of the cushions from which, in a moment of threatened consciousness she had turned her head, lay the young woman, heavy and disheveled.
>
> (Barnes 2007, 30–31)

As Rohman points out, the sense of smell that the passage evokes locates Robin in the "realm of animality" (2007, 66). This could be expanded to the nonhuman in general, not veering far from the text: she is said to exude an odor with a "quality of that earth-flesh, fungi [...] texture of plant life" (Barnes 2007, 31); even the birds are brought close to the world of things by the lengthy evocation of their usually covered cage. As in "Dusie," the narrating voice of *Nightwood* seems to lose itself in details of things, plants, fabrics, and birds in cages, evoked in a multisensory manner. The result is a tableau vivant that could be a parody of "The Sleeping Beauty" or a painting by Henri Rousseau where human and nonhuman agencies are further mixed: "she seemed to lie in a jungle trapped in a drawing room (in the apprehension of which the walls have made their escape), thrown in among the carnivorous flowers as their ration [...]" (ibid.). The picture constructed by these words features the figure of a female human being, but the sheer amount of sensory information from nonhuman elements in general overrides (and "oversings") the human form.

Similar patterns of character presentation emerge in many of Barnes's short stories. "A Boy Asks a Question" (1923) has as its human center Carmen la Tosca, a famous actress spending her holiday in a village. The main event of the short narrative occurs when a neighborhood boy of fourteen approaches Carmen, a well-known "woman of the world" (BCS, 346), with a question vaguely related to the nature of love. The resulting discussion is equally ambiguous, and the aesthetic focus of the story is, again, rather on a spatial tableau than on temporally organized action. Like Robin, and like Dusie at the end of her story, Carmen is pictured in bed, surrounded by a multitude of materialities:

> Carmen la Tosca breakfasted in bed, and late. Having caught herself out of sleep in a net of bobbin-lace, she broke fast with both food and scent, lazily dusting her neck and arms with perfumed talc, lolling on the bed (which stood between two ovals of pear-wood, framing versions of Leda and the swan), ripping through the

wrappers of Puerto Rican journals and French gazettes with the blade of a murderous paper-cutter, and finally, in the total vacancy of complete indulgence, her hand sprawling across a screaming headline, would stare out into the harsh economy of russet boughs, pranked out in fruit. (346–347)

Carmen, too, is surrounded by fabrics, furniture, art, small objects, and plants. The structures of agency suggested by the verb forms of the passage are ambiguous: Carmen has "caught herself out of sleep," in a net of lace, whose way of participating in the action is not specified. This description evokes the sense of smell like the one from *Nightwood*, but it also introduces sounds that foreground the very materiality of the words of the passage as well as the things and actions they denote: there is "ripping through the wrappers" that resonates with the trills of "Puerto Rican," "sprawling," and "pranked out"; there is also a "screaming headline."

In "A Boy Asks a Question," as in *Nightwood* and "Dusie," the description of the surrounding space does not simply support the construction of the character around whom all the things would be gathered—rather, the mass of things is what gathers action, affect, and attention. The things, in fact, may appear as more vivid than the character itself and override the human agent by their sheer volume. Thereby they have more potential for affective agency in relation to the reader. On the other hand, it is the body of the character and the thing-bodies together that make the vivid tableau. The richness of different materials invites the involvement of the reader's sensory imagination, and the human body among the things, while providing itself as a lived body, is also a thing-like body occupying space with a virtually imaginable surface and dimensions. None of these bodies in Barnes's assemblages needs to be seen as an agent in itself; it is the whole that makes up the tableau, which in turn makes what matters in the story. In a stagnant, descriptive scene like the list of "Dusie," or the two renderings of women in bed, the thing-likeness of human elements is readily noticeable, yet even characters who are presented as "animated" and who perform actions as part of the more traditional, narrative plots retain a close relationship with the nonhuman. In *Nightwood*, as Robin wakes up, rises from the bed and begins to move about in the fictional world, she never sheds the sense of being a mixture of human, animal and thing. Dusie, too, remains pronouncedly a body occupying space, an appearance of a surface: more than anything human, she is a doll, an idol, a "pet" and a "beast," and her movements are "like vines growing over a ruin" (BCS, 406,407; see Chapter 2).

As affective agents, Robin, Carmen, as well as the women of "Dusie" and the family of "Finale" are characters the reader follows and experiences as lived bodies, even though they are foregrounded as thing-like. In these stories, the structures of focalization can be what takes readers beyond the clear-cut human/nonhuman, subject/object divides. The imaginary experientiality of the characters emerges in the phenomenon of reading together with readerly reactions to the characters chiefly as bodies, a condition they share with the nonhuman things surrounding them. These bodies are material in themselves and networked and intermingled with and even penetrated by other nonhuman bodies of different shapes and sizes around them; everything in these stories is "changing and being," leading a life that only partly adheres to traditional narrativized ideas of a *human* life. This is what I will focus more closely on when reading Katherine Mansfield's stories in what remains of this chapter.

Katherine Mansfield Writing a Nonhuman Life

As has become clear in all of the preceding readings of Rhys's and Barnes's fiction, anthropomorphism and the animation of things and the occasional dehumanization and thingification of people go hand in hand. Magical and intense experiences as well as the dehumanizing effects of different social structures such as capitalism and the mass culture are, of course, crucially modernist thematics.[6] However, what is remarkable and too little acknowledged is the extent to which these phenomena are intermingled, and how this complicates their ethical implications. Here I will read Katherine Mansfield's short fiction to continue exploring my hypothesis that modernist authors' portrayals of humans as thing-like do not always mean that the human characters would be experientially inaccessible or trapped in the alienated position of objects in the fictional world—rather, human bodies too become "animated" as *part* of a vivid world of things, as bodies among bodies.

In the following, I wish to show how Mansfield's stories present their readers with magically animated thing-worlds, as well as other forms of blurring the boundaries between human and thing.. From the point of view of modernism and the short story, finding similar strategies and thematics to Rhys and Barnes in Mansfield's short fiction brings these observations closer to the "heart" of Anglophone modernism, if we want to accept that such a place exists, by virtue of the popularity of her stories during her lifetime, the critical attention and acclaim they have received since, and the fact that she explicitly focused on the short story form as a means of expression (see Head 1992; Kaplan 1991; Mitchell 2011). On the other hand, my aim here, too, remains to discuss the modernist aesthetics of the stories to arrive at a more general understanding about what literature can do with lived things, and show the more lasting value and effects of this "modernist" endeavor.

In a similar way to Rhys's and Barnes's short fiction, the worlds of Mansfield's most read and researched stories are populated with a curious and at times magical presence of nonhuman agents, which is not quite given the credit it deserves in research. This, like that on Barnes and Rhys, has remained focused on readings hailing from the symbolist (e.g. Kimber 2015) and post-structuralist (e.g. Fullbrook 1986; Head 1992; Kaplan 1991) traditions, and heavily interested in the cultural-historical and biographical contexts of Mansfield's work (e.g. Robinson 1994). For Mansfield, the descriptions of a lively material world come across in moments of dream and hallucination, but also and especially when the world is observed and narrated from the perspective of children or young people, which sets her apart from the other writers discussed here. In this way, the animation of the thing world is connected with but not reduced to the sphere of the imagination, as well as the simple imprecision of perception, which are recognizable traits of experience to most readers.

Like that of Barnes's fiction, the focalization of Mansfield's stories spills over the boundaries of the human individual and claims impersonal properties. These strategies create the "blazing moments" (see Chapter 1, Kimber and Smith 2014) of human experience that Mansfield is after, and my reading of them suggests the extent to which nonhuman agencies are in fact responsible for this effect. As in Rhys's case, I argue that it is not enough to approach the animation of the nonhuman world as a projection of the "inner" mental states of the characters, even though it is used by the author to generate socioculturally relevant meanings and critical commentary that goes beyond the simple presentation of matter. In the following, I will look at how this manifests in the dialogue and polyphony of different ideas of "life" that the stories bring forward. Focusing on the perspectives of children to the material and social worlds, I will read stories that address some socially determined turning point in the human life and use the material world to shift the readers' perspectives on it. I shall begin with stories that use the event of a party to create a quasi-magical sphere in which such surprising things may happen.

"The GardenParty" (1922) is one of Mansfield's stories set in New Zealand and arguably the most heavily read, taught, and discussed one of her stories. Its reader is thrust from the start *in medias res* (starting with "And") amid whirlwind-like party preparations and invited to align with the focalization of Laura, a girl on the threshold of adulthood. Laura's experience of the event is rendered in characteristic third-person narration that often resorts to free indirect discourse, typical of Mansfield, which creates the impression of proximity to her experience, while maintaining a distance that often lends itself to irony (e.g. McHale 2014; Ramazani 1988). The party, especially as it is used by Mansfield, is akin to the modernist motifs of magic and spiritualism in that it creates a sphere of particular intensity within the confines of everyday life, transforming the appearance of material everyday things. As Kate McLoughlin observes, both the intensity of experience and the everyday are of interest to modernist literature, making the party a fruitful topos to be revisited by a number of authors (McLoughlin 2013, 18). Laura is shown breathlessly participating in and marveling at the spectacle of flowers, marquees and fine foods that make up the party. The preparations are described with what appear as standard metaphorical expressions, yet the descriptions lean slightly toward a more concrete and at the same time more poetic tone. "The house was alive with soft quick steps and running voices" (Mansfield 1973 = MCS, 249), the narrator states, using an ordinary metaphor for human activity. However, as this joins an intratextual chorus of expressions throughout her fiction that in different ways refer to the world of things leading a life of their own, it becomes clear that Mansfield, too, is employing an aesthetics of vivid materiality that deserves to be read in more detail.

Mansfield's short stories are model pieces of texts built around an epiphany, in which a character experiences a sense of clarity in terms of how they view the world and a moment of recognition or understanding is offered to the reader (Harrington 2007, 6; Hanson 1985, 55). However, these moments of clarity tend to be followed by a moment of "anti-epiphany" in which the realization is bluntly shown to be illusory and a totalized knowledge of the world is in one way or another presented as impossible or at the very least incommunicable (see Drewery 2011, 108; New 1999, 106, 124). In "The Garden Party," the party appears as a sphere of illusion that first becomes shattered in the epiphanic moment, and then is reconstructed as its culturally accepted, grown-up version, as Laura negotiates the discrepancy between the tragic death of a carter living nearby and the excited preparations and lush celebration of the garden party in her home. As Angela Smith, for instance, has pointed out, the target of the satirical tone in which this discrepancy is rendered is the illusion of the classlessness of New Zealand society compared to the Old World (Smith 2013, 91), in addition to the equally apparent commentary of gendered norms and roles. In such readings, the material things that make up the party become markers of illusion and vehicles of satire and irony. I agree with them but wish to see what a closer attention to the materiality, and in this case, the agency of the things as it appears in the story, adds to the understanding of the stories' critical edge.

After Laura has reconciled her ambivalent feelings about the party with the help of her mother and a new, becoming hat that seems to transport her into the adult world, the experience of the party itself is passed by relatively quickly, represented as a litany of kind and courteous phrases mostly complementing Laura and her hat. The crux of the story occurs when she visits the bereaved family afterward, still in her party clothes, with a basket of leftovers, a gesture suggested by the mother and doubted by Laura. The grieving wife seems to be intimidated by the visit, and Laura wants to escape, but she is asked to look at the body of the young deceased. Instead of the horror she anticipates at the spectacle of the body, following her mother's earlier allusion to some-thing unsaid that she is to avoid at all costs, the sight provides her with a sense of blissful remoteness from the drama of guilt she has been living through: "What did garden-parties and baskets and lace frocks matter to him? He was far from all those things" (MCS, 261). Laura marvels at the dead man, borrowing from him the sense of contentment and distance that seems to set the preceding events in a new light for her.

The anti-epiphany begins to form right after, when Laura's realization that "all the same you had to cry" brings her back into the sphere of convention: feeling the need to say something before leaving the room, she blurts out "Forgive my hat" (ibid.) and escapes the house. Meeting her brother Laurie outside, she makes an attempt at communicating the earlier experience in response to his inquiry about whether it was awful, but nothing quite comes out of this. The exchange constitutes an ending typical of Mansfield's stories:

> "It was simply marvellous. But, Laurie—" She stopped, she looked at her brother. "Isn't life," she stammered, "isn't life—" But what life was she couldn't explain. No matter. He quite understood.
>
> "Isn't it, darling?" said Laurie. (Ibid.)

Readings of the ending have foregrounded the failure in communication (e.g. Childs 2016, 59–60; Smith 2013, 92), an instance of double dis-illusionment, in which even the potential opening toward some kind of higher consciousness, hinted at by Laura's encounter with the corpse and the fleetingness of life displayed by it, becomes negated by the fact that such experiences cannot be communicated in the socially conditioned language that the siblings share, and they are thus destined to become platitudes. In the relatively blunt terms used by Smith, Laurie "has not quite understood," and "Laura gets it wrong" (ibid.) already in ima-gining the dead man as dreamy and content, ignoring the pain and loss attached to the situation. This is a fair reading, yet looking at the af-fective dynamics of the story and the succession of material images that creates them, another narrative emerges beside this one. This narrative supports the critical reading on an experiential and performative level, but in fact makes a claim that goes further into how Mansfields rewrites social norms than the interpretations that foreground the ironical and critical functions of the story.

The scene of the visit to the cabin uses flowers, clothes, and food, things that have added to the liveliness of the party, as symbols of class difference and Laura's privilege, which she ends up apologizing for. From the point of view of affective materiality, however, the scene be-comes an intriguing interplay between things that simultaneously are and are not party to the human sociocultural systems of class, for instance, that the party signifies. On the one hand, the blissfulness of the corpse is marked, as Laura observes it, by its remoteness from "all those things," and Laura encounters the body as a beautiful thing—or an aestheticized and objectified spectacle similar to her vision of herself in a mirror wearing her charming new hat, except out of tune stylistically (cf. Childs 2016, 110). On the other hand, the comical absurdity that arises from the near-anthropomorphic gesture of apologizing for the unfitting hat reveals another undercurrent of the text, namely that the hat, in its materiality, is equally indifferent to the party and the significations and complications assigned to it as the corpse. In fact, I want to read its presence as a gesture that the text makes in the direction of the reader, sneaking past the more immediately available critical interpretation that reads sociocultural meanings into things. The preceding party assemblage of flowers, lace, hats, and sandwiches can thus be read to speak simultaneously of bourgeois privilege including a normative, narrow view of life, *and* of the nonhuman indifference that comes from a shift of perspective beyond these structures. As Mansfield herself suggests in a letter, quoted by Smith: "Laura says, 'But all these things must not happen at once' and Life answers 'Why not? How are they divided from each other.'" (Mansfield 1973, Smith 2013, 92.)

Looking at "The Garden Party" as a performance that subtly offers the reader a change of context and perspective, by way of an encounter with the indifference of material things to the oppressive and inequal social norms, makes its comic elements less ironical and more affirmative, similarly to what we noted of Rhys's parodic rewritings of the gothic, for instance. I suggest that even though this is not a popular interpretation in relation to Mansfield's story, it is a plausible one that in fact accounts for both the allure of the story and its critical potential. In this reading, the final dialogue quoted above in fact becomes less about failed communication and more about indirect communication, both in the fictional world and in the transitional relationship between the text and the reader. Laura's failure to voice her realization of what life is, and Laurie's affirmation that seems to be without content, could equally be read as a statement from the story to the reader: indeed, what life is cannot be expressed in total in the language of convention that the siblings have been initiated into with the help of the ritual of the party.

However, the story has just presented the reader with an array of lively things, including the corpse that, similarly to the one in Barnes's "Finale," is removed from human life but very much part of the intra-active, trans-corporeal life of things that keeps happening regardless of the turns the human life has taken. Readers are invited to see them, aligning with Laura's perspective, as images that condense some meaning otherwise inexpressible. That life is not reducible to the terms of human language or indeed to a propositional statement implies an ontological stance that is in line with the way the stories extend life to material things and their assemblages—and parallel these things with the occasionally thing-like bodies of the human characters, who thereby come to share in the indifferent stance. Furthermore, by doing this, the story ends up making a statement about the power of literature: Laura cannot communicate her epiphany about life, yet the story does something in this direction, not by propositional statements ("Life is …") but by what literature does best, namely taking the readers through an affective experience evoked by images of material things that have their own, unvoiced but felt perspective on the issue.

What life is, as an enduring philosophical question, has been discussed widely in posthumanist and new materialist contexts. A central issue is the distinction evoked by for instance Giorgio Agamben, between "bare life" *zoe*) and "good" or cultured life (*bios*), which has formed the basis of Western politics since Aristotle. *Bios* is what *zoe* develops into in a society, something more than bare existence, while the exclusion of the latter is how the human sphere of politics and society is formed (Agamben 1998, 8). For Rosi Braidotti (2011, 16, 21), *zoe* is a central posthuman concept and signifies "nonhuman life": a cyclic process of different becomings that refuses to be contained within the straight lines of human thinking. In this, Braidotti draws on the Deleuzean notion of "*a* life" (*une vie*) as an impersonal force acting in, upon and between human and nonhuman bodies alike: "immanent life carrying with it the events or singularities that are merely actualized in subjects and objects" (Deleuze 2001, 29). I would like to expand on this statement by noting that the categories of subject and object do not seem necessary for this kind of life to actualize; rather, the indifference of bodies as I read it in the short stories makes such categories useless. This is also implied in how Braidotti uses the concept of *zoe*, as well as in Jane Bennett's new materialist reading of Deleuze's "*a* life" as "restless activeness, a destructive-creative force-presence that does not coincide fully with any specific body" (2010: 54, 57; Deleuze 2001). In my reading of Mansfield, the normative, human-centered sphere of life with its signposts, arcs of development, ambitions, and hierarchies seems to be undermined by the simple but powerful processes of living and dying that go on regardless of the human party and expand beyond its boundaries.

Looking more closely at "The Garden Party," it seems obvious that the garden is full of nonhuman life and that the dead body contains it in some ways, but what about inorganic things such as hats as expressions of *zoe*? The shift of perspective called for by the story as well as the thinkers exploring *zoe* and *a* life in the indifferent singular calls for the abandonment of this distinction as well. Furthermore, it is necessary to remember that we are dealing with *literary*, fictional hats, flowers, bodies, and sandwiches. A reader may assign them into categories of organic and inorganic, natural and artificial, but as observed in the previous readings, before this the things appear to us as images or experiences. In short, they appear as things in the world—in phenomenological terms, the life-world—and their common denominator is their materiality, made imaginable and virtually tangible by their presentation in the medium of language. Life, which Laura struggles to express and Laurie thinks he knows, which the stories leave unexplained but express indirectly and experientially, works against the normative social structures as well as the anthropocentric ontologies, which on an apparent level control the bodies in Mansfield's stories but on this other level, equally present in the material "surface" of the narrative, are shown to have no significance. This is an ethical gesture that the story performs beside its critical and ironical meanings.

As Daniel Aureliano Newman has pointed out, a distrust of developmental, linear and progressive narratives of life is a shared trait of many modernist works, and is present on a formal level in experimental solutions that resist chronological plots, for instance (Newman 2019, 3–4). Short stories are in a useful position regarding such experiments, in that they are rarely expected to convey a life story, and rather focus on the unit of the moment. Reading from a different theoretical backgrounds, several researchers, such as Dominic Head and Sydney Kaplan, have called attention to the "impersonality" that is characteristic of Mansfield's aesthetics (Head 1992, 138; Kaplan 1991, 169). Kaplan, for instance, connects this trait in Mansfield with an experiential realization of a multiplicity of selves (instead of the term "fragmentation" that is more commonly used in the modernist context), which is manifest in Mansfield's life especially as experimentation with gender and sexuality identities and the masquerade-like "trying on '*all* sorts of lives,'" as she puts it in a letter (Quoted in Kaplan 1991, 170), and in her art as the sense of loss of self of the author. This Kaplan shows to form a tension with the confessional tendencies of Mansfield's fiction and a more general modernist search for an "authentic" self (179). In my exploration of life, lives, and *a* life in Mansfield's stories, I wish to expand the meanings of anti-linearity, "all sorts of lives," and the multiplicity of selves, and see how the nonhuman world plays into the modernist dynamics of impersonality and the associated criticism of the structure of life narratives.

For instance, in "Sun and Moon" (1918), another story with the setting of a party and its preparations, the magical change that takes over lived space and things is observed by Sun, a child much younger than Laura, whose perspective Mansfield evokes by employing more overtly animistic language than in "The Garden Party." Extra chairs "arrive" in the house, "their legs in the air," followed by flowers, who also simply "come" (MCS, 153). Sun's view of the situation all but erases the human activity behind the appearance of the things: "When you stared down from the balcony at the people carrying them the flower pots looked like funny awfully nice hats nodding up the path" (153–4). For Moon, his little sister, the illusion is even more convincing: "Moon thought they were hats. [...] But she never knew the difference between real things and not real ones" (154).

Importantly, this rendering of perception that is characteristic of Mansfield's children is not only about animation of the inanimate but also about the blending of categories of things. In fact, the blending of categories contributes to the same sense of a vivid world independent of the human observer: plants become hats, in a process of thingification, but the hats are "nodding up the path," leading an animated life of their own. Similar blends between phenomenological and ontological categories occur as the party preparations proceed and the children's movements in space are directed by them, as though the event, too, was an agent in itself. While it mostly displays a negative power to push the children out of its way, there is also a power of attraction to the quasi-magical sphere of the party, manifested in particular by the image of an ice pudding in the form of a little house with a nut for a door knob—a testament to Mansfield's attention to detail and its significance from a child's perspective. In general, the story offers detailed accounts of the decorations of the children's home, filled with flowers, "winking glasses," bird-shaped salt cellars and napkins that look like roses. As in Barnes's descriptions, the material abundance appears as an expression of affective thing-power and of the party as an assemblage whose power is derived from the interaction or intra-action of its elements, the vast majority of whom are in fact nonhuman and even traditionally considered as nonliving.

The children themselves, while they are the human witnesses to the scene, are subject to similar metamorphoses and affective entanglements as the material world they are observing. These are rendered indirectly in the way the children are placed somewhere between human, animal, and thing, as they are dressed up in the spirit of the masquerade: Moon is clothed in a white, fur-lined dress, with "fluffy stuff on the legs of her drawers" and white shoes with "big blobs on them" (MCS, 156). Looking at her, the nurse exclaims: "And you look like a sweet little cherub of a picture of a powder-puff? [sic.]" (ibid.) Her mother echoes, "What a picture!" (ibid.), a word that is also used by the housemaid about the dining room display. In the nurse's comment that confuses both syntax and semantics, the little girl becomes an angel who is a picture and also a powder-puff, all this leading to a question mark as if to underscore the child's ontological instability. The thingification of the children is accentuated as they are put on display for the guests of their parents, who seem scarcely more human ("sweet-smelling, rustling ladies and men with funny tails on their coats—like beetles," 157), and whose quoted comments recall the earlier blends of ontological categories: "what a picture! [...] Oh, the ducks! Oh, the lambs! Oh, the sweets! Oh, the pets!" (ibid). Even the names of the children associate them with the nonhuman world and, arguably, display their parents' original attitude toward them as intricate objects of art. After being paraded around, they "fly" back to their room, and are no longer welcome in the magic sphere of the party. When the children wake up to witness the remains of the celebration, the ruin of the pudding house, and their drunk parents, the experience turns tragic, as Sun in particular is upset without being comforted.

In the modernist party of "Sun and Moon," as it has been read by Smith (2013, 86–87) and Jacqueline Bardolph (1994, 167), for instance, the children's perspective reveals the spectacle of the grown-ups' pretense and carelessness in relation to both the material world and their offspring. However, like in the case of "The Garden Party," when looking at the narration of the whole story, while the objectification of the children and the illusions offered by the world of things are certainly used as a vehicle of critique, they also present themselves as an integral part of perception of the world—and the world, come alive for the children and thereby for the reader, extends beyond and is ultimately indifferent to the commodified spectacle that their parents seem to make of it, a parody of a cultured "polis." In this story, I argue that the mixing of categories of human, plant, thing, and animal is not a symptom of the children being entrained into the order of the spectacle, but as much a product of cultural influences as a "natural" phenomenon. Furthermore, like the natural and artificial things of "The Garden Party," the thing-like elements of "Sun and Moon" are all just things appearing to the fictional children and displaying their affective power. The animating language of the children in fact underlines their position as proxies for the reader, in front of whose eyes flowers and chairs indeed appear and disappear, on par with the appearances and disappearances of characters, in the enchanted sphere of the story that the magic circle of the party echoes.

Thus reading the story with the notion of *a* life in mind rids it of some of the stark oppositions of nature and culture, child and adult, human and thing: in "Sun and Moon," as in "The Garden Party," the counter-narrative for the patterned and structured "good life" that the story satirizes is actually already contained within the material properties of the party, which is also the central metaphor for these structures. Story elements such as the costumes and the eponymical names of the children can be read not only as denominators of their parents eccentric tastes, but also as elements that bring the association between the children and the world of things to an ontological level, on which the children's affective bodies are not different from the heavenly bodies after which they are named. Even though they are affected by the dynamics of the party event, on this scale their existence remains indifferent to it. Furthermore, this shift has already taken place considering the fact that the children are purely fictional bodies that appear for and affect the reader of a fictional narrative, which is an artifact in itself.

Another story with children as its focalizers and centers of attention, "The Doll's House" (1922), lends itself to a similar understanding of fiction as a sphere of enchanted, lively materiality, and a "flat" ontology of humans, things, and works of art. In this story, the Burnell children, who also appear in "Prelude" and "At the Bay," are gifted a huge doll's house. This, like the spectacle of the pudding-house in the previous story, allows for the curious situation in which a house is observed as a miniature thing, deliciously mysterious because of its detailed resemblance to the "real" but also because of its distance from the real, as the description from the point of view of a child suggests:

> Its two solid little chimneys, glued on to the roof, were painted red and white, and the door, gleaming with yellow varnish, was like a little slab of toffee. Four windows, real windows, were divided into panes by a broad streak of green. There was actually a tiny porch, too, painted yellow, with big lumps of congealed paint hanging along the edge. (MCS, 393)

In the eyes of the children, it is a "perfect, perfect little house" because of all the various elements it includes, but also because it contains pure forms ("slabs" and "lumps") that look edible, like the nut-handle or the dress accessories in "Sun and Moon" (ibid.). The scene becomes more marvelous, however, as the house front is opened, and the children gaze into the little rooms. The opening up of a house is a powerful gesture and may resonate in a reader's mind with other stories in which Mansfield presents houses as confined spaces for the women in them and the children share the imagery of their mothers' fears—a pattern I will discuss shortly when reading "Prelude." Another interpretation might foreground it as a metaphor for the literary work, affording a look inside the lives of others, or even the Jamesian "house of fiction." Kaplan, for instance, reads this story too as a display of thinly veiled class differences in New Zealand, as the house as an object exposes the inequality of the children admiring it (Kaplan 1991, 14).

All these ways of reading are completely justified, yet the presence of the doll's house in the story is not reducible to them. Its material detail is not exhausted by one explanation, and while supporting several, it also extends beyond them. Readers learn about the detail in the doll's house, like the little realistic lamp on the dining-room table that Kezia "likes frightfully" (MCS, 394). In the lamp, the story creates a stronger affinity between a human character and a clearly nonhuman thing than between the character and the anthropomorphic dolls, for instance: the doll father, mother, and two children seem too big for the house, and do not look "as though they belonged" (ibid.). On the scale of liveliness, they are contrasted in Kezia's eyes with the lamp: "But the lamp was perfect. It seemed to smile at Kezia, to say, 'I live here'" (ibid.). The house belongs to the lamp at least as much as to its "human" inhabitants; similarly, the life and liveliness in the story is a property equally of fictional things and people, all equally unreal like the furnishings and dolls in the doll's house.

The metaphorical meanings of the house become played out further in the story, which however is not set up as an allegorical whole but as a subtle interplay of connections between material organization of space and the gendered and socioeconomical norms thus enforced. The children are allowed to have two friends at a time come look at the house—with the exception of the Kelveys, children of a washerwoman. Kezia disobeys and shows them the house, until discovered by her young aunt Beryl. Beryl is shown to feel trapped by on the one hand by her position as the spinster sister and on the other hand the pressure from a man to meet with him, and scolding the children and slamming the doll's house shut seems to offer her some relief. Thus, the opening and closing of the house become parallel with Beryl's sense of double entrapment, and one form of social inequality has led to the enforcement of another, as it is the little Kelveys who suffer from her anger. The story, however, gives them the final word: having escaped, they stand looking over the fields and Our Else, the little sister who rarely speaks or smiles, ultimately does so to mark the special occasion: "I seen the little lamp" (401). The norms of life create gaps between children and grown-ups, but the experience of a material thing works to bridge the gap and, furthermore, bring all characters parallel with the readers, while maintaining their fictionality: because the children have seen the lamp, a material metaphor for the epiphany or the "isolated" moment of the story (Robinson 1994, 6), the reader becomes alive to it too—even if it at the same time was a "sham," a symbol of illusion and privilege (cf. Van Gunsteren 1990, 179).

Read like this, Mansfield's stories of parties and childhood are not primarily ironical observations of the discrepancy of the spheres of human and nonhuman, bare and cultured life. Rather, they can be read as a celebration of their intermingledness: a party will inevitably be crashed by the haunting presence of *zoe*, and writing about the party will carry the nonhuman influences with it. These influences are another side of the impersonality and fragmentariness of the human self exemplified by the stories that previous critics have pointed out, and focusing on them is a chance to expand these critics' observations in an anti-anthropocentric direction. I wish to keep making a case for this kind of reading and further examining the narrative techniques that give rise to it in Mansfield's work by turning to another story that pairs lively things with the critical exploration of received sociocultural narratives of the life of women, through the intense yet potentially impersonal experience of a focalizer on the threshold of adulthood.

"Her First Ball" (1921) is another account of a "blazing moment" and an initiation. Leila, a young girl from the countryside, is introduced to the heavily regulated sphere of social relations, the ball, with the help of her more experienced cousins, the Sheridans of "The Garden Party." The story is narrated from Leila's point of view, beginning with the cab ride; from its first lines it blends categories of agency, presenting the ball as a magical power that animates nonhuman material things:

> Exactly when the ball began Leila would have found it hard to say. Perhaps her first real partner was the cab. It did not matter that she shared the cab with the Sheridan girls and their brother. She sat back in her own little corner of it, and the bolster on which her hand rested felt like the sleeve of an unknown young man's dress suit; and away they bowled, past waltzing lamp-posts and houses and fences and trees. (MCS, 336)

Leila's perception is transformed into an anthropomorphizing power by the approaching event, in a way already familiar from the other stories read here. She is waltzing with the cab, the bolster, lamp-posts, houses, fences, and trees. Leila continues her observation, failing to be "indifferent like the others": "But every single thing was so new and exciting ... Meg's tuberoses, Jose's long loop of amber, Laura's little dark head, pushing above her white fur like a flower through snow" (ibid). Again, the rendering of vivid and vibrant details of the material world are paired with a dehumanized image of the human body, as they all blend together into a lively assemblage. This is a notable characteristic of all stories discussed in this book: the simultaneous tendencies to anthropomorphize the nonhuman world and to dehumanize the human challenge habitual ontological categories even in the stories of Mansfield and Rhys, which are less obviously experimental than Barnes's.

The intensity of Leila's experience is ironically paired with the apparent shallowness of the Sheridans' interactions: "I've never known your hair go up more successfully than tonight!" (337). On the other hand, a moral reading in which a character is judged as "shallow" would not do justice to the affect that accompanies the depictions of regulated female experience in the story. The impersonal narrator as an agent who selects these quotes for satirical perusal invites ironical reflection on the part of the reader, but the lived experience of the material details of the story that the focalization evokes calls for a recognition of an acute emotional reality: the reader is asked to live through this reality before or while reflecting on the ironies of the situation. In this story, the dynamics of impersonality are not reducible to the dynamics between narrator, focalizer, and reader; rather, as we have seen, even the acute experience, as it is entangled with the material world, becomes impersonal in the sense of the intensity of *a* life, an affective current running through bodies that encounter each other in spaces regulated by both social and material forms.

The intensity and the blending of the human and the nonhuman in a fantastical tone continues, as Leila enters the venue:

> Leila put two fingers on Laura's pink velvet cloak, and they were somehow lifted past the big golden lantern, carried along the passage, and pushed into the little room marked "Ladies." [...]

> A great quivering jet of gas lighted the ladies' room. It couldn't wait; it was dancing already. When the door opened again and there came a burst of tuning from the drill hall, it leaped almost to the ceiling. (ibid.)

In another vision with an ironical pointer toward the social order, the young women appear thing-like as they are shoved into the "ladies' room" for embellished in front of mirrors before being sent to the ball room to encounter the young men waiting there. The array of lively things, however, is again necessary for the full effect of this critical gaze to manifest. The things act as the basis of the affective, experiential power that is unique to fictional works' performative potential as political acts in the world. There also seems to be an affective surplus: as in Barnes's stories, the things are so plentiful that they all but engulf the human characters, who themselves are not far from being treated as thing-like by other characters in the fictional world as well as by the narrator. Furthermore, as in the other party stories, the things can be read as symbols of an oppressive, even if aesthetically enchanting, social order. However, I want to suggest that the things in this story, too, in fact have a double duty: they also act as carriers of a counter-narrative, not in spite of their material otherness to the human that would signify the dehumanizing effect of the society, but because this otherness affords a change of perspective in relation to the norms of the human life, conceived of as a story. This becomes even clearer as we look at the form of the entire story and the roles that things take throughout its development.

As the vivid description continues, Leila gets her hands on a "darling little pink-and-silver" program leaflet with a pink pencil, in the noisy ball room where she feels "that even the little quivering coloured flags strung across the ceiling were talking," and she is filled with a "rush of joy" (338). This feeling is shown to replace an earlier "rush of longing" recounted in an analeptic step into Leila's experience "forsaken up-country home." The girls wait for the men to approach from the other side of the room to claim their slots in the leaflet, which for instance Head reads accurately as another signifier for the commodification of the young women (Head 1992, 129). As they go through the motions of the dances and exchange comments about the quality of the floor and other balls, Leila wonders why her partners are not more interested in her thrilling experience of newness. One of Leila's partners is an old, "fat" and "shabby" man, who, uniquely, does take an interest in this matter and makes it the subject of a sermon that changes the appearance of the whole scene for Leila, in the epiphanic crux of the story. The man reveals that he has been going to dances for 30 years, but adds that Leila "can't hope to last anything like as long as that," painting a picture of her future as one of the maternal on-lookers on the stage, smiling at their daughters but sad to be no longer participating in the performance itself. Leila is shocked, becomes homesick and does not want to dance—but does so out of politeness, and is again quickly drawn into the magic of the event, aided by various forms of materiality: "The lights, the azaleas, the dresses, the pink faces, the velvet chairs, all became one beautiful flying wheel." (MCS, 343.) When she again bumps into the "fat man," she no longer recognizes him. Another lighting of a "little lamp" of epiphany has been negated. But is this disillusionment all that the story's critical voice conveys?

"Her First Ball" reads as a grim commentary of a social environment that glorifies female bodies as aesthetic objects—but only for a few years, after which they become maternal generators of new girl-objects. The whole narrative is bound to Leila's point of view, following her excitement, disillusionment, and re-entry into the sphere of what appears as an illusion. On the other hand, as Head (1992, 130) points out, it would be a simplification to read this story as a moralist account of a young girl's frivolous mind, rather than as a commentary of impersonal social structures that she is part of and that partly negate the agency of an autonomous, individual subject. This kind of structural reading is in an intriguing tension with the affective intensity of the story. A symbolist reading, on the other hand, might note the fairytale qualities of the milieu and the curious archetypal tinge of the old "fat man," whose presence at the ball seems curious if read in a realist framework. Yet this kind of reading does not quite account for the affective and material richness of the story, either, which I claim its critical potential rests on.

As seen in the quotations, Leila's experience of the ball is copiously framed with lively, human-made, that is, artificial things, often composed into frantic lists reminiscent of the catalogues that decentralize the human in Barnes's stories. On the other hand, her memories of her country home that punctuate the dance, even though they are located on the liminal space of the veranda, offer images of nonhuman nature: crying owls, moonlight, and stars. Thus, the story toys with the opposition of "real" and "illusion," exploring how Leila's perception is tricked by the dance spectacle to attribute the liveliness of natural things to lamps, dresses, and cab seats, and frames this as fetishist trickery, another instance of modern "table-turning" (see Chapter 2). However, in my reading the story displays a further polyphony in its blending of perceptual and ontological categories of human and nonhuman, natural and artificial, subject and object, which occurs in Leila's descriptions of both "worlds": the glittering normative fairyland of the dance, where things come to life and humans look like flowers (just as in Rhys's stories), and the liminal space of the veranda, where baby owls cry "more pork" and stars have "long beams like wings" (MCS, 338). The *zoe*-full natural world, here exemplified by Leila's home and childhood, becomes opposed to the *bios* of the ball, but the sphere of artificial, human-made, and culturally coded things in fact shares in the indifferent materiality of the rustling forest—as it does in relation to the dead body in "The Garden Party" and the children as heavenly bodies in "Sun and Moon." We are shown how Leila is seized, helped by her more experienced friends, into a ritualistic dance of life (in the sense of *bios*) that accompanies the actual dancing activity; she quickly learns the steps of the first, as she has already learnt those of the second at boarding school dance classes. She is enjoying herself, but the epiphanic encounter reveals how restricted and transitory her enjoyment is. The whole performance aims at marriage, which will swiftly lead to her becoming one of the on-looking ladies, who have done their reproductive duty and are no longer needed on the dance floor. The man, on the other hand, even when he is aged and unappealing, keeps frequenting dances apparently just to be close to young girls; his presence is made disturbing both by how it reveals the basic normative rules of the game, grotesque in themselves, and how he seems to be able to abuse them.

This annihilating vision of a woman's life is presented in a language that attributes something like "a life" to everything, including the nonhuman elements that make up the dance event. Seen this way, Leila's perceptions of the lively clothes and furniture are parallel with the lively memories of the "up-country" home; they respond affectively to the liveliness in her, however objectified her body may appear, both as the stimulation of her senses and her imagination and as an affective body in the world with potential for more than she is "used" for. Again, to foreground the character as a material being does not mean seeing her as merely an object. This vibrant life, which a reader can easily resonate with even without much interpretive effort, is posed against the objectifying logic that governs the life of a woman, the normative story that we can see scripted for the young girl, in which a short "blazing moment" is followed by drabness and isolation, and both phases are always already marked by a biopolitical control of bodies. While the sociocultural commentary of the story is poignant, I maintain that the description of the vivid experience of the material world need not be seen in opposition to it, as focus on a "personal" illusion that would lead to the reading of the events of this story, too, as an account of equally personal disillusionment and re-entry into illusion. Rather, the experiential liveliness can also be read as "impersonal," as expressive of *a* life that is not commensurate with the restrictive and oppressive, discriminating boundaries attached to "a human life." Therefore, its impersonality extends to an ontological level, beyond the sociological one that most readings of Mansfield's stories remain on.

Furthermore, this reading avoids trying to fit the story that has a cyclical structure of a whirling ballroom into a linear mold in which its last word would also *have the last word*, create a totality of meaning and judgment. This, like my previous ones, is an affirmative reading that uses the vitalist and nomad notion of *zoe* in a manner similar to Braidotti, who sees such interpretations as politically indispensable and envisions ethical opportunities in shifts of perspective on life. As Braidotti writes, "the process of confronting the thinkability of a Life that may not have 'me' or any 'human' at the center is actually a sobering and instructive process" (Braidotti 2011, 333). In what remains of this chapter, I wish to test such affirmative reading on a story that, unlike the enchanted accounts of a lively world of things discussed so far, combines thing-power with negative affects such as fear and anxiety.

In "Prelude" (1918), Mansfield makes a maximal use of the alternation between different focalizers throughout its twelve sections. The sections with Kezia's point of view are another example of her use of the perception of a child to create a lively material world that seems to bleed out of tacit categories. However, the same is true of the sections focusing on Kezia's mother Linda's relations with the world, and thereby this reaches beyond the oppositions of the adult world of *bios* and the "natural" bare childhood experience. The story starts with an evocative scene of another house turned inside out, as it were, as the family is moving to a new location. Here, too, the categories of humans and things become mixed in the focalization and narration of both Kezia and Linda. The children are looking at furniture that has been removed from its home and is now scattered in the yard, "tables and chairs standing on their heads on the front lawn" (MCS, 11), which echoes the lively furniture in the party stories. Linda, who seems distressed by but also passive in the face of the project of moving, has chosen an array of "absolute necessities" in bags and boxes to be taken with the first load—and the readers learn, in an instance of authorial irony, that the children are not among such necessities and are to follow in a later carriage. "We shall simply have to cast them off," Linda says, with a "strange little laugh." (12). She continues in her mind, in free indirect discourse, repeating the anthropomorphic illusion of the furniture on the lawn in Kezia's perception:

> How absurd they looked! Either they ought to be the other way up, or Lottie and Kezia ought to stand on their heads, too. And she longed to say: "Stand on your heads, children, and wait for the storeman." (Ibid.)

The situation of moving house, like the parties in the previously discussed stories, acts as an enchanted, enchanting sphere in which the world becomes defamiliarized and thereby its phenomena intensified. Harking back again to the previous chapter, the tables standing on their (nonexistent) heads recall Marx's famous fetish table standing on its head. However, the way they function in the story makes them more than a clever metaphor with cultural-historical allusions: the topsy-turvy tables and chairs are a product of a style of perception and experience that seems to be shared between the child and the mother and that the narrative asks its readers, too, to share in.

The beginning image is amusing, but the characters' experience of the lively world soon gains more sinister tones. Waiting for the storeman, wandering in the empty house and looking out one of the windows, Kezia experiences a moment of dread in which she senses the presence of a mysterious "IT" right behind her (15). In a parallel scene later in the story, left alone in her new bedroom, Linda stares idly at the wallpaper and feels the poppy pictured on it come alive:

> She could feel the sticky, silky petals, the stem, hairy like a gooseberry skin, the rough leaf and the tight glazed bud. Things had a habit of coming alive like that. Not only large substantial things like furniture but curtains and the patterns of stuffs and the fringes of quilts and cushions. How often had she seen the tassel fringe of her quilt change into a funny procession of dancers with priests attending. ... For there were some tassels that did not dance at all but walked stately, bent forward as if praying or chanting. How often the medicine bottles had turned into a row of little men with brown top-hats on; and the washstand jug had a way of sitting in the basin like a fat bird in a round nest. (27)

Here, the sense of the world of things being alive that was part of the experience of the children and even the young Laura in the previously analyzed stories is explicitly named in Linda's reflection: she is aware of this being perhaps an abnormal experience, yet she also reports it in a relatively disinterested manner, instead of framing it as weird or unnatural. The scene invites the reader to pay attention to these intense experiences and presents them as a part of everyday life, open for readerly identification, but also as another intensified, enchanted sphere of experience. It would be easy to label this experience as hallucination and to connect its central motif intertextually with Charlotte Perkins Gilman's "The Yellow Wallpaper" (1892), for instance. This is a justified reading, but I wish to turn the attention elsewhere. Remaining on the level of fictionality instead of psychology, a more relevant question is what kind of work the presentation of such experiences does in the story, and in relation to the other, plentiful presentations of lively things in other stories by Mansfield. Linda's experience of the wallpaper certainly has a central role in the story's critical commentary on the normative human life with its categories of gender, domesticity, and the family, but as with the previous readings, I want to investigate more closely how exactly the lively things contribute to such aims, and what post-anthropocentric by-products they might have.

The first lively thing in Linda's experience is a reference to the "nat-ural" world, but the rest of the items in her description are firmly human-made things housed in the domestic interior. As they come alive, however, they recall elements that are outside the home, either as part of the organic nonhuman world or the lively human world of performance and rite: the illustration becomes a real flower, the tassels and bottles become performers or priests, and the jug becomes a bird. Throughout the story, this kind of perception, be it the work of imagination or hallucination, is tied to Linda's problematic feelings about her marriage and motherhood and her occasionally voiced desire to escape the con-fines of the home. It seems like the loss of control over her own body that she experiences in relation to having children is linked to the sense that the thing-bodies surrounding her are also beyond her control, and lead a life of their own. In this sense, their liveliness appears as malevolent, as in the passage following the one quoted above where they become an ominous "THEY," parallel to Kezia's "IT":

> But the strangest part of this coming alive of things was what they did. They listened, they seemed to swell out with some mysterious important content, and when they were full she felt that they smiled. But it was not for her, only, their sly secret smile; they were members of a secret society and they smiled among themselves. Sometimes, when she had fallen asleep in the daytime, she woke and could not lift a finger, could not even turn her eyes to left or right because THEY were there; sometimes when she went out of a room and left it empty, she knew as she clicked the door to that THEY were filling it. And there were times in the evenings when she was upstairs, perhaps, and everybody else was down, when she could hardly escape from them. Then she could not hurry, she could not hum a tune; if she tried to say ever so carelessly—'bother that old thimble'—THEY were not deceived. THEY knew how frightened she was; THEY saw how she turned her head away as she passed the mirror. (27–28)

The sinister characteristics of the lively things seem to have to do with their independence and their pairing with inactivity, stillness, and even paralysis in Linda. They also connect with masculine and phallic motifs, resonating with her dream of a bird that swells up and becomes a baby. Linda feels like the things want something from her, and if she does not stay still enough "something" will happen. This section of the story ends with her being engulfed by experiences of the liveliness of the world that take a multisensory form: "everything had come alive down to the minutest, tiniest particle, and she did not feel her bed, she floated, held up in the air," as she is "listening with her wide open watchful eyes" (28).

This bleeding of experience over the categories of living and dead causes bodily disorientation and horror instead of the bliss experienced by Laura when faced with similar categorical blending. In "Prelude," another crossing of boundaries occurs when the children witness the decapitation of a duck and the grotesque aftermath in which the headless corpse waddles toward the stream. The children's reactions display different, learned and spontaneous attitudes in front of death: Lottie laughs, Kezia panics and begs Pat to "put head back," while Isabel, the eldest, borrowing a simile from the world of things, "squeals" a quaint and detached observation: "It's like a little engine. It's like a funny little railway engine." (MCS, 46). Enchantment and horror blend as death and a boundary-crossing body disrupt the everyday.

Linda too seems enchanted by the things come to life, but also assigns to them the role of THEY, a sort of recalcitrant superego that watches her and inhibits her actions. In this regard, the things could be read to stand for the social order that Linda experiences as oppressive: the domestic things have power over her by virtue of the patriarchal power they represent. Yet she is also shown as attached to her things, more than she is to her children. In any case, she is affected by them, and through her focalization the reader is also invited to be. The dead duck can be an enchanting spectacle and then suddenly a terrifying reminder of some life power beyond the confines of the human self; taken outside of the sphere of childhood, in Linda's experience, the lively things become similarly associated with the fear of a loss of self, a sociocultural construction. This is the sphere of epiphany that the blends of ontological categories create in the other stories discussed in this chapter. In "Prelude," however, the force of convention that in other stories waters down the enlightening experience of a world without subjects and objects is shown in a more threatened, protective stance, whereby the shaky position of the ideal of human subjectivity, scaffolded by the patriarchal norms and structures of the home, becomes more visible and uncanny. Like the children, Linda experiences as frightful not only the enchanted world of lively things but also everything that is supposed to guard her against it; Kezia seems to share parts this adult experience, even though she is still part of the sphere of childhood. The focus on liveliness of the thing world as a threat to the unified self recalls the fantastical and gothic elements used by Rhys as vehicles of social critique by way of undercutting the subject positions of patriarchal characters such as the Commandant of "A Spiritualist" (see Chapter 2).

Other women in the story are shown to be in an equally problematic position in relation to the categories of subjects and objects. Beryl's friend Nan Pym comments that men are interested in Beryl because she has "got so much animation" (57), which seems ironical especially as compared to the spectacle of the automaton-like dead duck. In the context of sociocultural normativity her "animation," meaning her interest in life and sensuality, swiftly leads to the commodification of her body, its acquisition, and thereby the kind of stagnation that her older sister in the married situation is feeling. As in Rhys's critical stories, animation of the object world and objectification of the human body run parallel to each other and become mixed: the objectified bodies of women can also appear as "animated," in the same way as the wallpaper of an oppressive home, or a dead duck. By way of such grim comparisons, Mansfield makes a critical point, but at the same time, the relentless blending of categories in the story actually does performative work against obvious divisions of the world into subjects and objects.

Reading the theme of impersonality from a postanthropocentric perspective, the "blazing" characteristics of the moments Mansfield writes can be seen as the product of a life force that cannot be fit into the big, linear, and end-focused narratives of human life, defined by events and sequentiality. These events also define fictional stories: the event of marriage, for instance, as the end point in the story of any female character, and correspondingly the undue importance granted to the endings of stories (see Nash 2013, 5). Mansfield's "Prelude" is not a prelude to this grand event and a testament to its power, narratively, to end fictional female lives. Rather, in the case of Linda, the story explores what happens after the marriage, and the continuity of life in the biological sense of procreation that becomes an area of shapeless, uncontrollable horror by virtue of the counter-narrative of animation that it houses. For Beryl, the marriage narrative is one she lives by; this, like the order of the social dance in "Her First Ball," is shown to feed her "animation" but also feed *on* it and use it up. Importantly, as in Rhys's stories, the patriarchal ideology is presented as dehumanizing and objectifying, but the female characters affected by it are presented as subjects full of life, or rather, *a* life. They are bodies beyond the logic of subjects and objects, who remain carriers of experience that reading them merely as victims of objectification and commodification would not do justice to. The sociocultural meanings that loom behind the things affect the way the characters' perception of them is rendered, but the experiences described and evoked in the stories are not reducible to these meanings. Like Mansfield's party stories, "Prelude" and "A Doll's House" draw on a perceived vividness of the world that the story, like the sphere of the events and emotional states it describes, can ascribe to things, "making the stone stonier." Children in "Sun and Moon," and "A Doll's House" are delighted by simulacra, the little lamp, and the hazelnut doorknob, because these things reproduce the magical power that is inherent in their life-size domestic models—this can be seen as one analogy to how Mansfield's stories harness and amplify the power of things by presenting us with fictionalized versions of them. That they "seen the little lamp" remains significant for the experience and thereby the understanding of the reader, even if the following events and statements seem to discredit the blaze of the epiphanic moment.

In Mansfield's stories, the liveliness of things exposes the inconclusiveness of normative life events that more traditional narratives with for instance a marriage plot or an omniscient narrator characterizing people and events from a stable point of view might help to sediment. The impersonal, polyphonic assemblage of life in stories like "Prelude" keeps happening in its many forms, from children being born to a dead duck walking to the things in the house taking control of its visitors or inhabitants. Through different perspectives and thereby different relations to material things, readers are invited to share in this chorus of experiences without ascribing to it a totality of significance or morality. In "Prelude," the impersonal effect of traveling focalization is paired with and strengthened by the impression that not only the human characters but also the whole world around them seems to be alive, and the children and grown-ups share the experience of this lively presence between them. On the other hand, they could be said to make a counterforce to the tone of impersonality, namely the acutely affective power of the experience, as the characters' encounters with the material world are rendered in experiences of bodily and affective intensity that invite the involvement of the embodied reader. As I showed in relation to Barnes's stories and as I will keep pointing out in the next chapter, impersonal, nonhuman life-forces and embodied affective involvement are not in opposition to one another, but in fact act together. The stories bring the "bare" quality of life, which Laura fails to articulate in a propositional statement, to play in the form of experiential knowledge created in category-blending assemblages of the affective, affecting, and affected bodies of readers, books, fictional characters, and motifs. The essential presence of the nonhuman is a significant discovery in relation to Mansfield's stories, as it brings this presence also closer to the heart of canonized modernism.

Notes

1 Barnes 1958, 8.
2 Some observations of this chapter about "Dusie" and "Finale" were made while writing earlier articles (Oulanne 2016; 2020).
3 At the background of this view, also influenced by Latour's actor network theory, are empirical findings in the field of quantum physics. However, Barad shows how the approach is applicable to a wide array of philosophical questions, including ones pertaining to society, ethics, art, and literature. The

entangled phenomena she is referring to are mixtures of what we might habitually call material and cultural; in this vein of thinking, the distinction may cease to matter. Barad emphasizes the importance of nonhumans in distributive agency (Barad 2007, 32), yet she also specifies that the use of the term 'posthumanism' in denoting a "posthumanist performative account" "marks a refusal to take the distinction between 'human' and 'nonhuman' for granted" (Ibid.), a will to see them as profoundly entangled, and to investigate the very practices in which these poles are enacted (139).
4 As Bill Brown (2016, 29) notes, the Germanic origin of the words "thing" and "ding" refers to a gathering, a political assembly.
5 I thank Heta Pyrhönen for initiating this observation.
6 See McLoughlin 2013, Wilson 2013, Armstrong 2005.

Works Cited

Agamben, Giorgio. 1998. *Homo Sacer: Sovereign Power and Bare Life.* Stanford: Stanford University Press. DOI: 10.1515/9780804764025.

Alaimo, Stacy. 2010. *Bodily Natures: Science, Environment, and the Material Self.* Bloomington: Indiana University Press.

Armstrong, Tim. 2005. *Modernism: A Cultural History.* Cambridge: Polity Press.

Banfield, Ann. 1987. "Describing the Unobserved: Event Grouped Around an Empty Centre." In *The Linguistics of Writing: Arguments between Language and Literature*, edited by Nigel Fabb, Colin MacCabe, Derek Attridge, and Alan Durant, 265–285. Manchester: Manchester University Press.

Barad, Karen. 2007. *Meeting the Universe Halfway: Quantum Physics and the Entanglement of Matter and Meaning.* Durham, NC: Duke University Press. DOI: 10.1215/9780822388128.

Bardolph, Jacqueline. 1994. "The French Connection: Bandol." In *Katherine Mansfield: In from the Margin*, edited by Roger Robinson, 158–172. Baton Rouge: Louisiana State University Press.

Barnes, Djuna. 1936/2007. *Nightwood.* London: Faber & Faber.

Barnes, Djuna. 1996. *Collected* Stories. Los Angeles: Sun & Moon Press.

Barnes, Djuna. 1958. *The Antiphon.* New York: Farrar, Straus & Giroux.

Bennett, Jane. 2010. *Vibrant Matter: A Political Ecology of Things.* Durham, NC: Duke University Press. DOI: 10.1515/9780822391623.

Boscagli, Maurizia. 2014. *Stuff Theory: Everyday Objects, Radical Materialism.* New York: Bloomsbury.

Brown, Bill. 2016. *Other Things.* Chicago: University of Chicago Press. DOI: 10.7208/chicago/9780226283166.001.0001.

Braidotti, Rosi. 2011. *Nomadic Theory: The Portable Rosi Braidotti.* New York: Columbia University Press.

Caracciolo, Marco. 2014. *The Experientiality of Narrative: An Enactivist Approach.* Berlin: DeGruyter. DOI: 10.1515/9783110365658.

Childs, Peter. 2016. *Modernism.* New York: Routledge. DOI: 10.4324/9781315679679.

Deleuze, Gilles, and Félix Guattari. 1980/2013. *A Thousand Plateaus:. Capitalism and Schizophrenia.* Translated by Brian Massumi. London: Bloomsbury.

Deleuze, Gilles. 2001. "Immanence: A Life." In *Pure Immanence: Essays on A Life*. Translated by Anne Boyman, 25–33. New York: Zone Books.

Drewery, Claire. 2011. *Modernist Short Fiction by Women: The Liminal in Katherine Mansfield, Dorothy Richardson, and Virginia Woolf*. Farnham: Ashgate. DOI: 10.4324/9781315595948.

Fludernik, Monika. 1996. *Towards a 'Natural' Narratology*. London: Routledge. DOI: 10.1515/jlse.1996.25.2.97.

Fullbrook, Kate. 1986. *Katherine Mansfield*. Brighton: Harvester Press.

Hanson, Clare. 1985. *Short Stories and Short Fictions, 1880–1980*. Basingstoke: Palgrave MacMillan. DOI: 10.1007/978-1-349-17685-4.

Harrington, Ellen Burton. 2007. "Introduction." In *Scribbling Women and the Short Story Form: Approaches by American and British Women Writers*, 1–14. New York: Peter Lang Publishing.

Head, Dominic. 1992. *The Modernist Short Story: A Study in Theory and Practice*. Cambridge: Cambridge University Press. DOI: 10.1017/CBO9780511735356.

Kaplan, Sydney Janet. 1991. *Katherine Mansfield and the Origins of Modernist Fiction*. Ithaca: Cornell University Press. DOI: 10.7591/9781501736841.

Kimber, Gerri. 2015. *Katherine Mansfield and the Art of the Short Story*. Basingstoke: Palgrave Macmillan. DOI: 10.1057/9781137483881.

Kimber, Gerri, and Angela, Smith, eds. 2014. *The Poetry and Critical Writings of Katherine Mansfield*. Edinburgh: Edinburgh University Press.

Mansfield, Katherine. 1973. *Collected Stories*. London: Book Club Associates.

McHale, Brian. 2014. "Speech Representation." In *The Living Handbook of Narratology*, edited by Peter Huhn et al. Hamburg: Hamburg University. Accessed November 5, 2020. http://www.lhn.uni-hamburg.de/article/speech-representation.

McLoughlin, Kate. 2013. "Introduction: A Welcome from the Host." In *The Modernist Party*, edited by Kate McLoughlin, 1–24. Edinburgh: Edinburgh University Press. DOI: 10.3366/edinburgh/9780748647316.003.0001.

Mitchell, J. Lawrence. 2011. "Introduction." In *Katherine Mansfield and Literary Modernism*, edited by Janet Wilson, Gerri Kimber, and Susan Reid, 1–10. New York: Continuum.

Nash, Katherine Saunders. 2013. *Feminist Narrative Ethics: Tacit Persuasion in Modernist Form*. Columbus: Ohio University Press.

New, William. 1999. *Katherine Mansfield and Metaphors of Form*. Montreal: McGill–Queen's University Press.

Newman, Daniel Aureliano. 2019. *Modernist Life Histories: Biological Theory and the Experimental Bildungsroman*. Edinburgh: Edinburgh University Press. DOI: 10.3366/edinburgh/9781474439619.001.0001.

Oulanne, Laura. 2020. "*Djuna Barnes and Queer Interiorities*." In *How Literature Comes to Matter: Post-Anthropocentric Approaches to Fiction*, edited by Marlene Karlsson Marcussen, Sten Pultz Moslund, and Martin Karlsson Pedersen, 153–171. Edinburgh: Edinburgh University Press.

Oulanne, Laura. 2016. "Affective Bodies: Nonhuman and Human Agencies in Djuna Barnes's Fiction." In *On_Culture: The Open Journal for the Study of Culture 2*. http://geb.uni-giessen.de/volltexte/2016/12351.

Ramazani, Vaheed. 1988. *The Free Indirect Mode: Flaubert and the Poetics of Irony*. Charlottesville: University Press of Virginia.

Robinson, Roger, ed. 1994. *Katherine Mansfield: In from the Margin*. Baton Rouge: Louisiana State University Press.

Rohman, Carrie. 2009. *Stalking the Subject: Modernism and the Animal*. New York: Columbia University Press. DOI: 10.7312/rohm14506.

Rohman, Carrie. 2007. "Revising the Human: Silence, Being, and the Question of the Animal in *Nightwood*." *American Literature*, 1: 57–84. DOI: 10.1215/00029831-2006-071.

Shklovsky, Viktor. 1917/2004. "Art as Technique." In *Literary Theory: An Anthology*, edited by Julie Rivkin and Michael Ryan. Malden: Blackwell Publishing, 15–21.

Smith, Angela. 2013. "Looking at the Party With You: Katherine Mansfield's Party Stories." In *The Modernist Party*, edited by Kate McLoughlin, 80–94. Edinburgh: Edinburgh University Press. DOI: 10.3366/edinburgh/9780748647316.001.0001.

Taylor, Clare L. 2003. *Women, Writing, and Fetishism 1890–1950: Female Cross-Gendering*. Oxford: Oxford University Press.

Taylor, Julie. 2012. *Djuna Barnes and Affective Modernism*. Edinburgh: Edinburgh University Press.

Van Gunsteren, Julia. 1990. *Katherine Mansfield and Literary Impressionism*. Amsterdam: Rodopi.

4 Touching Things

> It was odd, she thought, how if one was alone, one leant to things, inanimate things; trees, streams, flowers; felt they expressed one; felt they became one; felt they knew one, in a sense were one; felt an irrational tenderness thus [...] as for oneself.
>
> Virginia Woolf: *To the Lighthouse*[1]

Feeling for and being touched by material things is not easily expressed in the language of literary studies. Emotions tend to be attributed to readers, characters, and possibly (implied) authors, while things are there for support, projection, and mediation: like in Woolf's passage quoted above, they are leant to "if one is alone" and felt for "as for oneself." But as the previous readings in this book have suggested, there is more to things than this kind of role as the surrogates of human contact and self-reflection. In Barnes's, Mansfield's, and Rhys's stories, material things appear in affective assemblages with the human characters. They resonate with the senses of characters and thereby readers; they participate in the social circulation of feeling, and in relations of empathy and sympathy; they are present, either silently and invisibly or conspicuously, in the affective progression of a story. They are entangled with the human characters, but like in the cases of power and agency, not only to be used by them and to support them. In this chapter, I examine to what extent material things are there for human bodies and minds to "lean on" and to what extent they call for more ontological investigation implied by Woolf's "became one" and "knew one."

Touch is an intriguing example of the intermingledness of agency, materiality, and affects. "Touching" refers equally to physical contact and emotional effects, like its cousins "feeling" and "moving." Its use in the context of affective phenomena calls attention to the embodied characteristics of affective experience, which also connects it with the material world: it suggests that emotion or affect happens when two surfaces meet. Following Eve Kosofsky Sedgwick, "a particular intimacy seems to subsist between textures and emotions" (Sedgwick 2003, 17).

Touching is also in a curious relation to agency: as Merleau-Ponty famously suggests, touching and being touched occur simultaneously to both parties in the event, and consequently, it becomes harder to distinguish between the subject and object, active and passive party of the event, even though the two surfaces touching one another remain separate instead of merging together (Merleau-Ponty 1968, 133, 147). In Sedgwick's words, touch "makes nonsense out of any dualistic understanding of agency and passivity" (Sedgwick 2003, 14). Touch can be a means to experience one's own body as other and thereby a potential postanthropocentric gesture (Barad 2015, 1), but touching things and the sense of resistance they offer is seem to be partly responsible for the experience of the corporeal boundaries of embodied phenomenological subjectivity (Colombetti 2013, 9).

To study how the things in Barnes's, Mansfield's, and Rhys's short stories touch their readers, I turn to a variety of approaches to touching and feeling. Instead of the more cognitively and socially oriented notion of "emotion," I generally rely on "affect" and "affectivity" as umbrella concepts that can encompass emotional phenomena as well, or even denote the general "interestedness" and value ladenness inherent to all life (Colombetti 2013). This usage draws on different approaches to affect theory, especially the Spinozist-Deleuzean branch that aligns with new materialism (Deleuze and Guattari 2013; Coole and Frost 2010; Bennett 2010). However, as the interaction between materiality and sociocultural norms and meanings is of central interest here, my discussion will also draw on the feminist phenomenology of feelings in Sara Ahmed's work. As this chapter looks more closely at the ways the texts potentially engage and interact with their readers, I will further develop my method of reading affective materiality, using 4E approaches to cognitive science and phenomenology, especially to find ways of addressing the reader as an embodied, feeling mind. According to Karin Kukkonen (2014), the focus on the embodiment of the reader adds to the "implied reader" by accounting for the ways making sense of fiction relies on how the body functions in the material world: how it uses predictive processing and the affordances of the world in sensorimotor actions. This also resonates with David Herman's reframing of modernism as the art of evoking experiential, lived worlds (Herman 2011). I will investigate what an anti-anthropocentric perspective to bodies—thing and human alike—means for the study of affective interactions in fictional worlds and in reading.

The chapter will begin and end with Mansfield's stories, proceeding from tea time as a locus of normative happiness and homeliness to affective travels with touching things that become incorporated into human experience. In between, I will discuss the problematic expressions of happiness, belonging, and empathy in relation to real and imaginary things in Rhys's stories, the universalizing empathy of Mansfield's "Miss

Brill," and the way Barnes's stories are structured around touching and feeling that seem to escape psychological definitions of affective phenomena. Beside a way of reading affective materialities, what emerges in this chapter is a further confirmation of how the materiality and affectivity of things, even as they appear to be in the service of oppressive structures (and are thereby employed as vehicles of irony by the authors) requires us to try on shifts of perspective that may have profound consequences on the categories through which we see the world, including the worlds of modernist short stories. My way of reading affective materialities means bringing into focus the ways stories use the sensory experiences of the material world to touch their readers, and how this, like their experiments with nonhuman agency, has so far unexplored ontological and ethical consequences.

Nice Things: Materiality and Positive Affect in Katherine Mansfield's and Jean Rhys's Stories

"Don't get excited. You know what happens when you get excited and exalted, don't you? [...] And then you know how you collapse like a pricked balloon, don't you?" Sasha Jansen warns herself in Jean Rhys's *Good Morning, Midnight* (Rhys 1985, 351). It is almost a commonplace that Rhys's heroines are unhappy, alienated, and down-and-out. Her characters are usually set away from any home, in hotel rooms, streets, or cafes of a city that they seem to be only visiting, even if indeterminately. Their attitude toward the world outside is marked by a sense of alienation and even hostility. When the characters experience positive feelings, it often comes with a caveat for the risk of overdoing it, and an acute sense of its fleeting nature. However, as Laura Frost notes, pleasure is a "dominant concern" in Rhys's texts, although it has been overlooked in favor of negative emotions (Frost 2013, 163). In fact, moments of pleasure and happiness, belonging, empathy, and sympathy are notably intense even in the bleakest stories, and they often seem to come about with the help of material things. Rhys herself, interviewed in *The Paris Review*, states: "I've never written when I was happy. I didn't want to" (Vreeland 1979, 224). On the other hand, in *Harper's Magazine* a year earlier, she attempts to defy the role of a victim ascribed to her, largely based on her heroines; an assumption that "I have never had any good times, never laughed, never got my own back, never dared, never worn pretty clothes, never been happy, never known wild hopes or wilder despairs" (Rhys 1979, 70). This comment suggests a Rhysian connection between "pretty clothes" and "good times" as well as the recognition of the inherent complexity of both.

Similarly, in Katherine Mansifeld's short stories, material things are connected with problematic and ambiguous feelings often attached to belonging, domesticity, and the gendered norms that accompany them.

Things offer comfort, but they may also gesture toward a sense of imprisonment and alienation. Her stories are often, rightly, read through the idea of a "double discourse," in which earnest and touching expressions of feeling are always undermined by irony (Dunbar 1997), or through the existentialist notion of alienation, as opposed to authentic selfhood, including the gendered alienation and victimization of women in particular (see Kaplan 1991, 118–119; Kokot 2011, 71). Yet, some readers also pay attention to the way the affectivity of the stories engages readers in spite of the irony (Besnault-Levita 2011). As my previous analyses have shown, things are often read as vehicles of such irony, but they also carry the affective load of the story, and thereby a surplus of meaning that prevents them from being exhausted by an ironical reading. Through reading first Mansfield and then Rhys, I suggest that a focus on materiality and embodiment added to the sociocultural discussion of emotion can help in acknowledging the latter dimension without it undermining the first, to appreciate the critical aspects of both Mansfield's and Rhys's work without ascribing excessive victimhood to their characters, or limiting the discussion of the stories to an assessment of the characters' social worlds, but rather taking further the discussion of interaction between levels of sensory imagination and interpretive meaning making in reading fiction.

Things in Katherine Mansfield's stories evoke social and political norms and issues recognizable to readers, often accompanied by an affective charge that exceeds the everyday use connotations of the thing. The stories invite a reading in which emotional phenomena are located in the intersubjective, social sphere, as an effect of the "circulation" of signs and objects, as Sara Ahmed puts it (2004, 45). In Ahmed's approach, emotions are not reducible to objects, nor are they a subjective phenomenon, but in constant movement between the two, something shared and socially defined. Social groups are defined by an orientation toward the same "objects" as "happy" ones (Ahmed 2010, 35). These include such conceptual objects as family and marriage, but also manifest in concrete things that provide the material frames for these institutions. As we saw in the party stories, for instance, Mansfield's material things build communities and support norms but also invite readers to see the cracks and conflicts inherent in them. They complicate feelings of belonging located in the sphere of domesticity, for instance, as the home becomes the locus of both normative life and impersonal life forces.

The Burnells' house in "At the Bay" (1922), as well as in the other stories of the same cycle ("Prelude" and "The Doll's House," both discussed in Chapter 3), functions as an expression of the gendered divide of the home space and the affective dynamics it gives rise to. Close to the beginning, after finishing a frantic process of getting Stanley Burnell on his way to work, the women of the house appear thankful and relieved: "their very voices were changed as they called to one another; they sounded warm and loving and as if they shared a secret" (MCS, 213). Beryl ceremonially offers another cup of tea to her mother, while Alice, the servant, "used the precious tank water in a perfectly reckless fashion" when washing the dishes: "'Oh, these men!' said she, and she plunged the teapot into the bowl and held it under the water even after it had stopped bubbling, as if it too was a man and drowning was too good for them" (ibid.). The teapot explicitly stands for the man, but it is not necessary to look for formal or symbolical connections between the two. Rather, the effects of the image rely on a combination of sociocultural meanings inscribed on them and their material presence: Alice takes revenge on the teapot, because that is what she is holding at the moment, just like Beryl's gay tea-pouring is the readiest material expression of her relief in the moment. On the other hand, the fact that the women are holding teapots is itself a result of a normative system that ascribes forms of service both to female family members and paid employees. The women are touching teapots, and in the story they become vehicles of an affective charge as physically recognizable everyday things and partici-pants in scenes in which gendered structures are played out. For the reader, they appear in contact with the human bodies of characters, whereby normativity is paired with materiality.

Following Kukkonen and Caracciolo (2014, 261), characters' fictional minds should be considered as embedded in the material and social reality, and engaged in by readers with embodied reactions: the char-acters' feelings and attributions of meaning make sense as rooted in the material world. Furthermore, what is of interest here is the way the material world often seems to not only house these feelings but also add to them and even act against them. For example, "All Serene" (1923) also stages a scene around an affective teapot, depicting a married couple having breakfast:

> He leaned over the back of her chair, his hands on her shoulders; he bent down and lightly rubbed his cheek against hers, murmuring gently but with just enough pride of proprietorship to make her flush with delight, "Give me my tea, love." And she lifted the silver teapot that had a silver pear modelled on the lid and gave him his tea.
>
> (MCS, 482–483)

The story pairs the crudely explicit reference to proprietorship with the lived joy the couple is shown to experience playing the socially accep-table parts of husband and wife, sharing in the "happy objects" of matrimony that condense in the detailed image of the teapot and the transaction it allows for. There are hints that the happiness is not without cracks: the husband seems to be obviously lying about the contents of a letter. At the end of the story, the man again leaves the house, but this time Mona, the wife, without a supporting presence of her partner, suddenly feels forlorn and out of tune with the material surroundings:

> The grey chairs with the fuchsia-coloured cushions, the black and gold carpet, the bright green silk curtains might have belonged to anybody. It was like a stage setting with the curtain still down. She had no right to be there, and as she thought that a queer little chill caught her; it seemed so extra-ordinary that anything, even a chair, should turn away from, should not respond to her happiness. (487)

The teapot obediently plays its part as a prop in the breakfast arrangement, ready-to-hand and thereby almost invisible—were it not for its presence in the literary assemblage presented to the reader. In the latter scene, the materiality of things exposes the constructedness of Mona's happiness: left alone with the things, she feels alienated from the ideas of life they help build, and the house that she fantasizes about showing to "the self she had been before him" (486), to experience her happiness more fully. In the end, the things seem to exceed their role as set pieces and in their irresponsiveness suggest that the narrative of happiness that Mona is weaving is somehow lacking. The furniture becomes present-at-hand instead of ready-to-hand in Heideggerian terminology. This might tempt a reading in the spirit of Bill Brown's thing theory, also in the Heideggerian tradition, in which the thing exerts recalcitrance as their means of agency (Brown 2004, 4–5). Things indeed remain others and thus to an extent mute in their materiality in relation to the human characters, but I would argue that they are not impenetrable to the affective shifts between bodies. This is especially true as we remember that we are dealing with *fictional* things, whose presentation in the story evokes a set of potential sensations in addition to and as a basis of the sociocultural meanings of happiness they are attached to.

Recalling Iser's notion of the "repertoire" (Iser 1978, 70; see Chapter 2), literature never shows us either things or norms "as they are," but rather recontextualizes them, while also evoking what we are already experientially familiar with. As in my readings of Mansfield's stories in the previous chapter, I want to view the things in her fiction not so much as recalcitrant and receding from the sphere of human emotions, as they seem far too entangled in it for this. Rather, they appear as a presence of affective materiality that nevertheless remains indifferent to the repertoire social norms ascribed to it, while the frame of fiction also actively recontextualizes both the things and the norms. The furniture, unlike the teapot, fails to participate in Mona's happiness, not because of an inherent difference in its being, but because of the way the story highlights its otherness in opposition to its use as a culturally embedded and ready-to-hand thing. The things remind Mona of the limits of the social affect of happiness, because they bring with them into the house, and into the story, not only their normative significations as "happy objects" but also their material presence that is not reducible to the normative role—and still reaches the embodied reader on an affective level, lending weight to both the norms and the detachment from them. The same is ontologically true of the teapot, which introduces this indifference to norms covertly even into the "serenely" normative breakfast scene, like we saw other things do in relation to the event of the party in Chapter 3. As Besnault-Levita (2011, 89) suggests, the affective charge of the things cannot be reduced to their ironic function: even as obstinately mute and material, they can't help remaining affective things in the interaction between the text and the reader.

Rhys, like Mansfield, presents a satirical array of such "happy objects" in her stories. At the same time, the stories show the immediate affective power of the things and the ways their materiality in fact complicates the assignment of meanings such as alienation and victimhood to the relationships between women and things. Rhys's "Tea with an Artist" (1927) is another story that connects happiness and belonging with tea drinking. Its British narrator meets a Dutch painter called Verhausen in a Paris café and goes to look at paintings in his apartment, where a surprisingly nice tea service is offered: "On the table was spread a white cloth and there were blue cups and saucers and a plate of gingerbread cut into slices and thickly buttered" (LB, 76). The narrator describes the artist's personality as "comfortable and comforting" (ibid.). The reader is invited to imagine the tokens of "Englishness" and Dutch homeliness in an artist studio in Paris and react to them either by sharing the feeling of belonging, or possibly being amused by this description of precarious belonging and nationalism, with a hint of pity for the characters. But both readerly positions can exist simultaneously. The comfort and happiness depicted are acutely imaginable, but there is always also an ironic touch that exposes the normative dimensions of the characters' taste in what makes a good life. This results in a more affirmative reading than is common in Rhys-criticism (cf. Maslen 2009; Britzolakis 2007; Zimring 2000).[2]

For some of Rhys's characters, happy things are the stuff of daydreams. "He will buy me roses and carnations and chocolates and a pair of pink silk pyjamas and heaps of books" (LB, 111), the narrator of "A Night" (1927) describes a fantasy of a man she is conjuring up in her imagination. These are normative things that are socially acceptable for a young woman to dream of (perhaps with the exception of "heaps of books"). The reader of the stories is invited to experience what it is like to have such dreams, while they are also recontextualized by the fictional frame. The sensory cues given by the mentions of things makes them experientially "real" and lends the feeling of "realness" to the potential emotions experienced alongside them, if we follow cognitive studies about emotions induced by fictional accounts of experience being similar in quality to ones produced by real stimuli (Gibbs 2017). Thus, readers can get a relatively complex sense of emotional activity even within a very short piece of writing like "A Night." The acuteness of the experience thus created exists alongside the readers' ability to distance themselves from the feelings ascribed to the character and see them as presented in an ironical light, for instance. The crux of my argument here is that an ironically sensitive reader does not exist separately from one affectively engaged in some form of sensation and preconscious feeling evoked by the story. In their affective materiality, the things refuse to be read only symbolically or symptomatically. Instead, there is an acute sense of happiness, however short-lived, that the reader has to encounter and feel in some form while reading and interpreting the text. As Jenefer Robinson (2005) suggests, when reading we cannot avoid feeling the emotions evoked by the text, even if we do not agree with the propositional content that gives rise to them. Their cognitive judgment comes later and is always colored by the initial affective appraisal.

To further exemplify this, let us look at another story that plays with the thematics of happiness, belonging, and alienation. Ahmed (2010, 137) calls someone who is "out of line" with the affective community, not oriented toward the same objects, an "affect alien." Rhys's characters are close to this position: they are pictured wanting similar things as the communities around them, but also distancing themselves from them, ironically or out of economic necessity. In "At the Villa D'Or," the Villa in Southern France, which Sara, a writer from Paris's Montparnasse is staying at, is filled to the brim with objects that imply conspicuous material well being. Sara is the "affect alien" of the story, even though she is first shown to enjoy a feeling of belonging in "the depths of a huge arm-chair," observing the room and its people, thinking benevolently: "and very nice too" (LB, 155). However, she also thinks: "At the Villa d'Or life was something shallow … that tinkled meaninglessly … shallow but safe" (159). In the middle of the story, there is a moment of serenity as Sara, while listening to Mrs. Valentine, imagines the "silken caress of the water when she would bathe next morning," meaning either swimming in the sea or taking a bath (159). The story ends with Sara retreating to her bedroom:

> She opened the windows wide and looked out on the enchanted night, then sighed with pleasure at the glimpse of her white, virginal bathroom through the open door: the bath-salts, the scents, the crystal bottles.
>
> She thought again: "Very nice too, the Villa d'Or." (164)

The sensations of the imagined caress of water and the night air create moments of pleasure that are rendered in the materiality of language, in waves of rhythm and rhyme (wide-night-sighed-white). Water as an enjoyable element is reified and brought into the interior in the bathroom bottles that contain salt and scents and simultaneously banalized by these things. This opposition between the natural and the artificial adds to the ironical dimensions of the story. Then again, the sensory pleasure the toilette items are able to create does not need to be questioned in order to appreciate the irony and ambiguity. They are smaller in size, artificial, and conventionally feminine, but none of these features justifies considering them any lesser as affective things that seem to produce an effect that is the opposite of alienation in the human character. The Villa d'Or may be a banal and dehumanizing environment, and staying in it may mean becoming an affect alien, yet Sara's "very nice too" not only denotes an ironical submission to normativity but also the actual pleasure that the Villa affords. Through the enactment of this pleasure, the reader may be more likely to sympathize with Sara's point of view in the ironical and critical sense on an experiential level. This way, a focus on the interaction of material "lived things" with the character and reader as lived bodies adds to a reading that would only be based on Ahmed's phenomenology of social structures. The things are the force with which this repertoire of social norms is presented, and they also become, in their indifferent affectivity, the force that recontextualizes the norms once they have been brought into the sphere of affective interaction with the reader.

To examine the complexities of social and embodied affects of happiness and alienation further, let us look at Rhys's "La Grosse Fifi" (1927), another story set in the *Côte d'Azur*, published in *The Left Bank*. The character of Fifi, a large, rich woman entertaining a gigolo in the hotel, is introduced as a very thing-like woman to the reader through the bewildered eyes of a young man in the company of the focalizer, Roseau. Roseau's answer, however, suggests that Fifi is a more complex figure:

> "Oh my Lord! What's that?"
> "That's Fifi," answered Roseau in a low voice and relaxing into a smile for the first time.
> "Fifi! Of course—it would be—Good Lord!—Fifi!" His voice was awed. "She's—she's terrific, isn't she?"
> "She's a dear," said Roseau unexpectedly. (166–167)

Depending on the point of view, Fifi is either a "who" or a "what." She is presented as a thing, a terrific and awe-inspiring, grotesque apparition of femininity that is well beyond the norm. Nevertheless, Roseau feels "unexpectedly" warmly toward her, while she participates in the objectifying discourse and at times sees Fifi as an abject part of the seedy hotel surroundings. Sympathy and empathy between focal characters and grotesquely presented figures of "bad" women is part of Rhys's stories' general tendency to disrupt notions of sexuality and femininity. Fifi is an especially complex, both lively and thing-like example of such character. When Roseau is crying in her room in a fit of desperation following a large dose of Veronal,[3] Fifi enters to console her with an array of comforting things. She is "[...] wonderfully garbed in a transparent night-gown of a vivid rose colour trimmed with yellow lace," with a "dirty dressing-gown" thrown around her neck (173); she helps Roseau dress in a lace nightgown and hands her a pocket handkerchief; Roseau clutches the flannel sleeve of Fifi's garment, begging her to stay.

Endowed with consoling things, Fifi becomes both a mother figure and a subject of apotheosis, "as kind as God" (175). This is, once again, an ironical statement, but the feelings of affection that accompany it are acutely imaginable, and they form part of the cultural work done by the story to complicate the stereotype of a "bad woman." At the same time, Fifi remains the "terrific" object of a patriarchal gaze until the end of the story, which is also her own melodramatic as well as tragic end, in which she is stabbed by her lover. Roseau's affection toward Fifi makes her temporarily an "affect alien" in the eyes of her acquaintances. Roseau's feeling itself appears complex as well, expressed equally as sympathy toward another suffering woman and as admiration of her appearance as a thing, her kitsch aesthetics and the comforting things she has to offer, possibly also her physical size. Curiously enough, her thing-likeness is part of what renders Fifi a subject in the story. The mentions of corsets, night gowns and dressing gowns wrapped around Fifi's fictional body are cues for the reader to imagine her as a feeling, lived body. She may be a thing, but she is not an object.

In her analysis that combines new materialism and cultural criticism, Maurizia Boscagli reads the striptease scene in the "Nausicaa" episode in Joyce's *Ulysses* (1922) affirmatively, as a description of means for resisting commodification and objectification, in which "the object is alive and has lots of fun" (Boscagli 2014, 91, 94–95). I would argue that this is exactly what Fifi is doing, in Rhys's story, besides her suffering and eventual death in the fictional world. *Ulysses* is intertextually linked to Rhys's work,[4] and Rhys employs many literary devices that resemble Joyce's and also develops them further, at least in the problematic case of the representation of male gaze/female spectacle. When the reader is offered a position that enables embodied identification, the characters, although objectified, become subjectively "alive," and the "fun" they are having can be felt as real. The reader is invited to imagine the embodied being of the characters *by* being shown them as things, as bodies that engage with and incorporate other things. All this can be read and understood on parallel with the ironical, critical tones in relation to normative ideas of happiness, for instance. Furthermore, there is no question of the agency of the female characters: they are not only experiencing bodies but also active ones that use the material means and affective orientations available for the purposes of self-definition, survival, and pleasure.

Abreast all the objectifying gaze and talk, the stories foreground their characters as material bodies surrounded and supported by material things, whose very materiality, albeit fictional, makes them experientially real to a reader. Besides recognizing and enacting embodied sensations and emotions and attributing these to a character, readers can resonate with the way material things participate in such emotions. As Marco Caracciolo argues, referring to the faculties of imagination employed in reading fiction, "If perception is embodied, then mental imagery must be embodied, too. [It is] deeply rooted in our real body and in memories of our past sensorimotor interaction with the environment" (Caracciolo 2014, 160). Clothes are a constant companion in our sensorimotor interactions; they are unusual in their position of partly belonging to that environment, partly incorporated, as it were, to the sensing process and the body itself—a phenomenon that will be examined more closely in the final part of this chapter. Furthermore, from an anti-anthropocentric perspective, it makes sense to see things as incorporated in emotional experience, because our bodies are always already permeated by and embedded in the world of things, and on an ontological level, not that different from them. Read this way, the "thingification" of characters in fact does work against a disproportionate focus on alienation. The thing-like presentation of Fifi's body does not make her any less party of the currents of affectivity in which bodies intra-act with one another—and the same applies to Roseau, Sara of "Villa d'Or," and the narrators of "Tea with an Artist" and "A Night." The stories expose happiness as a socioculturally constructed normative orientation, yet make their reader live through simultaneously enjoyable and uncomfortable feelings, attributable to lived bodies embedded in a world of lived, material things. This is an invitation for the reader to recognize experientially the ways we care for and feel with such things, however "artificial" and however indifferent to our human struggles with norms and orientations they are.

"Feeling with," that is, experiencing empathy towards the nonhuman world, is a special case that merits study in both Rhys's and Mansfield's stories. In her seminal account of narrative empathy, Suzanne Keen (2007, 4) defines it as "vicarious, spontaneous sharing of affect" that occurs between readers and fictional characters, which can then, possibly, lead to *sympathy* ("feeling for") or *personal distress* (feeling upset because of another's suffering). However, the relevance and possibility of "sharing an affect" for empathy has been contested by contemporary phenomenologists, who draw on the embodied tradition stemming from Merleau-Ponty. For instance, Dan Zahavi and Philippe Rochat (2015) suggest that empathy is not about the blurring of borders between the self and other and experiencing the "same" emotion, but accessing or grasping the mental state of the other *through its embodied expression*, while the other remains to some extent other. These accounts, of course, assume a minded creature and an experience, fictional or actual, to empathize with, and things get slightly more complicated when we address empathy and fictional things.

In my reading, acknowledging the conceptual and experiential complexity of both "empathy" and "sympathy" and the general embeddedness of affective phenomena in the material world brings out a variety of tones in relation to them in the texts studied here. If we look back to early discussions of empathy and sympathy, in which their definitions are especially entangled, the focus is surprisingly often on nonhuman, even inanimate entities. Empathy, as well as its German originator *Einfühlung*,[5] was in fact first used in the domain of aesthetics. Vernon Lee uses the concept to refer to an emotional, embodied reaction that occurs in a viewer of a scenery, an object or a piece of art, and the subsequent effect that this reaction has on the perception of the object (Lee 1913, 61–69). The process described by Lee is located between a perceiving subject and a perceived object as an affective relation, in which both actually emerge as active parties, even though there is an assumption that it is always human feeling that is projected into the environment. Sympathy, on the other hand, has been shown to appear problematic for modernist writers because of its implications of inequal power relations (Hammond 2014, 1–2, 20; Martin 2013). However, as Jane Bennett points out, even the concept of "sympathy" stems from earlier uses denoting impersonal affective intensity and is used as such in the work of Walt Whitman, for instance: "currents of 'affection' circulating in the atmosphere to connect different types of beings and things" (Bennett 2020, 29). These etymologies form the starting point of re-reading empathy and sympathy in Rhys's and Mansfield's stories and observing how these phenomena, too, are possibly reimagined by the presence of the affective, material world.

"Let Them Call It Jazz" (1962), in Rhys's later collection *Tigers Are Better-Looking*, begins with an encounter between the first-person narrator Selina, a Caribbean immigrant, and her landlady, who is turning Selina out of her apartment for badly masked racist reasons. As if to make her point more concrete, the landlady kicks Selina's belongings: "When I tell her no, she give my suitcase one kick and it burst open. My best dress fall out, then she laugh and give another kick" (Rhys 1972, 44), she narrates in her dialect. Later, touching the dress evokes an emotional reaction in Selina:

> [...] but it's a funny thing—when I take up that dress and remember how my landlady kick it I cry. I cry and I can't stop. When I stop I feel tired to my bones, tired like old woman. (45)

There is a metonymical relationship between Selina and the dress: one is dumped out of a suitcase, the other out of an apartment, and the imagined proximity of the dress to the surface of Selina's body makes it expressive of something that she feels "to her bones." Readers are invited to imagine that the dress has traveled a long way with Selina, from Martinique, and carries residue of its wearer and their common past. In the story as a whole, the motif of the dress has a structural function: after several misfortunes and a period in prison, Selina finds a job as a seamstress in a department store ("altering ladies' dresses," 62), meets a man who is interested in a prison song she is singing and who sells it forward, not leaving Selina more than five pounds. However, the story ends with a retaliation: "I buy myself a dusty pink dress with the money" (63). The story thus shows the multiple ways dresses are entangled in economic and social inequalities, but the effect of the ending rests on the empathetic, affective connection between Selina and the dress established in the very beginning.

In "Illusion," there is a parallel case of sympathy between character and clothes. The narrator finds a stunning array of beautiful dresses in the restrained Miss Bruce's wardrobe. In a sudden epiphany, she realizes the meaning the clothes have for their owner, but she is also moved by the dresses themselves:

> I went to lock the wardrobe doors and felt a sudden, irrational pity for the beautiful things inside. I imagined them, shrugging their silken shoulders, rustling, whispering about the *anglaise* who had dared to buy them in order to condemn them to life in the dark ... and I opened the door again.

> The yellow dress appeared malevolent, slouching on its hanger; the black ones were mournful, only the little chintz frock smiled gaily, waiting for the supple body and limbs that should breathe life into it ... (LB, 35–36)

The narrator is first shown to imagine the dresses displaying anthropomorphic gestures and attitudes, but then she *sees* the clothes as expressive of personalities, each with its own "appearance" of malevolence, mournfulness, or gaiety, which affects her emotional reaction to them.

In light of our understanding of empathy and sympathy, does it make sense to suggest that these passages as exemplify one or the other? Nonhuman things such as dresses are indeed others to us, and we cannot have the experience of being a dress. In phenomenological accounts, empathy in relation to them would be regarded as based on an illusion, because there is no actual mental state to perceive, yet the experience of empathy as cognitive and affective activity can still be seen as "real."[6] As regards literary fiction, readers are by default in the domain of illusions, as denoted by the title of Rhys's story, quite wittingly, and still capable of being immersed in feelings evoked by them; this experiential proximity between humans and nonhumans is something that literature, as Caracciolo (2016, 140) for instance suggests, is especially equipped to bring about.

Humans constantly communicate with the things around us in a bodily way that does not rely on projection but a tendency to perceive affective tones in the environment and to act out affectivity in collaboration with the environment. Bennett (2010, 120) suggests that a moderate dose of anthropomorphism might in fact work against anthropocentrism, by bringing some aspects of the things closer to human experience and, consequently, suggest that the human is not located above or outside the nonhuman world. This effect, in my reading, is strengthened by the ways the fictional texts locate affectivity and even empathy somewhere in-between human and nonhuman bodies, by making readers live through experiences like Selina's. "Let Them Call It Jazz" stages an encounter in which the perception and expression of emotion become intermingled. A reader can imagine, and respond to, Selina's engagement with the dress. Anna Gibbs (2010) suggests that the contagion of affects in mimetic communication is neither a property of a subject or an object, but a multisensory synchronization of bodies, the capacity for which humans develop in early infancy (cf. Tomkins and Izard 1966, vii). We see emotions we can grasp in human bodies in other things and visual media because of a cross-sensory resemblance in expressive gestures, and these gestures in turn make us go through a mimetic affective experience on a very basic level.

We can imagine that Selina knows, at least figuratively, how it feels to be kicked and to fall like the dress, and sees the dress as expressive of her feelings of disappointment and fatigue, but we can also imagine her as mimicking the dress, experiencing feelings parallel with and in response to its form and tactile feel. The two make up an assemblage toward which readers can be pulled as they engage with the scene and draw on their own experiential traces in doing so. A reader's empathy might be consciously directed toward Selina, a lived, experiencing body, but it is induced by the entire assemblage, as an intensity that is more impersonal than psychological. Readers can identify Selina with the nonhuman thing on both a minimal preconscious level and a level of metonymical interpretation that can also result in narrative empathy.

In "Illusion," the narrator is shown to feel pity and amazement, which distance her from the dresses, but also to imagine what it is like to be a beautiful thing shut in a dark wardrobe. These dresses are not merely metonymies for her experience, or their absent owner's; they are given their own fictional lives. These lives are expressed by the material properties of the dresses. They follow the shape of a human body, but they also remain clearly other, distinctly nonhuman and inanimate, like the chintz frock that waits for a human body to "breathe life into it." Part of the affective communication in the passage is produced by the personification of the dresses, but part is due to their expressive qualities *as material things*. The passage invites mimetic, kinesthetic enactment of the expressive forms of the dresses, with an affective content of its own.

A form of readerly narrative empathy, again, could be evoked by the whole scene, but it is important to note the vitality of the things as affective players in it.

Jean Rhys is clearly among modernist writers skeptical of the power-relations implied by the notion of sympathy. As we have seen, Rhys is associated with stories of alienation and separation between humans, instead of moments of emotional connection. However, my reading has revealed more affirmative political tones in Rhys's writing and surprising possibilities for empathy between characters and things, including thing-like characters. With the help of a brief example I wish to suggest that the same is true of Mansfield's stories,[7] in which emotional connections not always between human minds and bodies, but with nonhuman ones, to look more closely into what J. Lawrence Mitchell (2011, 7) calls "sympathetic magic": the ways in which Mansfield "identifies wholly with an object or animal or gives life to the inanimate."

In one of her popular stories, "Miss Brill" (1920), the eponymous character, an English teacher, is taking a Sunday walk in a French park. She is wearing a fur, which she strokes affectionately and calls "dear little thing" (MCS, 331). In the park, listening to a band, she fantasizes about herself as an actor who is part of a scene enacted every Sunday in the park; reacting to the music, she experiences an intense moment of what seems like universal empathy, encompassing all people and things, coming one by the power of the music: "And Miss Brill's eyes filled with tears and she looked smiling at all the other members of the company. Yes, we understand, we understand, she thought—though what they understood she didn't know" (335). This seems to be an anti-epiphanic moment characteristic of Mansfield, in which a cosmic realization stops short and becomes a platitude when put into words. This is further highlighted by the ending in which Miss Brill hears a young couple make derogatory comments about her and her fur, returns home and lays the accessory back in its box: "But when she put the lid on she thought she heard something crying" (336).

Like Rhys's dresses that are shut in cupboards and suitcases and even get kicked around, the fur becomes a carrier and expression of the emotion of the human character. However, set in the context of the whole story, there is more going on than the projection of emotion: the fur works as an expression because it has an animal form, but also because of a structural, experiential, and embodied parallelism that is there before sociocultural significations are attributed to it. It is contained in a box, taken out and forced to enter again, just like Miss Brill's embodied being escapes her cupboard-like apartment and lonely mindscape, only to be forced back in. In the meantime, however, the fur has been out, and the character has experienced an inexpressible unity with the world beyond her human being. In an intriguing parallel to "The Garden Party" (see Chapter 3), I suggest that the epiphany as the turning point of the story (the encounter with the dead man and the failure to put the experience into words; the inexpressible experience of connection cut short by a mean comment) lingers beyond its negation. The fur may be playing a proxy to Miss Brill, but it is also objectively part of the world of human and nonhuman bodies that she resonates with in the park. The reader can appreciate the irony in the character's failure of communicating her experience, but also receive the experience as communicated indirectly by the whole of the story, with its openings and closures, not just a linear progression that would place undue weight on the end in which everything shuts down. I propose that it is right to view Mansfield as critical of moments of sympathy and illusions of mind reading, but her stories also rely on something like an impersonal, universal empathy to become understood, and thereby complicate the ways of reading empathy in the first place.

A reader of Mansfield's and Rhys's stories is drawn into affective relations between different kinds of bodies and given both human and nonhuman agents to "communicate" and empathize with. It has proven enlightening to look at the things and characters as assemblages, in which they generate the affective engagements together.[8] In my interpretation of the stories discussed here, the boundaries of the self can be transcended not by knowing an "original" mental state in the nonhuman other, as there is none, but by the very fact that mental states are constructed in the assemblage of things and humans, and between fictional assemblages and the reader. In fact, I wish to make the bold suggestion that any instance of narrative empathy on its basic level relies on our everyday experience of being-with-things. The sensory and expressive cues provided by the references to materialities act as suggestions of feeling, in which case it is the entire assemblage of fictional characters and things that solicits the potential basic empathic response, intermingled with cultural issues and interpretations. Navigating these notions and theories around fellow-feeling, we can investigate how literature evokes the relations of self and other in a material, embodied way, and provides readers not only "the experience of the embodied mind of the other" (Zahavi 2014, 55) but also an understanding of this embodied mind as embedded in and extending into the material world.

To sum up, the way material, inanimate things contribute to the affective unfolding of Mansfield's and Rhys's stories shows the texts' complex relations with happiness, belonging, and empathy. Often, reading with materiality in mind, the affective whole changes and some new shades of positive affect in relation to the thing-world emerge beside grim and ironical tones highlighted in earlier research. Paradoxically, the issue of agency becomes more complex as even objectified characters come across as agent-like, mimetically identifiable, lived bodies, in all their thing-likeness. Human and nonhuman bodies become intermingled and take various positions of subjects and objects, and their affectivity is enacted in encounters between the body of the reader and the body of the text. This way, the stories show more varied tones in relation to positive affect and empathy, for instance, than if they were read merely from the point of view of the social relations signified by the things; still, the complexity of emotional phenomena remains. At the same time, they retain their power to recontextualize and invite us to reimagine the oppressive norms at the root of the negative affect also portrayed. In the second part of this chapter, I will look more closely into how fictional material things and their interactions with human bodies contribute to the affective dynamics of stories as a whole.

The Affective Journeys of Djuna Barnes's and Katherine Mansfield's Stories

The previous readings have shown how the meaningful events and actions in the stories of Djuna Barnes, Katherine Mansfield, and Jean Rhys often arise from the affective power or arrangements involving humans and nonhumans. In Djuna Barnes's work, this often takes the shape of *tableaux*, instead of actions, plot or even psychological interest; in Mansfield's, the characters and the world of things become mixed up as the categories of perception refuse to hold up. In the following, I will look more closely into how both writers' stories are structured around this impersonal affectivity. Compared to Rhys's relatively sparing and restrained presentation of emotion, Djuna Barnes's "passionate prose" (Miller 1999, 121) bulges with dramatic affectivity, grand gestures, and intense pleasures. Julie Taylor (2012) argues convincingly that Barnes's writing acts within canonized high modernism as a reminder of the embodied sides of reading. Mansfield's presentation of affect is often more restrained, and the more overflowing emotional passages are often ironically motivated (New 1999, 18–19; Dunbar 1997, 72). Mansfield also criticized other writers for their characters' lack of emotion and interiority, but also complained about the domain of psychology invading literature—emotion, as depicted by her, is crucially embodied and acted out in the world (Hammond 2016, 56–57; Hanson 2016, 23).

In both cases, the stories invite readers to engage with a series of experiences and affects. As Susan Lohafer (1983, 159) observes, the invitation for readers to "go through" an experience can be more prominent in short stories than other fiction. Therefore, they could be said to underscore the "what-it-is-like" characteristics with which all fiction creates knowledge (see Herman 2009, 2). Following philosopher Daniel Hutto, to undergo an experience either actually or imaginatively is the only way to gain this kind of phenomenological knowledge:

> The only way to understand "what-it-is-like" to have an experience is to actually undergo it or re-imagine undergoing it. Gaining insight

into the phenomenal character of particular kinds of experience requires practical engagements, no theoretical insights. This kind of understanding 'what-it-is-like' to have such and such an experience requires responding in a way that is enactive, on-line and embodied or, alternatively, in a way that is re-enactive, off-line and imaginative—and still embodied.

(Hutto 2006, 52)

It is noteworthy that for Hutto, too, both actual and imaginative experience are embodied. To fully appreciate the role of affective things in the stories, and to understand how the kinds of interactions between social and embodied affects examined in the previous section come about, we need to look at how affective connection with "touching things" manifests on a formal level, beyond the psychology of individual characters.

Two of Barnes's stories published in the collection *Spillway*, "Spillway" (1919) and "Aller et Retour," the latter of which was discussed in Chapter 2, begin with an unconventional homecoming of a mother and a transgenerational encounter that is shadowed by death. These concrete and metaphorical journeys are formulated on the level of narrative discourse as a succession of clothes and accessories to be put on and removed and of different surfaces to be touched. Even if the visual sense has a priority for humans and may dominate the cognitive experience of reading, haptic imagination also plays a part (Cave 2016, 35). "Spillway" begins with Julie and Ann, a mother and the daughter, traveling home from a tuberculosis sanatorium in a carriage. Their illness manifests itself in synchronized coughing fits. Its bodily location is highlighted by details of Julie's clothing that evoke haptic sensations: "She took a deep breath, stretching the silk of her shirtwaist across her breasts" (BCS, 268). When they reach the destination, Julie picks Ann up from the carriage, "thrusting her black gloved hands under the child" (269). The movement of the hands seems rapid and slightly violent ("thrusting"), and they are denoted as being one with the black gloves covering them, whose color is transferred to an attribute of the hands. The blackness forms a parallel with the black horses (a standard motif for Barnes) in front of the carriage, and so becomes associated with muscular power that agrees with the force of "thrusting." The child has already been cast as fragile and pale from the illness she is carrying, while Julie seems to be a combination of frailty and exploding strength.[9] The gloves come between the mother and the child, but more as an object incorporated in the sensation than as a boundary.

They enter the house and meet the husband, Paytor, who is aware neither that his wife is coming home, nor that she has a child. After a heated exchange, he disappears in anger into his shooting loft and she is left leaning on her hand by the window. The different senses are painstakingly evoked in this passage:

> Darkness was closing in, it was eating away the bushes and the barn, and it rolled in the odors of the orchard. Julie leaned on her hand by the casement edge and listened. She could hear far off the faint sound of dogs, the brook running down the mountain, and she thought, "Water in the hand has no voice, but it really roars coming over the falls. It sings over small stones in brooks, but it only tastes of water when it's caught, struggling and running away in the hands" [...]. She could hear Paytor walking on the thin boards above, she could smell the smoke of his tobacco, she could hear him slashing the cocks of his guns. (275–276)

A synesthetic affective whole combines vision, sound, touch, and smell out of which Julie composes the aphoristic emblem about running water. The pause in the movement of the main character in the fictional space leads her to an imaginary space that evokes powerful experiences and meta-phorical references to various directions, including the Catholic faith. Between sensations, Julie encounters remembrances, such as of kissing the cheek of the dead priest of her community. Metaphors, emblems, and memories that rely on haptic experience are followed by the action of touching in the storyworld, as Julie begins to rummage through the items of clothing in a chest: "She turned over the upper layer of old laces and shawls until she came to a shirtwaist of striped silk ... the one she had worn years ago, it had been her mother's. She stopped." (ibid.). Here she takes off her gloves, and the way she wonders about not having done that before may surprise a reader with a realization that the gloves have been incorporated in all the previous sensations described in the story. The intensity of these sensations is stored in the motif of the gloves, while removing them exposes Julie's hands to even more acute sensation.

The affective frenzy of "Spillway" may lead to dizziness in the reader, and a similar sensation is evoked in the main character at its ending:

> What could she do, for God's sake, what was there that she could do? [...] "Because I am cold I can't think. I'll think soon. I'll take my jacket off, put on my coat ..."
> She got up, running her hand along the wall. Where was it? Had she left it on the chair?
> "I can't think of the word," she said, to keep her mind on something. [...] She became dizzy.
> "It's because I must get on my knees. But it isn't low enough," she contradicted herself, "but if I put my head down, way down—down, down, down, down ..."
> She heard a shot. "He has quick warm blood—"
> Her forehead had not quite touched the boards, now it touched them, but she got up immediately, stumbling over her dress. (277–278)

In Julie's experience, thinking and doing, abstract ideas and embodied actions seem to fly in different directions, up and down. In the conceptual metaphors that involve verticality, a reader can recognize the folk-psychological idea of mind and body as two separate, vertically arranged areas, yet at the same time the text complicates this vein of thinking. The mind-body dualism becomes fuzzy, and the story makes more sense if we consider its affectivity to arise from the sensation of the materiality of the things. The illness, the child, the house of the husband, and all the material things that Julie touches make an assemblage that drags her down and makes her dizzy; Julie is not only feeling her environment and thinking about it, but "feeling with" and "thinking with" it, looking for her coat not as a metaphor but as a practical means of looking for material support for the socially acceptable emotion that she does not seem to be able to find for a situation that transgresses the norms of marriage and family, and even life and death.

All the affective intensity might be difficult to comprehend on psychological terms, as the case often turns out to be in Barnes's work: there is no conceptualized "explanation" for the excessive affectivity, as Julie Taylor notes (2012, 152–157). The feeling is there, available to readers for grasping and reacting to, in the heated thoughts and sensations evoked by the text. It is possible to read Julie's character in a naturalizing manner, in the sense of attributing to her an interiority or apersonhood composed of knowledge, beliefs, attitudes, and intentions, and besides understanding all of these as fictional constructions (Palmer 2004, 38). In such an approach that follows a cognitivist paradigm, emotion is connected causally with beliefs or judgments and thus can be demonstrated as plausible or not: "cognition causes emotion" (116; see also 113). Barnes's stories do not follow this paradigm, not only in that cognitive states leading to emotion are not described, but in that such states fail to provide a cause or a justification for the overall affectivity presented. The lack of cause does not diminish the affects that resonate in the text, between its animate, inanimate, concrete, and abstract subjects and objects.

The previous passages have offered the reader some scenes of touching in the fictional world, both actual and imagined or remembered by the character, to be interpreted more or less symbolically in relation to illness, death, and motherhood: the water in the hands, kissing the cheek of the dead priest, the mother's shirtwaist, the forehead on the floorboards. In the last passage, the symbolic meanings that could be reached by thinking have escaped, and Julie's hands are bare. Her body seems to struggle for balance and to replace thinking by doing. Approached thus, the jacket, the coat, the wall, the chair, the floorboards, and the dress refuse to yield to symbolism. In "Spillway," the dramatic gesture of bowing down is also an action afforded by the form of the story, the tragic culmination that Barnes teasingly leaves slightly twisted, even awkward, like Julie's gesture of repentance that has not quite finished before it falls apart in her stumbling: has someone been shot and died, is there a punishment or a redemption?[10] All is left open and conceptual explanations miss their mark, yet the affective composition has grasped something that resonates phenomenologically with readers. There is a normative assumption of what Julie is supposed to feel, and she tries out a theatrical and religious gesture of repentance, but its failure and her stumbling create a nonnormative affective surplus. Psychological interpretations simply fail to grasp the affective assemblage that the passage creates.

This cryptic unreachability of Barnes's characters has been characterized by Deborah Parsons as follows:

> Her protagonists resemble silhouettes, or marionettes, who present angular and impenetrable exteriors. Often bizarre and emotionally or physically abusive, and frequently involved in mysterious relationships of strange intensity, they seem to respond to forces which remain inaccessible to the reader.
>
> (Parsons 2003, 23)

According to H. Porter Abbott, characters with "unreadable" minds, common in short stories, tend to be "naturalized" or made more readable by classifying them as types, catalysts for understanding other characters, or symbolic (Abbott 2008, 450–452, 458–459). There are undeniably typified and symbolic dimensions to Julie, Ann, Paytor, and Madame von Bartmann. However, neither symbolism nor typification suffices as an explanation for the *affectivity* of the characters. As Abbott notes, such explanations should not "displace the experience of unreadability" (463), which is ultimately an experience of the unattainability of the other. Indeed, as I have suggested in the previous part of this chapter, the *minds* of the characters may be *unreadable* and other, depending on how we imagine a mind, while *the characters* as fictional agents imaginable as lived bodies remain to some extent open for the reader's experience, exactly like the half-anthropomorphic things that elicit forms of empathy in Rhys's and Mansfield's stories. They function in the texts as bodies that react to other bodies in a shared, lived world, whereby the line between character and a "lived" thing becomes quite thin.

The affective content circulates between things, involves readers, and leaves them with no clear meaning or explanation, but a sense of having touched something beside the book object they are holding. According to Cheryl Plumb (1986, 65), readers are inclined to be sympathetic to Paytor as the one who has been wronged in the story. I would argue that in spite of this potential bias of sympathy, readers are invited to imaginatively and enactively go through Julie's confused and confusing feelings that arise in interaction with the material world around her. Julie is the focalizer of the story, while Paytor remains a distant and archetypal character, standing for the patriarch around whom the whole scheme of family crumbles, like the roof of their living-room. A reader may not feel *for* either of the characters, but the affective structure of the story is a strong invitation to feel *with* Julie, even if only by imaginatively engaging with the fictional surfaces she touches. The intensity of feeling becomes more approachable if we relinquish the search for its psychological cause in an "inner" mind and consider the vibrant material world as an equally plausible source of affect.

"Aller et Retour," as its name suggests, is also constructed around a journey. The narrative begins with a woman on a train from Marseilles to Nice. To be more exact, readers are first given the train, then told that it "had on board a woman of great strength" (BCS, 362). The woman, Madame Erling von Bartmann of Paris, is firmly located in and tightly framed by her material surroundings. Recall the description cited briefly in Chapter 2:

> Her bosom was tightly cross-laced, the busk bending with every breath, and as she breathed and moved she sounded with many chains in coarse gold links, the ring of large heavily set jewels marking off her lighter gestures." (Ibid.)

Her "great strength" is made tangible in her contact with things such as her high boots; she "control[s] the jarring of her body with the firm pressure of her small plump feet against the rubber matting" (ibid.). In the space of half a page, the reader of the story is presented with a tightly packaged parcel of a character, with the sense of a muscular, heavy body resonating in contact with a multitude of materials.

As Madame von Bartmann leaves the train in Marseilles, a cavalcade of experiences for different senses begins. "Noting every object," holding her skirts, she goes from "foul odors" of side streets, by a woman in a doorway "holding a robin loosely in one huge plucking hand," to a ship-chandler's, where she "smell[s] the tang of tarred rope" and on to a side alley, where she "touche[s] the satins of vulgar, highly colored bed-spreads" laid out for sale (363). Again, readers encounter many sensory experiences, but their affective significance for the character remains obscure. Unlike Julie in "Spillway," Madame von Bartmann as a focalizer is, insofar as possible, a detached observer. Readers are only told that she "looked neither pleased nor displeased" (ibid.). When she reaches her hotel, the narrator reports that she is "trying to think," while removing her clothes and washing her hands with a "large oval of coarse red soap" (364). Things and their haptic, visual or olfactory qualities are precisely and experientially described and graspable, and readers are invited to attribute a consciousness to Madame von Bartmann, even if the alleged contents of her psychological mind are out of reach; her thoughts refuse to be formulated completely, apart from the effort of "trying to think" that resonates with Julie's struggles at the end of "Spillway." Madame von Bartmann is constructed as another character whose mind is unattainable for the narrator and the reader, but whose experience can be to some extent imagined via the embodied expression of her body.

The following day, before reaching her destination, the house on the outskirts of Nice, Madame von Bartmann visits a church, where she, too, kneels down: "She turned the stones of her rings out and put her hands together, the light shining between the little fingers; raising them she prayed, with all her vigorous understanding, to God, for a common redemption" (ibid.). This is the first idea of the content of her thoughts that readers are given, and its abstract grandeur resonates with "Spillway." After she has got up, "feeling the stuff of the altar-cloth," the narrative jumps to Nice and the gate of the garden around her house, which she opens "with a large iron key" (ibid.). In the garden she meets her daughter. This meeting, like almost everything that has preceded it, is mute and mediated by a thing—and a glove—and without psycho-narration or other references to nameable emotions: "She still held the key to the gate in her gloved hand, and the seventeen-year-old girl who came up from a bush took hold of it, walking beside her" (365). Madame von Bartmann has been first introduced as a thing seen from without, and now her daughter emerges from a bush, as tightly connected with her surroundings as the mother, and grasping at the same thing, the key. It is easy to see that Barnes suggests a version of an oedipal scheme, a composition that involves a mother, a daughter, and a phallic object; yet it is definitely a variation that may challenge the theme itself.

In fact, the triadic composition is not static, nor are its components even strictly recognizable as separate units. They become enmeshed in each other as well as embedded in the textures of the garden and the shifting positions of bodies and things inside and outside the house. First, the mother answers Richter's questions about Marseilles (not very large but dirty) and Paris ("Paris was Paris") while sitting down on a knoll "warm with tempered grass" that Richter begins to pluck (366). The following, now explicitly emotional exchange is framed once again with gloved gestures:

> Madame von Bartmann drew off one of her tan gloves, split at the turn of the thumb, and stopped for a moment before she said: "Well, now that your father is dead—"
> The child's eyes filled with tears; she lowered her head.
> "I come flying back," Madame von Bartmann continued good-naturedly, "to look at my own. Let me see you," she continued, turning the child's chin up in the palm of her hand. "Ten, when I last saw you, and now you are a woman." With this she dropped the child's chin and put on her glove. (366–367)

Unlike Julie, Madame von Bartmann takes off her glove to touch her child. The mother's response to the child's affective reaction to the mention of death continues her portrayal as strong, brisk, and detached. If there was for a moment a direct contact between two skins, coinciding with an affective burst on the other's part, the more neutral state and a focus on physical touch is restored as the hand returns into the glove. The mother's indifference, however, does not come across in a scandalous or tragic tone. She has been absent for quite a significant time, and while the period of absence itself is not explained, it is in no way presented as a tragic motif, as one would perhaps expect, especially with the death of the father. This is another example of the stories' apparent incompatibility of form and content, affect and circumstance, which reflects a rebellious attitude especially in relation to family norms. Madame can be seen as another empathetically material human body that partakes in the "indifference" of the world of things to such norms.

Madame's lessons in life, which I will discuss in the following chapter, are interrupted by a scene with her playing the piano ("the sparkles of her jewelled fingers bubbled over the keys") and Richter listening in the garden, "shiver[ing] in the fur coat that touched the chill of her knees." Later, Richter plays, "touchingly, with frail legs pointed to the pedals, [...] with thin technique and a light touch" (371). The mother and the daughter are set as opposites: heavy, sparkling, and round versus light, frail, and thin; warmth versus chill. All this is done with the help of haptic expression: a coat touching knees, fingers touching keys and feet touching pedals, all of which result in "touching" music. The gestures of touching reach mostly toward things and from the story toward the reader, while the two characters remain distant from one another. The narrator reports that for the next few days Richter avoids her mother, and then suddenly announces her engagement to an older neighbor. Madame von Bartmann has urged her daughter to experiment and experience the beauty and ugliness of life, an ambition that now seems to be thwarted with the engagement. An ellipsis replaces the event of the wedding and the "*retour*" closes the story in a similar passive description as the "*aller*":

> Within two months Madame von Bartmann was once again in her travelling clothes, hatted and veiled, strapping her umbrella as she stood on the platform [...].
> Once the train was in motion, Madame Erling von Bartmann slowly drew her gloves through her hand, from fingers to cuff, stretching them firmly across her knee.
> "Ah, how unnecessary." (373)

Madame von Bartmann is clothed and placed on the platform as if making visible the hand of the author that has again packaged her in her attire and dropped her in the appropriate place to be transported. The story ends with another gesture of the gloves from another strong and thing-like lady. The feeling behind her sigh is again expressed as (hatted and) veiled, unnamed, and somatic, something to grasp by taking in the pointed event of drawing the gloves through the hand and stretching them across the knee rather than the propositional content of her utterance.

Structurally, "Spillway" and "Aller et Retour" resemble a succession of *tableaux vivants*. Their characters are set in a variety of situations, in relation to and affected by different others in the form of characters or things. The affective charge of "Spillway" seems exaggerated and disconnected from the story and its characters, if the story is read looking for unity of content and form, credible causality, or imaginable minds. In "Aller et Retour," the principal feeling is perhaps one of strain and tension, constrained by corset laces and tight boots, but sparking out when different materials come into contact with one another. None of the affective flashes in the two stories have their grounds in a clearly imaginable mental state of a character. I venture a claim that to do justice to the texts, such grounds need not be looked for. I suggest that we read the affective states of Barnes's characters as not inner states of characters, but as "states of things" in the world. Terence Cave's cognitive poetics could be applied to these stories, too: he sees a poem not as a "rarefied conceptual thing, a creature of the transcendental imagination," but "an ingenious gadget, or a small, compact box that delivers, when one opens it, an explosive cocktail of responses" (Cave 2016, 38). The texts remain affective, even when a reader can have a hard time accounting for the affectivity by way of any imaginary idea of the mind or subjectivity of a character. In Barnes's case, it might simply be too much to ponder upon characters as minded subjects at all: they are bodies with agency, but so are the inanimate objects surrounding them.

One of the features Katherine Mansfield's short stories share with Barnes's is their structuring around affective shifts that arise from and reside in sensory interactions between characters and the details of the material world. They, too, constitute invitations for the reader to undergo an experience, not necessarily to attain a final totality of propositional knowledge or even an epiphany that has a final word. Akin to the intra-actions of Barnes's unconventional women and their worlds, Mansfield's stories harness affectivity and the material world for the purposes of satire and meta-commentary of forms such as the conventional narrativizations of human life we explored earlier in this chapter. This way, the form of her stories indirectly expresses a vision of affective structures as cocreated between human subjects and the material world, while they provide critical explorations of how affects circulate in the social sphere.

"Taking the Veil," (1923) for instance, thematizes and satirizes the power of fictional, narrative experience, and its attachment to both the material world and normative social structures. The story is narrated in third person, focalized by Edna, a young girl who has decided to enter a convent for what come to appear as rather nonsubstantial reasons. From the start she casts herself as the heroine of a story she tells of her life-world, sometimes aligning with her concrete surroundings, sometimes going against them. "It seemed impossible that anyone should be unhappy on such a beautiful morning," she narrates, while making an effort to look "as unhappy as she felt" (MCS, 417). The reason for her grief is that she has fallen in love with an actor when visiting the theater the previous night with her fiancé Jimmy. Edna is reminiscing about these events and imagining future ones while sitting in the garden of a convent—this environment is what leads to her decision to become a nun. In her imagination, she weaves a conventional story that involves the dramatic reactions of her fiancé and her family to her solemn decision, and her subsequent tragic death after saving a stray animal: now she is fondly remembered as Sister Angela. However, as she reaches the end of her narrative, featuring a devastating scene of white-haired Jimmy crying at her grave, she is shaken by the tragedy and fraught with remorse for causing such (fictional) suffering, and swiftly, extatically resolves to return to her life, which is dedicated to fulfilling another conventional narrative that involves Jimmy, a house, a garden, and two children.

Edna goes through the whole affective journey while sitting in place in the garden, and this fictional world within the story is framed by material details of the actual environment. The sacred tone of her fantasy is set by the singing she hears from the convent, and by the black-bound book she is clasping, "as though it were her missal" (420). On the other hand, the environment is also set against her conventional narrative, and she has to make an effort to ignore it. This becomes highlighted when the unfolding of the imaginary tragedy in her mind is interrupted by a nonhuman agent:

> A big bee, a golden furry fellow, crept into a freesia, and the delicate flower leaned over, swung, shook; and when the bee flew away it fluttered still as though it were laughing. Happy, careless flower!
> Sister Angela looked at it and said, "Now it is winter." (421)

As Janet Wilson, for instance, has argued (2014, 219), the assemblage of the bee and the flower is positioned by the ironic narrator as an antidote to Edna's solemn story-within-the-story, but the end of the passage suggests Edna employs the happiness and carelessness to highlight the tragedy of her destiny by contrast. However, for a reader of "Taking the Veil," the material environment unavoidably frames the story. The descriptive passage, along with shorter allusions to the garden surrounding Edna, suggests a continuous potential for a broader vision of life than the one she entertains in her conventional dream.

For Edna, undergoing a fictionalized experience is enough to make her see her present life in a new light and transform the strong emotion governing the beginning of the story. This is a testimony to the power of fiction that can be taken as a cue for reading; however, *Mansfield's* story is different from its character's fantasy in that for its reader, the otherness in the form of the material environment constantly affords a polyphony of meanings and readings, as we have seen the world of things do in the stories discussed in the previous sections of this book, and this plays against the effortless unfolding of a sentimental story with a simple affective outcome. The reader of the story will undergo Edna's affective journey, which can be felt as "real" regardless of its being based on "fictional" stimuli even within the fictional world, but this journey remains punctured with encounters with a material world that both supports the affective shifts and extends beyond them. Following David Herman's re-evaluation of the understanding modernism as the art of interiority (Herman 2011), the goal of "Taking the Veil," too, seems to be the creation of experiential worlds instead of an illusion of interiority. Even though Mansfield's stories are more readily approachable by psychological interpretations and naturalizing readings of characters than Barnes's, they too seem to turn away from attributing emotion simply to human cognition. Rather, affect and emotion appear as complex products of social structures, which the narrative spun by Edna adheres to, and of enactive encounters with the material environment, which extend beyond such simple narratives.

Descriptive passages like the one quoted above offer relatively specific detail of the nonhuman world, as if to encourage the reader's imagination to stray from the story Edna is telling. Correspondingly, this story appears all the more stereotypical because of the lack of such detail. Edna imagines "[giving] away her jewellery *and so on* to her best friends," and the animal she rescues in her fantasy will be "a kitten or a lamb or—*well, whatever* little animal might be there" (MCS, 420, 421, emphases mine). This kind of story is capable of creating an affective outcome in Edna, but in its form and progression and thereby its effect it differs significantly from the more distanced, yet still engaged reading invited by "Taking the Veil" itself. Mansfield offers Edna's feelings as "real" but pairs them with a sense of ambiguity that is not defined by either the beginning or the end, but rather the continuous presence of open possibilities. The material environment can give rise to, enhance and sustain affects but also maintain its own impersonal level, communicating an affective polyphony in the direction of the reader who embarks on the journey offered by the story. Taking an anti-anthropocentric attitude to affects and things seriously means seeing such journeys as co-constituted by different actants, or put more simply, bodies. In my reading, the form and feel of the story rest not so much on a series of actions undertaken by protagonist, or even on a series of things that happen *to* the protagonist, but on affective assemblages and encounters between bodies.

This way a reading of affective materialities supports and expands the view of the short story as an impressionistic form beyond the more traditional forms of arcs and closures, which feeds into its experimental potential also in a political, feminist sense of reshuffling *social* structures (see Hanson 1985, 5–6, 55; Harrington 2007, 4).

Another example of such reconfiguration of structures that merits a closer look is "The Voyage" (1921), which is explicitly structured around a journey. This is also another story focalized by a child. It opens with the image of a boat, to move to sense experience and action prompted by an encounter between the environment, material things, and a human character:

> The Picton boat was due to leave at half-past eleven. It was a beautiful night, mild, starry, only when they got out of the cab and started to walk down the Old Wharf that jutted out into the harbor, a faint wind blowing off the water ruffled under Fenella's hat, and she put up her hand to keep it on. (MCS, 321)

Fenella, the young girl about to make a journey to Picton, in New Zealand, with her grandmother, is introduced first and foremost as a lived, sensing body, yet the descriptive and affective focus the story from the beginning also foregrounds lively thing-bodies, whose contact with human bodies sparks the most meaningful moments of the story. The description of the dark wharf continues: "Here and there on a rounded wood-pile, that was like the stalk of a huge black mushroom, there hung a lantern, but it seemed afraid to unfurl its timid, quivering light in all that black-ness; it burned softly, as if for itself" (ibid.). The passage is one more example of the blending of categories in a child-focalizer's imaginative perception, recognizable in the comparison of wood piles to mushrooms. This creates a poetic sense of the world of things being alive and vibrant, "for itself." The description of the lanterns does not need to be read as a projection of Fenella's state of mind but rather as an aid in creating a sense of her affective, experiential world that becomes enacted in encounters of bodies in lived space. Quoting Herman, modernist narratives suggest that "mental states have the character they do because of the world in which they arise, as a way of responding to possibilities (and exigencies) for acting afforded by that world" (2011, 253). Here I wish to follow this premise while seeing what follows when we foreground the fact that the world Herman is referring to is of necessity a material world that is ap-proached through the senses and which, as we have seen in numerous readings above, is alive and in an independent, affective contact with the reader.

The most important thing-body in the story is Fenella's grandma's umbrella, which she is described carrying from the beginning. The constant physical contact between Fenella and the thing makes it stand

out, but also remain incorporated in the affective experiences: "[...]
Fenella carried clasped to her grandma's umbrella, and the handle, which
was a swan's head, kept giving her shoulder a sharp little peck as if it too
wanted her to hurry" (ibid.). The form of the umbrella affords another
instance of "as if" in Fenella's focalization, to create a blend of thing and
animal with a will of its own and a way of showing it—like the little fur
in "Miss Brill." Fenella can clearly tell the difference between an umbrella and a swan, but the action of the thingly actant gives form to her
state of mind: the feeling of being hurried. When Fenella and her
grandmother look for their cabin, the old woman seems to offer the
umbrella as an anchor, in a manner of a Winnicottian transitional object
(Winnicott 2005), something that resides both in the shared material
world and in the child's imaginary, to help Fenella with the traverse of
the water and into a new period in her life. She urges the child to take
care it does not get caught in the rails when they move about. Fenella,
though, grasps the rail and forgets about the umbrella, yet the readers are
still kept aware that she keeps holding it, carrying the sensation along
with the description of the journey.

When the travelers settle into their cabin, helped by a friendly stewardess, through whom readers also indirectly learn that Fenella's mother
has died, which may shift the affective tone of the story and make readers
reconsider the movements they have observed so far in a new light. The
situation is conveyed to the stewardess indirectly by the travelers' gar-
ments that signal mourning. After the conversation between the stewardess and the grandmother, we also learn that Fenella has spent the
whole time standing shyly against the door, clasping both her luggage
and the umbrella. In bed, when the boat starts to rock violently, Fenella
worries about the umbrella, but her grandmother is again on top of
things and asks the stewardess to lay it down. The description of the
arrival in Picton is interrupted by the grandmother, referring to the
umbrella without the need to name it: "'You've got my—'" / 'Yes,
grandma'" (MCS, 329). When they reach the grandparents' home,
Fenella kisses her grandpa, who brings the umbrella to the readers' attention for the final time: "What's that she's holding? Her grandma's
umbrella?"—at which Fenella smiles and hangs the swan-necked
umbrella over the bedrail, to mark arrival and the end of the story.

The presence of death gives "The Voyage" an affective undercurrent,
which in fact is not so much under as on the sensible surface. It is present
in Fenella's and grandma's black clothes, which blend with the dark
night of their port of departure and the dark waters they cross, being
physically tossed by them, and the ambiance of the spaces that Fenella
grasps, wondering when everything will become less sad. Here the story
is not occupied with using death to disrupt the representation of life
narratives, as in "The Garden Party," for instance; rather, death seems to
already be accepted as part of the structure of a voyage that the story

follows, whereby there is also less observable tension between what could be read as master and counter-narratives. The end of the story is untypically comforting and affirmative, and the grandfather seems to suggest life instead of death in his affectionate manner and white hair, which contrasts with to the dark tones that dominate the story until then.

"The Voyage" has been read extensively in light of its symbolism of darkness and light (see Hanson and Gurr 1981, 96; Rohrberger 1977, 109, Tyler 1991, 44), and it is intriguing to look at how these meanings rest on the materiality of the symbolic elements—a topic that will be studied more closely in the following chapter. Black, of course, as a color of mourning is based on a cultural agreement, but the way it is used in the story in conjunction with crammed spaces, clothes that are not only black but physically constraining (as shown in the lengthy process of taking them off), and the night with its half recognizable, hybrid things, brings an experiential component to support it. In the world, as experienced by Fenella, there is a *feeling* of darkness, and a transition toward light. The umbrella, however, is capable of traversing both worlds and helping Fenella with her own traverse.

Recalling the enactivist paradigm of the cocreation of experience, I wish to suggest that the umbrella is an essential part in producing this feeling in the first place. This is also apparent if we read the story in light of the accounts of distributed agency and affective assemblages and follow the definition of affect as an intensity occurring in-between bodies, human or nonhuman. It may seem intuitive look for support for a similar claim in the phenomenological accounts of affective in-corporation and scaffolding, to address the specific case experientiality of reading, which is exclusive to human bodies. Giovanna Colombetti, for instance, suggests that material objects can be incorporated in the experience, sustenance, and expression of affective states (Colombetti 2016). For example, a coffee cup can be habitually grabbed in need of strength or support; a nice suit can be used to gain self-confidence; a musician's capacity to express emotions and create affective response depends on her interaction with the instrument.

Applied to the study of literature, analyzing experiences of in-corporation becomes complicated. We may approach fiction as a tool that highlight the experiential phenomenon of incorporation by re-presenting occurrences of it, like the relationship between Fenella and the umbrella in Mansfield's story. Her movements, the agency of her body, and her negotiation of the affects involved in the journey are sustained and also potentially toned down by the umbrella. However, as has been maintained throughout the analyses in this book, it is fruitful to view literature as not only a tool for making observations and gaining pro-positional knowledge of the world. Its power relies in readers' affective engagement and participation, and the meanings it communicates are of an experiential kind. When reading "The Voyage," we go on a fictional journey with Fenella. Most of the journey is framed by an interaction with the fictional umbrella, which becomes incorporated in our experience of reading. This, however, is a different case of incorporation than the "real-life" experience that the story draws on, as I maintain that this thing appears to the reader as more similar than different from the character's body. The two together form an assemblage that creates the affective ground on which the meaning of the story rests, instead of the reader fully identifying with the character and "sharing" her experience.

What I suggest is that the story indeed conveys experiential knowledge of what it is like to live in a world of things and taps into experiential phenomena such as affective incorporation. However, besides doing this, it displays a more profound connection between affect and the non-human world, one that opens up for an anti-anthropocentric reading and the shifts of scale required by it. In the phenomenological accounts, the role reserved for nonhuman things is clearly subordinate to the human subject, which also means that they remain in the ontology of "objects" and "subjects" even if they do work toward blurring the line between humans and things as participants in affective phenomena. Thereby they stop short of the aims of my reading to investigate the basic level of meaning making that literary works engage in with material things and bodies. In "The Voyage," the grandmother's umbrella is incorporated in Fenella's affective state, but we can also say that especially considering the reader of the story, the whole affective structure is produced jointly by the fictional bodies of Fenella and the umbrella. As in the example of a musician, both the "instrument" and the human body are needed for the experience to arise in the first place, which is why we can consider them both as its agents if not its experiencing subjects. In the arguably more complicated case of reading fiction, the human lived body, central to the phenomenological approach, is necessarily accompanied by a "lived thing": a fictional locus of experience and affectivity that intra-acts in an assemblage with the human. On a basic level of reading, both appear as "things in the world," and it is the literary form that especially invites such leveled ontology. A study of affects in reading does not need to stick to human-centered approaches; in fact, it can both complement and further complicate them.

From an anti-anthropocentric perspective, we could say that Fenella's body is engaged in trans-corporeal or intra-active relations with the material world, including the umbrella. This makes sense especially when looking at her body as a fictional one, as it is does not appear so clearly removed from the stuff of the nonhuman world around her. Whatever the text evokes is produced jointly by these collections of agencies. Compared with the phenomenological accounts, this angle presents the story as a world of bodies in which affect is not located in the human interiority but manifests in the in-between spaces of assemblages and encounters. Thereby the experiential worlds that Herman ascribes to the modernist interest appear even less focused on interiority than when observed from the phenomenological or 4E point of view that Herman shows to interact fruitfully with the modernist context. What I am proposing is a different scale of observation, which exposes ontological similarities between entities that tend to be considered fundamentally different even in phenomenological accounts.

As we have seen in the previous chapters, fictional accounts of the world can awaken us to these similarities. More specifically, as David Rodriguez (2019, 95) suggests, the effect of scale shifts in literary description in particular invites the realization that human perception is not the only way of accessing the world and thereby works against anthropocentrism. In the case of Mansfield's stories, the shifts of scale are not necessarily tied to the concrete position of the character in the environment, yet they remain tied to the presentation of perception and the techniques of focalization, as it is in this process that the constant shifts between ontological categories take place, without being explicitly thematical. The human experience, even if associated with a character sitting in the garden or leaning against the wall in a boat cabin, is always already "elsewhere" and "other" as well, in a world of distributed affects and agencies, which the literary artifact is capable of highlighting by slight shifts of perspective and voice and interruptions from the nonhuman world that call the reader's attention. "The Voyage" does position Fenella as the focalizer and the subject of experience, but while doing so it leans entirely on the presence animated nonhuman agencies, which destabilize her position as the only meaningful, affective body in the assemblage of the story.

Things such as the umbrella are indeed building blocks of experiential worlds in short stories as well as in real life, but the readings in this chapter show that their affective presence exceeds such functions. Even such crucially "human" emotions as happiness, belonging, alienation, and empathy, as well as the phenomena of touch and affective incorporation, are located quite firmly in the world of things—which does not exclude the humans. Thereby the presentation of affects in these stories requires a scalar shift to the level of the basic constitution of the world as one filled with affective bodies. This kind of reading may also call for a shift in the ways we read modernism: in Brian McHale's influential account (1987), for instance, modernism is seen as primarily engaged with the epistemological questions of interpreting and understanding the world, while postmodernist fiction moves to question the modes of being themselves. Once again, we should remember that Barnes's, Mansfield's, or Rhys's modernist stories are not precociously postmodern, or postanthropocentric, for that matter, but reading from the point of view of the latter approach shows how they tempt questions such as "what is a world?" and "what is the mode of existence of a text?" cited by McHale as postmodernist concerns (10). The following, final chapter in this book will keep looking into the ways the texts make meaning with things and the ways things as they are perceived and presented in fiction invite basic ontological questions as well as epistemological and ethical ones.

Notes

1 Woolf 2004, 59.
2 Britzolakis and Zimring focus on the alienating effects of the capitalist society on women, while Maslen focuses on the conditions of depression and melancholia.
3 A brand name of a barbiturate commonly used as a sleeping aid in the first part of the 20th century.
4 For instance, the ending of Rhys's *Good Morning, Midnight* (1939), in which Sasha Jansen succumbs to the sexual advances of a fellow hotel guest, echoes (ironically) the end of Molly Bloom's monologue: "Yes — yes — yes ..." (Rhys 1985, 462.)
5 Coined in 1873 by Robert Vischer and first applied to social cognition by Theodor Lipps.
6 I thank Anna Ovaska for an especially careful reading and discussion of this section, and of conceptual suggestions in relation to empathy.
7 I develop this view at length elsewhere (Oulanne 2021Oulanne Caracciolo 2021).
8 This is something that Suzanne Keen's account of narrative empathy also recognizes, as she points out that narrative empathy is not merely about character identification, but also involves other actants and surroundings as well as the whole narrative situation (Keen 2013).
9 Susan Sontag has famously explored and challenged the habitual metaphorical connections of tuberculosis with unexpressed passion (Sontag 1978).
10 Kneeling and bowing also have intratextual significance: they are central motifs in *Nightwood* (with its evocative ending in which Robin crouches in front of Nora's dog and its chapter titles "Bow Down" and "Go Down, Matthew").

Works Cited

Abbott, H. Porter. 2008. "Unreadable Minds and the Captive Reader." *Style* 42 (4): 448–66.

Ahmed, Sara. 2010. *The Promise of Happiness*. Durham: Duke University Press. DOI: 10.1215/9780822392781.

Ahmed, Sara. 2004. *The Cultural Politics of Emotion*. Edinburgh: Edinburgh University Press. DOI: 10.4324/9780203700372.

Barad, Karen. 2015. "On Touching: The Inhuman That Therefore I Am (V.1.1)." Forthcoming in The Politics of Materiality, edited by Susanne Witzgall. https://planetarities.sites.ucsc.edu/wp-content/uploads/sites/400/2015/01/barad-on-touching.pdf. Accessed May 21, 2017.

Barnes, Djuna. 1996. *Collected Stories*. Los Angeles: Sun & Moon Press.

Bennett, Jane. 2020. *Influx & Efflux: Writing Up with Walt Whitman*. Durham: Duke University Press. DOI: 10.1215/9781478009290.

Bennett, Jane. 2010. *Vibrant Matter: A Political Ecology of Things*. Durham: Duke University Press. DOI: 10.1515/9780822391623.

Besnault-Levita, Anne. 2011. "'—Ah, what is it?—that I heard': Voice and Affect in Katherine Mansfield's Short Fictions." In *Katherine Mansfield and Literary Modernism*, edited by Janet Wilson, Gerri Kimber, and Susan Reid. Edinburgh: Edinburgh University Press.

Boscagli, Maurizia. 2014. *Stuff Theory: Everyday Objects, Radical Materialism.* New York: Bloomsbury.

Britzolakis, Christina. 2007. "This Way to the Exhibition: Genealogies of Urban Spectacle in Jean Rhys's Interwar Fiction." *Textual Practice* 21 (3): 457–82.

Brown, Bill. 2004. "Thing Theory." In *Things*, edited by Bill Brown, 1–22. Chicago: University of Chicago Press.

Caracciolo, Marco. 2016. *Strange Narrators in Contemporary Fiction: Explorations in Readers' Engagement with Characters.* Lincoln, NE: University of Nebraska Press. DOI: 10.2307/j.ctt1gr7dkd.

Caracciolo, Marco. 2014. *The Experientiality of Narrative: An Enactivist Approach.* Berlin: DeGruyter. DOI: 10.1515/9783110365658.

Cave, Terence. 2016. *Thinking with Literature: Towards a Cognitive Criticism.* Oxford: Oxford University Press. DOI: 10.1093/acprof:oso/9780198749417. 001.0001.

Colombetti, Giovanna. 2016. "Affective Incorporation." In *Phenomenology for the Twenty-First Century*, edited by J. Aaron Simmons and J. Edward Hackett, 231–48. London: Palgrave Macmillan. DOI: 10.1057/978-1-137-55039-2.

Colombetti, Giovanna. 2013. *The Feeling Body: Affective Science Meets the Enactive Mind.* Cambridge, MA: MIT Press. DOI: 10.7551/mitpress/ 9780262019958.001.0001.

Coole, Diana, and Samantha Frost. 2010. "Introducing the New Materialisms." In *New Materialisms: Ontology, Agency, and Politics*, edited by Diana Coole and Samantha Frost, 1–43. Durham: Duke University Press. DOI: 10.1215/ 9780822392996.

Deleuze, Gilles, and Félix Guattari. 1980/2013. *A Thousand Plateaus. Capitalism and Schizophrenia.* Translated by Brian Massumi. London: Bloomsbury.

Dunbar, Pamela. 1997. *Radical Mansfield: Double Discourse in Katherine Mansfield's Short Stories.* London: MacMillan. DOI: 10.1007/978-1-349-25910-6.

Frost, Laura. 2013. *The Problem with Pleasure: Modernism and Its Discontents.* New York: Columbia University Press. DOI: 10.7312/columbia/9780231152723. 001.0001.

Gibbs, Anna. 2010. "After Affect: Sympathy, Synchrony and Mimetic Communication." In *The Affect Theory Reader*, edited by Melissa Gregg and Gregory Seigworth, 186–205. Durham: Duke University Press.

Gibbs, Raymond W. 2017. "Embodied Dynamics in Literary Experience." In *Cognitive Literary Science: Dialogues Between Literature and Cognition*, edited by Michael Burke and Emily T. Troscianko, 219–37. Oxford: Oxford University Press. DOI: 10.1093/acprof:oso/9780190496869.003.0012.

Hammond, Meghan Marie. 2016. "Mansfield's Psychology of the Emotions." In *Katherine Mansfield and Psychology*, edited by Clare Hanson, Gerri Kimber, and Todd Martin, 56–67. Edinburgh: Edinburgh University Press. DOI: 10. 3366/edinburgh/9781474417532.001.0001.

Hammond, Meghan Marie. 2014. *Empathy and the Psychology of Literary Modernism*. Edinburgh: Edinburgh University Press. DOI: 10.3366/edinburgh/9780748690985.001.0001.

Hanson, Clare. 2016. "Katherine Mansfield and Vitalist Psychology." In *Katherine Mansfield and Psychology*, edited by Clare Hanson, Gerri Kimber, and Todd Martin, 23–37. Edinburgh: Edinburgh University Press.

Hanson, Clare. 1985. *Short Stories and Short Fictions, 1880–1980*. Basingstoke: Palgrave MacMillan.

Hanson, Clare, and Andrew Gurr. 1981. *Katherine Mansfield*. London: Palgrave Macmillan.

Harrington, Ellen Burton. 2007. "Introduction." In *Scribbling Women and the Short Story Form: Approaches by American and British Women Writers*, edited by Ellen Burton Harrington, 1–14. New York: Peter Lang Publishing.

Herman, David. 2011. "1880–1945: Re-Minding Modernism." In *The Emergence of Mind: Representations of Consciousness in Narrative Discourse in English*, edited by David Herman, 243–72. Lincoln, NE: University of Nebraska Press. DOI: 10.2307/j.ctt1df4fwq.12.

Herman, David. 2009. *Basic Elements of Narrative*. Chichester: Wiley-Blackwell. DOI: 10.1002/9781444305920.

Hutto, Daniel D. 2006. "Impossible Problems and Careful Expositions: Reply to Myin and De Nul." In *Radical Enactivism: Focus on the Philosophy of Daniel D. Hutto*, edited by Richard Menary, 45–64. Philadelphia and Amsterdam: John Benjamins. DOI: 10.1075/ceb.2.06hut.

Iser, Wolfgang. 1978. *The Act of Reading: A Theory of Aesthetic Response*. Baltimore: Johns Hopkins University Press.

Kaplan, Sydney Janet. 1991 *Katherine Mansfield and the Origins of Modernist Fiction*. Ithaca: Cornell University Press. DOI: 10.7591/9781501736841.

Keen, Suzanne. 2013. "Narrative Empathy." In *The Living Handbook of Narratology*, edited by Peter Hühn et al. Hamburg: Hamburg University. Accessed November 8, 2020. http://www.lhn.uni-hamburg.de/article/narrative-empathy.

Keen, Suzanne. 2007. *Empathy and the Novel*. Oxford: Oxford University Press. DOI: 10.1093/acprof:oso/9780195175769.001.0001.

Kokot, Joanna. 2011. "The Elusiveness of Reality: The Limits of Cognition in Katherine Mansfield's Short Stories." In *Katherine Mansfield and Literary Modernism*, edited by Janet Wilson et al., 67–77. New York: Continuum.

Kukkonen, Karin. 2014. "Presence and Prediction: The Embodied Reader's Cascades of Cognition." *Style* 48 (3): 367–84.

Kukkonen, Karin, and Marco Caracciolo. 2014. "Introduction: What is the 'Second Generation'?" *Style* 48 (3): 261–74.

Lee, Vernon. 1913. *The Beautiful*. Cambridge: Cambridge University Press.

Lohafer, Susan. 1983. *Coming to Terms with the Short Story*. Baton Rouge: Louisiana State University Press.

Mansfield, Katherine. 1973. *Collected Stories*. London: Book Club Associates.

Martin, Kirsty. 2013. *Modernism and the Rhythms of Sympathy: Vernon Lee, Virginia Woolf, D.H. Lawrence*. Oxford: Oxford University Press.

Maslen, Cathleen. 2009. *Ferocious Things: Jean Rhys and the Politics of Women's Melancholia*. Newcastle Upon Tyne: Cambridge Scholars Publishing.

McHale, Brian. 1987. *Postmodernist Fiction*. London: Routledge. DOI: 10. 4324/9780203393321.

Merleau-Ponty, Maurice. 1968. *The Visible and the Invisible*. Translated by Alphonso Lingis. Evanston: Northwestern University Press.

Miller, Tyrus. 1999. *Late Modernism: Politics, Fiction and the Arts Between the World Wars*. Berkeley: University of California Press.

Mitchell, J. Lawrence. 2011. "Introduction." In *Katherine Mansfield and Literary Modernism*, edited by Janet Wilson, Gerri Kimber, and Susan Reid, 1–10. London: Continuum.

New, William H. 1999. *Reading Mansfield and the Metaphors of Form*. Montreal: McGill-Queen's University Press.

Oulanne, Laura. 2021. "Containment and Empathy in Katherine Mansfield's and Virginia Woolf's Short Stories." In *Narrating Nonhuman Spaces*, edited by Marco Caracciolo, Marlene Karlsson Marcussen, and David Rodriguez. New York: Routledge.

Palmer, Alan. 2004. *Fictional Minds*. Lincoln: University of Nebraska Press.

Parsons, Deborah. 2003. *Djuna Barnes*. Tavistock: Northcote House.

Plumb, Cheryl J. 1986. *Fancy's Craft: Art and Identity in the Early Works of Djuna Barnes*. Selinsgrove: Susquehanna University Press.

Rhys, Jean. 1985. *The Complete Novels*. New York: W.W. Norton.

Rhys, Jean. 1927/1984. *The Left Bank & Other Stories*. Salem, NH: Ayer Company.

Rhys, Jean. 1979. *Smile Please: An Unfinished Autobiography*. London: André Deutsch.

Rhys, Jean. 1968/1972. *Tigers are Better-Looking*. London: Penguin Books.

Rhys, Jean. 1978. "Q&A: Making Bricks without Straw." *Harper's Magazine* 1978: 70–1.

Robinson, Jenefer. 2005. *Deeper than Reason: Emotion and its Role in Literature, Music, and Art*. Oxford: Oxford University Press. DOI: 10.1093/ 0199263655.001.0001.

Rodriguez, David. 2019. "Spaces of Indeterminacy: Aerial Description and Environmental Imagination in 20th Century American Fiction". Dissertation, Stony Brook University.

Rohrberger, Mary H. 1977. *The Art of Katherine Mansfield*. Norman: Oklahoma State University Press.

Sedgwick, Eve Kosofsky. 2003. *Touching Feeling: Affect, Pedagogy, Performativity*. Durham: Duke University Press. DOI: 10.1215/9780822384786.

Sontag, Susan. 1978. *Illness as Metaphor*. New York: Farrar, Straus & Giroux.

Taylor, Julie. 2012. *Djuna Barnes and Affective Modernism*. Edinburgh: Edinburgh University Press.

Tomkins, Sylvan, and Carroll E. Izard. 1966. *Affect, Cognition, and Personality: Empirical Studies*. London: Tavistock Press.

Tyler, Graeme. 1991. "Mansfield's The Voyage." *The Explicator*, 50 (1): 42–3.

Vreeland, Elizabeth. 1979. "Jean Rhys: The Art of Fiction No. 64." *The Paris Review* 76: 219–37.

Wilson, Janet. 2014. "Veiling and Unveiling: Mansfield's Modernist Aesthetics." In *Journal of New Zealand Literature*, 32 (Part 2): 203–25.

Winnicott, Donald W. 1953/2005. *Playing and Reality*. London: Routledge. DOI: 10.4324/9780203441022.

Woolf, Virginia. 1927/2004. *To the Lighthouse.* London: Vintage.

Zahavi, Dan. 2014. *Self and Other: Exploring Subjectivity, Empathy, and Shame.* Oxford: Oxford University Press. DOI: 10.1093/acprof:oso/9780199590681.001.0001.

Zahavi, Dan, and Philippe Rochat. 2015. "Empathy ≠ Sharing: Perspectives from Phenomenology and Developmental Psychology." In *Consciousness and Cognition* 36: 543–53. DOI: 10.1016/j.concog.2015.05.008.

Zimring, Rishona. 2000. "The Make-up of Jean Rhys's Fiction." *Novel* 33 (2): 212–34. DOI: 10.2307/1346080.

5   Making Sense of Things

"Is that all?" Said Julie.
"Isn't it enough?" Answered Wendell.
"And what does it mean?" said Timothy.
"Well," answered Wendell, "much and little, like all wisdom."
— Djuna Barnes: *Ryder*[1]

Stories like Barnes's, Mansfield's, and Rhys's invite readers to make sense of them on many levels. We have seen how the things and materialities they present resonate with our basic experiences as well as our cultural knowledge. The stories invite affective immersion as well as symbolic interpretation and a critical consciousness. We have also seen how these levels tend to be intermingled: critical, reflective considerations are built on and modified by embodied, pre-reflective affectivity. The stories' tendency to highlight similarities between things and people has affective, aesthetical, and embodied grounds, as well as ethical implications. In this chapter, these levels of meaning, reading, and interpretation are investigated further in all three writers' work. Based on the observations about the affectivity of stories in the previous chapter, I want to go further in developing a way of reading materiality that does justice to the varieties of sense-making called for by the stories of the three writers. I will suggest, further, that these observations apply to modernist short fiction more broadly and are valuable also for the continuing discussions about how we read fiction in general.

I start from a premise rehearsed throughout this book that reading is an embodied activity rooted in the material world. Rita Felski, in a contribution to the critical discussion around different ways of reading,[2] suggests we ought to see reading as an "embodied mode of attentiveness that involves us in acts of sensing, perceiving, feeling, registering and engaging" (Felski 2015, 176). Here I wish to examine how the evocations of things and materialities and their experientiality invite readers to engage in such acts. According to George Lakoff and Mark Johnson's embodied cognitive approach to literary metaphor (2003), our higher-order, metaphorical capacities of making sense of the world rest on the experience our body and the lived world of things afford in their interaction. We conceptualize the world though metaphors of directions (the future is forward, the past is behind), containers (the mind is a vessel with content), and things as individuals and in groups, based on our sensorimotor interaction with such phenomena. "Higher" capacities of meaning-making can be seen "as growing out of and shaped by our abilities to perceive things, manipulate objects, move our bodies in space, and evaluate our situation" (Johnson 2008, 11). Additionally, material things, even ones evoked in fiction, often come with "tacit meanings" based on the kind of use and interaction they have habitually afforded us (Määttänen 2015, 89). Here I wish to see the basic affective engagement with fictional materialities as expressive and meaningful, not as a separate phenomenon from conscious or intellectual activities to do with interpretation and understanding, but a ground on which the latter are built, or something that permeates it, if we want to avoid a spatially hierarchical metaphor. The aim of this chapter as a whole is therefore not to answer the question "what do the things in these stories mean?" but rather, "how do they mean?"

When looking at the phenomenon of literature, meaning is of course made by means of language. However, it is not an intrinsic property of language or words, but a relational phenomenon brought forth jointly by the text and its reader; as Louise Rosenblatt suggests, the kind of knowledge created by literature is never a transmission but always a result of a "transaction" between the text and a particular reader (Rosenblatt 1995). Seeing our relationship to language as grounded on our bodily being-in-the-world gives reason to view language itself as a set of affordances that restrict our thinking but also enable experimenting with different courses for it. As Terence Cave points out, importantly, language viewed this way does not ontologically precede or determine our thinking (Cave 2016, 54). Furthermore, for Gilles Deleuze, "sense" emerges as an effect or an event that is neither a property of linguistic or logical propositions nor a property of "things," but enabled by both (Deleuze 1990, 19–20, 70, 95). Applied to the task of this study, we cannot find "sense" exclusively in the things "represented" in the stories, in the words used to evoke those things, nor as propositional content in the mind of the reader who encounters these words/things; sense happens in an encounter.

"Sense" is a valuable notion for this investigation because of its evocation of the domain of *the senses* as well as the more reflective, conceptually organized parts of interpretation that in everyday use fall under its scope.[3] Ezequiel Di Paolo's enactivist definition demonstrates how a discussion of meaning can be enhanced by attention to sense-making as an activity:

To make sense is for a body to encounter value and significance in the world [...]. Sense-making is not something that happens *in* the body, or *in* the brain, but it always implies a relational and value-laden coherence between body and world—the world does not present itself as sense-data to be interpreted, but is itself a participant in the sense-making process and often the stage where my sense-making is enacted [...]. Sense-making is not primarily a high-level voluntary interpretation of the world (though it can take this form) but bodily and worldly activities of all sorts, from biological and pre-reflective to conscious and linguistic. In all these cases, sense-making is always affective.

(Di Paolo 2014, xii)

This definition asserts that sense-making can take the form of conscious, conceptual interpretation, but it also encompasses biological and prereflective engagement with the world, and that affectivity colors all of these "levels" (see also Colombetti 2013). In this chapter, different types of meaning and sense-making are discussed in relation to the literary works, with the overarching idea that they share a common basis in an embodied, affective activity in a material world with material things—and which literature, as per Felski, asks us to pay attention to. Our *feelings* of the qualitative dimensions of this world develop and acquire meaning, yet these are not experiences of an isolated subjective nature, but qualities "in the world as much as they are in us," as Johnson puts it (2008, 25). This "world" encompasses both the material world available to the senses and the cultural world of meanings and habits that we grow into, two spheres that should be seen as overlapping instead of separate.

This chapter will take different foci on aesthetic wholes and parts, moving from the discussion of one collection, through a section focused on the beginnings of two stories, to one that discusses sense-making within the confines of one story. First, I will discuss Jean Rhys's stories published in the collection *The Left Bank*. I examine how the materiality of both things and people and Rhys's ways of presenting them as uniform masses or as aesthetic detail affect readerly sense-making from the basic, embodied and affective levels to aesthetic and ethical considerations. Next, I will look at how the perspectival techniques that open and close two of Mansfield's short stories affect the way we make sense of the stories as a whole, including both the blending of ontological categories and the norm-critical epiphanies that have been brought up in the previous analyses. In the final section, the focus is on Djuna Barnes's short stories and their use of description and material detail. Allegorical interpretation is compared and combined with an "archaeological" one, which traces historical and cultural connections of material things, before these, too are read in the light of sense-making, meaning, and metaphor as embodied.

Masses and Vividnesses: the Aesthetics and Ethics of *The Left Bank*

In his preface to *The Left Bank*, Ford Madox Ford taunts Rhys (in an ultimately laudatory manner) on erasing even the few "words of descriptive matter as had crept into her work," for the benefit of "passion, hardship, emotions" (Ford 1984, 26). It is true that Rhys's stories are not filled with such rich descriptive passages as Barnes's for instance, yet the stories' equalizing, aestheticizing approach to both people and things, and their tendencies toward journalistic observation, seem to arise from a predominantly descriptive ethos. This leads to the stories' portrayal of their human characters as types and masses, which is a politically loaded gesture, but also an aesthetic one. "The masses" is a notion present in many discussions about phenomena of modernity contemporary to Rhys, from commercialism and entertainment to factory work and fascism (Kracauer 1995; Adorno 1991). I will look at Rhys's treatment of masses of people as well as masses of things, and how both things and people are picked out of these groupings for aesthetic effect and ethical consideration by the narrating agency that persists throughout the entire collection. While these are thematics frequently evoked in a variety of Rhys studies I have cited here, the aesthetics of the masses or the connections between experientiality, ethics, and aesthetics in Rhys's work have not yet been thoroughly discussed; nor has an analysis of *The Left Bank* as a textual whole been undertaken. Focusing on this collection allows me to investigate how the format of a collection of short fiction, which is made up of stories, anecdotes, and sketches loosely bound by shared themes, places, temporality, and repertoire of things, affects readerly possibilities of sense-making.

Viewing people or characters as "types" is a parallel phenomenon to describing them *en masse*. The tendency of early researchers to read Rhys's protagonists as *representatives* of a type such as "the underdog," as Ford's introduction already puts it, has been rightly criticized for its narrowness, reductionism and victimizing tendencies (Emery 2013, xi; Le Gallez 1990, 1–8; cf. Ford 1984). Like the masses, typification as an aesthetic device is such an important part of Rhys's writing that it needs to be studied here, and its relations to habitual ways of thinking through metaphorical things and masses, subjects and objects, pointed out. I see typification as a textual strategy with cognitive grounds and effects, instead of assuming a representative relation of the fictional type to one actually existing, while recognizing also the historical and cultural context of these textual choices.

During the models' lunch hour in "Mannequin," a story already discussed in Chapters 2 and 4, the young women come across as a uniform mass in that they are all dressed in identical black cotton chemises designed for their off-duty time. In addition, each is acting according to her "type," on the basis of which clothes are selected for the models to present in the shop: there is "the *gamine*," "the *blonde enfant*," "the *femme fatale*"; Anna is the "*jeune fille*" (LB, 64). Similarly, Rhys's writing classifies and typifies chorus-girls, artists, tourists, different nationalities, as well as men and women. Specific subclasses such as the *anglaise* (an Engliswoman in Paris) or the *cerebrale* (an intelligent woman) also emerge, always with a dose of irony—and the distancing effect of being quoted in French. In addition to its resemblance to surrealist photography and installations explored in Chapter 2, this stance taken in Rhys's stories toward their characters and things can be compared to early 20th century "humanist" photography by artists such as Brassaï, whose photographs of Paris are used to illustrate her *Complete Novels*, and Henri Cartier-Bresson, building on the work of street photographers such as Eugène Atget (see Chapter 2, Figure 2). In their pictures, there is a curious mixture of, on the one hand, the celebration of individuals and forms of life that are at the margins of social hierarchies, and on the other, a tendency to position the "subjects" of the pictures as objective specimens of a recognizable type; something that can be seen as *dehumanizing* rather than "humanist." A similar tension haunts Rhys's writing, which also engages in an intermedial borrowing of visual forms. What I want to emphasize here is the way Rhys's work not only reproduces but also reimagines these aesthetic forms.

At the very end of "Mannequin," following the description of Anna's newly acquired sense of happiness and belonging afforded by new clothes, it is as if the scope of the narrative "lens" was widened to encompass first her colleagues leaving the shop, then the whole street with other similar shops, to form an image of the streets near Place Vendôme that could be an iconic shot by one of the humanist photographers:

> Georgette passed her and smiled; Babette was in a fur coat. All up the street the mannequins were coming out of the shops, pausing on the pavements a moment, making them as gay and as beautiful as beds of flowers before they walked swiftly away and the Paris night swallowed them up. (70)

The ending repeats the flower metaphor that has already been used in calling the models' dressing room "an inadequate conservatory for these human flowers" (6). Georgette and Babette are named and singled out as individuals, but in the case of the latter we "see" more of the fur than of the woman inside. The rest of the passage shows a mass of mannequins as a spectacle of beauty and gaiety. We have already seen how such "thingified" presentations of human beings as bodies need not immediately equal representations of alienation and objectification, although these discourses are never far from Rhys's writing. What kind of sense-making is invited by a story that buries the human subject within a fur coat or presents her as a decorative flower in a public space?

If we take a step back and look at "Mannequin" in the context of the whole collection of stories, we begin to see a variety of "human flowers" scattered throughout the book. *The Left Bank* is constructed as a collection of both longer, sequential stories and shorter, "spatial," or "anecdotal" (Harrington 2007, 5; Frank 1991) glimpses into moments of life on the Paris *Rive Gauche*, with detours to the south of France, other European cities, and the Caribbean Antilles. Despite the alternation between intradiegetic, named character-narrators and extradiegetic third-person narrators, the style in which situations and human beings are perceived and commented on in the stories remains rather constant, which creates a sense of continuity in the narrating voice throughout the collection. The same is true of the focalizers, who do not always coincide with the narrators, but nevertheless retain a recognizable attitude to the world. The way the stories invite their readers to make sense of them is strongly guided by the way their focalizers are making sense of their surroundings; a focalizer, after all, tends to invite the reader to share her point of view more strongly than other characters (Caracciolo 2014, 173).

Before investigating the overall combination of voices or styles in *The Left Bank*, I begin with a single story with a continuous first-person narrator. "Vienne" (1927) consists of a cavalcade of people encountered by the narrator Frances during the few years depicted by the story. The section titles emphasize this impression: "André Parisien," "Tillie," "Fischl: Winter 1920–Spring 1921," "Dancing at Eisenstein's with Antoine Renault." André, for instance, is a "little man," who takes pains to disguise his height with the cut of his suits, and whose titling as a Parisian means not only coming from Paris: "One could tell a Frenchman, Parisian, a mile off. Quantities of hair which he had waved every week, rather honest blue eyes, a satyr's nose and mouth" (LB, 195). The image of the satyr that is used to brand André's physiognomy also introduces his most central characteristic, a ceaseless interest in women and games of seduction that are usually realized as simple plots of chase, conquest, and abandon. In the beginning, André dominates the games, but in the fourth section, he gets conned (a classic plot that involves supposedly missing pearls that he has to recompense for) and eventually abandoned by another typified character, Tillie. She is described by Frances as "the most complete specimen of the adventuress, the Man Eater, I've ever met" (200). Tillie is contrasted with Ridi, a "shy" girl mistreated by André. "Glory to the Tillies, the avengers of the Ridis!" (208) Frances exclaims, pushing both Tillie and Ridi further into the realm of specimen-like names that in the plural define a type instead of pointing to an individual. They have their places in a moral system constructed around Frances, expressed by her mind style that favors neat characterizations and a cynical approach to sexual and socioeconomic relations as a game of eat-or-be-eaten. The "Tillie" section ends with André's hope for reconciliation as imagined by Frances: "The next girl perhaps—will be sweet and gentle. His turn to be eater. / Detestable world." (Ibid.)

Many of the characters in "Vienne" are defined by national stereotypes verging on racist. Fischl, a casual acquaintance, is characterized as "like most Viennese, charming, and clever as hell" (217). Eisenstein, on the other hand, is described, this time in a newspaper article read by Frances, as "the typical Viennese aristocrat" (218): he has lost his fortune because of the war and become a dancing instructor to make ends meet. These characterizations sweep through the story, to the point of nagging repetition: "all Vienna was vulgar" (201); "Excessively good-looking, but, being a Prussian, brutal, of course" (203); "the Japanese thought a lot of the German army and the German way of keeping women in their place" (211); "the Viennese have nearly as much temperament as the French, the Hungarians even more" (213); "the attractive Englishman is a little bit stupid, a little bit 'thick', more than a little bit an egoist, and a hypocrite" (219).

All in all, the classifying style contributes to a sense of the presence of a large mass of people at the mercy of power structures and habits, divided into smaller masses that are exemplified by typical representatives. This mind style, combined with the ironic tone, reflects alienation and cynicism brought about in Frances by travel and a life based on spending her husband's money of dubious origin, what Judith Kegan Gardiner has called her moral downfall (Gardiner 1989, 29). However, if we look at the levels of embodied sense-making that the text invites, and the context of the whole collection, these small and large masses come across as a continuous way of tapping into a very basic experience in readers, and producing a certain aesthetic outcome. In my view, the reasons for such strategies of characterization are not reducible to the "moral" of the story exemplified by Frances as a "fallen woman." Like Rhys's thingifying gestures discussed earlier, they also conversely invite even empathetic rand affirmative readings.

A group or a mass that consists of individual things is one of the basic patterns created by experiences of bodily interaction with the world, "image schemas," that can be used by fictional texts to appeal to the reader's repertoire of experiences of being in the world (Johnson 2008, 81–82 Caracciolo 2012, 97–98).[4] Human bodies are a special case afford the possibility of social interaction (Froese and Di Paolo 2011, 21–25; Gibson 1979, 135–136), but they, too, can be seen schematically as bodies in space grouped in various formations. As James Gibson puts it, other animate beings appear to us as "animate objects," with their own affordances (Gibson 1979, 135–136). The way "Vienne" insists on its narrator grouping human "animate objects" into sets with one

defining property (German and French, shy dancers and ruined aristo-
crats, Tillies, and Ridis) solidifies the presence of the schema in the flow
of reading. The groups of people are considered as exemplary of a certain
narrator's world view and thereby serve to characterize her experiential
point of view constructed in the story.

This, of course, is not the only thing a reader of the story is made
aware of. When engaged in reflective interpretation, a reader can set
these experiences in a historical context and see them as gendered and
ethnic stereotypes. In any case, if we stop to consider the stories as
aesthetic arrangements that invite visual and multisensory imagining, it
becomes clear that humans and things play similar parts in the world-
making of the narrative, which tap into the way human minds are
capable of and often restricted to experiencing people as masses and
groups of things in the world. In the moment of reading, the schematic
arrangement of elements into groups is encountered within the frame of
fictionality (Polvinen 2017, 143). The discursive strategies and the
reader's situation when engaging with the story are likely to be recognized as part of a fictional, artistic whole, as an essential part of any
reading experience instead of a layer of interpretation added to it.
Thereby the perception of the aesthetic and rhetorical value of Frances's
stereotypical comments demands attention beside their ethical implications, which would be pre-eminent if her words were uttered by an actual
person in the real world.

The Left Bank as a whole calls forth various schemas that rely on
embodied being-in-the-world, but the tendency of grouping becomes
highlighted. Partly this is due to typification, as in "Vienne," partly to
other strategies such as the photographic description in the final scene
of "Mannequin." This scene is aesthetically unified in its presentation
of the human flowers that beautify the streets and its borrowing from
the visual arts. The stereotypes in "Vienne," on the other hand, have
no common aesthetic characteristics, but the very repetition of the
gesture of grouping constitutes the aesthetic experience of this story,
too. The stories solicit basic bodily schemas, along with socioculturally shared features readers can draw on; the repeated evocation
of such schemas becomes a stylistic device contributing to the aesthetic effect of the stories and part of the enactive experience of
readers schooled by reading fiction. Reflective considerations of the
stories' ethical implications are invited by interpretive connections
that can be made between the mind styles of the narrators and the
historical context of the stories, and these interpretations are colored
by the basic schematic experiences and the recognition of the
fictionality of what is being read.

In the impressionistic description of a prison visiting hour in "From a
French Prison" (1927), people are compared to spiders:

From the foot of the staircase leading down from the room in which they waited, ran a very long whitewashed corridor, incredibly grim, and dark in spite of the whitewash. Here and there a warder sat close against the wall looking in its shadow like a huge spider—a bloated, hairy insect born of the darkness and of the dank smell. (LB, 44)

In "The Grey Day" (1927), on the other hand, a depressed poet, one of the few male focalizers in the collection, sees nothing inspiring or beautiful around him: "Then his despair faded again to greyness in that dark, quiet café, where two men with hooked noses and greasy, curly hair, played draughts" (142). The human elements in these descriptions appeal to our ready ability to imagine a human figure, but at the same time these figures blend into their environment. In the café, the two men act as furnishings that heighten the "grayness" of the environment. In the prison, the narrator as the perceiver and experiencer of the scene retains their humanness, but the anonymous warders, "here and there," emerge not only as animals but as parts of the scenery, "born of" it.

Rhys blends a realist tendency to use the environment for characterization and a modernist vision of the interconnectedness of the experiencing being and its environment. In "The Grey Day," the environment is there not only to reflect the moods of the focalizer: it also participates in their emergence. The environment, in this sense, does not mean all that is left outside the human: it is composed of both nonhuman and human elements. In many of the stories in *The Left Bank*, the exploration of an individual consciousness does not seem to be of most importance. In the context of the whole work, moments of psycho-narration and other references to individual consciousness become parts of the descriptive ethos of the collection, is intensified by its title and preface that direct its readers to approach it as a documentary, although impressionistic account of contemporary Parisian expatriate life centered on the *Rive Gauche*, of which "Miss Rhys" has "profound knowledge" (Ford 1984, 23), and of which the different characters appear as specimens. The poet of "The Grey Day" unsuccessfully tries to conjure up inspiration and faith with the help of his imagination:

He shut his eyes and tried hard to think of blue seas in the sunshine, of the white, supple arms of a dancer dressed in red—of the throb that lives in a violin and the movement of flowers in the wind.
It was quite useless.
Besides, flowers have stupid faces and so have dancers for the matter of that. (LB, 142)

Almost all the "happy objects," in Sara Ahmed's definition (2010; see Chapter 4) that the poet imagines also appear in one or several other stories in the collection. Thus, an implicit intratextual reference lends some color to the otherwise "gray" passage, but offers the colors as illusory and gray as the tone of reality.

This textual strategy can be read as a defamiliarizing repetition-with-a-difference of gendered and aestheticized stereotypes, ironically presented by the implied author who seems to almost but not quite share the mind style of the character narrator. However, I want to emphasize that the interpretation of the repetitive strategy of grouping as such is built on ambiguous meanings lent to the people-as-things by the stylistic and aesthetic choices that borrow from imagery contemporary to the story and the evocations of basic bodily, cross-sensory schemas. I suggest that Rhys's schematic repetition of a mass of things in connection with the presentation of characters can create new affordances and tacit meanings in the reader's repertoire (see Määttänen 2015, 91; Gibson 1979). Such tacit meanings and affordances are also evaluative and form an affective basis for ethical considerations. They can lead readers to ponder interpretively whether the values the text invites them to share are sound ones, to be taken ironically, or to be contradicted. All this can occur simultaneously with the transactional and enactive engagements with the texts. All literature solicits such movement between levels of sense-making; what makes Rhys's massified people noteworthy is her texts' blend of ironical commentary, aesthetic experience and tacit, affective resonances produced by a mixture of human and nonhuman bodies—like café clientele and liquor bottles.

"In a Café" (1927), one of the briefest sketches in the collection, consists of the documentary-like description of a scene: another Paris café in the evening, with a five-person band playing. The customers are characterized as "stout business men" drinking beer, "neat women in neat hats," "temperamental gentlemen in shabby hats" drinking *fines à l'eau*, and "temperamental ladies" wearing turbans and drinking mint liquor, all enveloped in a "peaceful atmosphere" (LB, 50). The peace is disturbed by a visiting singer, who performs the song "*Les grues de Paris,*" the tragic story of a prostitute. This seems to cause some agitation among the clientele, continuing when the singer proceeds to sell records of the song. An American lady buys two, the usual orchestra starts playing once more without the singer, and "peace descend[s] again on the café" (52). The main "event" of the story is a change in the general ambience, and its protagonists consist of the general group sitting in the café; a protagonist given *en masse*. The narrator of this story, too, takes a typifying and distanced stance toward the mass protagonist as well as to the type of the *grue*:

> The grues are the sellers of illusion of Paris, the frail and sometimes pretty ladies, and Paris is sentimental and indulgent toward them. That, in the mass and theoretically of course, not always practically or to individuals. (51)

The *grues* "in the mass" may give rise to sentimental attitudes in an agent, and this agent is also massified by the synecdochical passage. The narrative itself echoes the attitude pictured in the quotation toward the *grues* in its description of the people in the café. This can be used as an example of Rhys's sympathy for the underdog, in Ford's words, this time the fictional prostitute. The story of the *grue* in the form of a song, a nonhuman agent, agitates the crowd. However, it is noteworthy that the peaceful and stagnant ambience of the café ("an atmosphere of a place that always had been and always would be," 50), and thereby of the story, is stirred even before the appearance of the singer:

> The only vividnesses in the café, the only spots of unrest, were the pictures exposed for sale, and the rows of liqueur bottles in tiers above the counter of the bar, traditional bottles of bright colours and disturbingly graceful shapes. (50)

In the storyworld, art induces unrest, which is a possible hint at the desired effect of the story. However, even ordinary material things in the form of "traditional" bottles above the counter are accepted into the realm of "disturbing" things or events. Moreover, calling these things "the only vividnesses" of the place contributes to the leveled ontology of vivid, vibrant thing bodies that I have explored throughout this book. They all make up to the aesthetic whole of the story: an impressionistic description of a place, the human and nonhuman bodies in it, and the subtle changes in its atmosphere, from stagnant to slightly stirred to stagnant again, like a drink poured from one of the bottles. Bottles and liquor, like flowers and dancers, create intratextual links within the collection as material metaphors. In the passage above, the bright colors and the graceful shapes of the bottles are presented as vivid and disturbing. They are also accompanied by an invitation to imagine the taste and intoxicating effect of their contents, some of which have already been brought forth in the descriptions of the café clients and their drinks at the beginning of the story.

In "Mixing Cocktails" (1927), one of the stories in the collection that are set on a Caribbean island instead of Paris, the frothing cocktails that the narrator remembers having been so skillful at making as a child are metaphorically paired with the highly affective vividness of the sea: "It was very difficult to look at the sea in the middle of the day. The light made it so flash and glitter: it was necessary to screw the eyes up tight before looking" (89). This vision recalls the parallelization of the sea, bath-salts and crystal scent bottles in "At the Villa d'Or" (see Chapter 4). In this story set by a different sea, Mr. Valentine becomes a spokesman for the aesthetics of bottles, quoted in a satirical manner:

> Now, for instance: Bottles—the curve of a bottle, the shape of
> it—just a plain glass bottle. I could look at it for hours ... I started
> life in a chemist's shop—I was brought up amongst the bottles. Now
> the pleasure I get in looking at a bottle makes me understand artists
> ... (163)

Mr. Valentine's childhood has taught him his aesthetic tastes, just like
"Mixing Cocktails" might suggest that the narrator's early affinity with
mixing cocktails is bound with the focus on bottles and drink in the later
collection, considering the sense of continuity that is produced by the
narrating voice. Many stories mention specific drinks, such as *menthes
of striking emerald*" (50) or *fines à l'eau*. Visually expressed vividness
and alcohol also come together at the start of Rhys's writing career:
according to her unfinished autobiography *Smile Please,* Rhys used black
note books to write out her first love affair that had just ended, with quill
pens of different colors that she had bought to "cheer up" her bare table.
The result was the manuscript of her first, unpublished novel, which she
titled *Triple Sec* after the citrus drink (Rhys 1979, 105). The colors were
cheerful, but the experience, as described by Rhys, was close to dying.
Johnson and Moran (2015, 1) see in this moment the beginning of an
"affective stance" that literally colors all of Rhys's work.

   While fictional bottles have a metonymical link to alcoholism and
melancholia or depression, the aesthetic choices in their presentation as
vivid, bright, and graceful things create a tension with these meanings.
The drinks have their place in the aesthetic whole of the collection and
the visual sensations it evokes, like the bright green absinthe in Henri de
Toulouse-Lautrec's paintings. The aesthetics tickle the more basic levels
of sense-making, too, evoking conceptual metaphors and affective values, especially as they are paired with people presented as thing-like,
lacking a spark of life: on a very basic level, bottles filled with sugary,
fermented liquid come across as life enhancing. This connection is enforced in the later collection *Tigers Are Better-Looking*, in "Till
September Petronella" (1968), when Petronella and her casual acquaintance order a bottle of *Veuve Clicquot* champagne and the man
remarks as though quoting an advertisement, "It puts some life into you,
doesn't it?" (Rhys 1972, 26). Drinks are also plausible objects of affective incorporation in that they directly, chemically participate in the
creation, enhancement, and sustenance of affective states. In Rhys's
stories, they are simultaneously connected to pleasure and sadness, depending on the interpretive distance. Both levels of meaning are present
and not completely separable. They are rather in tension than in
harmony with one another.

   Some things in Rhys's stories are literally more vivid than others, as
they are personified and given imaginary lines of speech, like the dresses
in "Illusion" (see Chapter 4). Such underlining is often done on aesthetic

grounds. The narrator of "In the Luxemburg Gardens," another depressed young man, observes children playing in the park. One of them is called by his name, Raoul, by his nanny, while the focalizer is "gazing morosely at all the other Raouls and Pierrots and Jacquelines in their brightly coloured overcoats" (LB, 71). The children are a mass, not saved from this outlook even by individual names. A woman in a green hat enters the scene and steals the young man's attention, and the park is given the last words of consolation: "Such a waste of time, say the Luxemburg Gardens, to be morose. Are there not always Women and Pretty Legs and Green Hats" (72). The children and the woman, multiplied and generalized at the end, become specimens of park goers and part of the visual world of this nonhuman, yet personified entity, with their brightly colored clothes as a shared feature (the woman is wearing a hat "as green as Raoul's overcoat," 71). The story tempts a visualization in which these bright colors light up the somber ambience of the park, the characteristic light gray of the Paris ground matching the gray mind-state of the focalizer. Thereby their aesthetic function is parallel with the colorful bottles of liquor. Readers leave the story having encountered the young man, Raoul, the other children, and the woman, but their most vivid recollections may well be of a green overcoat and hat, like splashes of color on a light canvas in an impressionist or post-impressionist painting (in which women indeed tend to be swallowed visually by their hats).

While the connections to impressionist art will be taken up again in conjunction with Mansfield's work, here I wish to keep it as a visual analogy and focus on the ethical considerations invited by displays of people and things as masses and specks of color in Rhys's collection. Many of the ethical implications have already been taken up throughout this book: the stories' consciousness-raising about the situation of women in the society and the possibilities and limitations within these frames of feelings such as belonging, empathy, or sympathy between people. At first sight, Rhys's critical "passion for stating the case of the underdog" and "sympathy for [...] law-breakers" (Ford 1984, 24) do not seem to be in line with the aesthetic strategies of thingification, typification, and massification. It is certainly not a simple case of the narrators performing the gestures of objectification and then with an ironical distance, the implied author showing the readers the related sociocultural problems, using the narrators as cautionary examples. Rather, the very gestures of objectification are often paired with affirmative meanings and feelings. The thing-like presentation of a human character does not seem to get on the way of empathy and sympathy, identification, or a sense of belonging and community—on the contrary, the thing bodies, human and nonhuman, are brought within these phenomena, by way of such aesthetic choices as I have described, and thereby new tacit connections of meaning are created.

Overall, *The Left Bank* challenges meanings based on dividing things into subjects and objects. In this case, a notion such as "objectification" all but loses its meaning, and "thingification" means merely being regarded as an animate or inanimate body in space, with aesthetic properties and affordances for interaction. People are presented mostly as opaque to one another, but this comes across as a basis for an ethics. The passages suggest an anti-anthropocentric version the Levinasian approach, in which the face of the other *as* other is seen as morally binding (Levinas 1969). In Rhys's fiction, there are no prerequisites as to what kind of subjectivity lies behind the face, or rather, the surface. Thereby they afford a broad scope of empathy, sympathy, and identification, which involves the nonhuman world. Furthermore, the opaque human bodies are fictional characters made of textual gestures, and a reader can be expected to engage with them as such. As readers of the collection are already positioned within the frame of fictionality, they remain capable of experiencing the opacity partly as a matter of course in a literary device, and of proportioning their ethical consideration of the stances taken by the narrating voice accordingly.

As regards the masses of people and things, a similar interpretation can be made. The modernist problematic of "the masses" rests on a belief in the primary nature of the human individual as the basis of ethics. Rhys's work keeps pointing to how the value of the individual is challenged by modern capitalism, and how the value of the female individual always seems to be slightly less than that of the male. However, the reciprocation that *The Left Bank* offers is *not* a newly-found celebration of individuality. It is a suggestion to see possibilities of recognition and identification regardless of how similar to or different from the surrounding minds and bodies one is. Individualism often rests on the notions of depth and interiority, and an anthropocentric preference of the *human* individual in possession of a disembodied self and a rational mind, who is essentially separate from the environment and who tends to appear as masculine. In contrast, if we see human cognition as embodied and embedded in and extended into its surroundings, the gap between the individual self and the world is made smaller. I hope to have shown that in Rhys's stories, too, characters feel and make sense *with* the world of things, instead of making sense *of* it while remaining separate from it.

Furthermore, the way agency and affect are distributed in the texts, as I have shown in the previous chapters, certainly does its part in challenging the idea of the human individual as the primary subject of action, and suggest a more inclusive account of subjectivity. I want to recall the view that even human agency is collaboratively constituted, and that human beings are molded by affective encounters with material things. As Karen Barad writes,

What if it is only in the encounter with the inhuman—the liminality of no/thingness—in all its aliveness/liveliness, its conditions of im/possibility, that we can truly confront our inhumanity, that is, our actions lacking compassion? Perhaps it takes facing the inhuman within us before com-passion—suffering together with, participating with, feeling with, being moved by—can be lived.

(Barad 2015, 8)

If we follow Felski's "post-critical" suggestion and experiment with focusing on the immediate effects that the stories afford, ways of thinking beyond the human individual quite necessarily emerge. The masses of people and things, as Rhys presents them, need not be seen primarily as agents of dehumanization in a sense that would be associated with racism, war, or the exploitation of labor, for instance. These concerns are undeniably and importantly present on the critical levels of reading that the stories invite. However, as a performative aesthetic act, the masses and sprinklings of people readers are invited to imagine, along with bunches of lively things, insistently generate affirmative and reparative spaces alongside the critical ones, again demonstrating the power of literature not only to criticize but also to reimagine. The affective and aesthetic whole of *The Left Bank* is a combination of sinister forebodings, critical considerations steeped in irony, and reparative instances in which people and things come together in assemblages that invite readers to enact sympathy, empathy, happiness, and belonging. Importantly, the latter meanings are not dependent on the human characters *surpassing* their embeddedness in the world of things, crowds, and masses. The mannequins sprinkled on the Paris streets as "human flowers" suggest a sense of belonging regardless of their dehumanization; vivid things on bar counters or brightly colored clothes in the Luxembourg Gardens induce happiness and pleasure primarily *as things*.

In other words, some of Rhys's typifications repeat sexist and racist stereotypes, and the aim of this study is by no means to present all of them in a light that would magically turn them into affirmative or reparative gestures. An important part of the meaning of the collection is built on tensions and contradictions of sameness and otherness, happiness and despair, agency and objectification, and instead of transmitting one positive or negative meaning or message it asks readers to interact with a variety of conflicting meanings, and come out the other side experientially enriched. I hope to have shown how a reading of affective materialities enables us to see the variety of different tones and colors that exist in the stories and has potential to exist between the stories and their readers; not in harmony, but in a movement capable of producing meanings on many levels, and supporting the critical with the affective. *The Left Bank* addresses topical concerns of alienation and the value of human beings, but it does so in a manner that is not preaching or didactic, but ambiguous and "disturbingly graceful," like the tempting liquor bottles in a Paris café. This is how the collection of stories surpasses its function as contemporary commentary of a specific time and place and reaches toward generating spaces for readers to reimagine ways of being in the world with other people and things.

At the Indifferent Bay: Nonhuman Perspectives and Meaning in Katherine Mansfield's Stories

After reading the impressionistic and expressionistic aesthetics and temporalities, the glimpses of humanist photography, and the rhythmic repetition of glasses and bottles in Rhys's *Left Bank*, it is intuitive to move on to Katherine Mansfield's short fiction, which is often explicitly called impressionistic. Her stories have been compared to the visual arts such as Monet's serial studies, to which her restricted "palette" is compared (Kimber 2015, 27; Van Gunsteren 1990, 15). According to Julia van Gunsteren, Mansfield was not directly influenced by French impressionistic paintings or painters, but rather shared some of their aesthetic principles that apply to literary as well as pictorial arts: a focus on immediate experience and its fluctuation over time, and on the sensations as "filtered through the intermediate minds of a narrator and a character" (Van Gunsteren, 1990, 12, 15). This creates an interesting tension between a focus on the mind and perspective of an individual and the *impersonality* that is also, justifiably, associated with Mansfield's fiction, yet I will suggest that this may in fact be a false opposition.

In a defense of impressionistic literature, Ford Madox Ford declares that a writer should "not narrate, but render." Instead of providing objective information of a scene or an event, what should be conveyed is the basic sensation of a character: "he saw a steel ring directed at him" instead of "he saw a man aim a gat at him." (Ford 1935, 31.) We have seen how a similar strategy manifests in Mansfield's use of especially free indirect discourse to bind the narration to characters' limited and "flawed" sensory experience of the world, without the narrator organizing it into interpretive categories. We have also seen how this kind of impressionism can create "flat" ontologies of people and things, subjects and objects, personal and impersonal. What remains to be discussed is what kind of readerly sense-making is invited by these perspectival techniques, and through what kind of process these aesthetic choices become ethical ones—something we saw happen in Rhys's collection of stories. In this chapter, I will look at how the opening parts of two of Mansfield's stories, "At the Bay" also read in Chapter 3 and "The Stranger" (1921), approach the problematics of perception, imagination, and the material world, and how they engage the readers in what becomes an aesthetics of open-endedness and impersonality.

Unlike its "sister" story, "Prelude," "At the Bay" does not start with the experience of its characters (in "Prelude," the children Lottie and Kezia, who do not fit in the buggy transporting their things to the new house). Rather, it starts with a view as distant as possible, with an impersonal descriptive statement that falls short of being a complete sentence: "Very early morning" (MCS, 205). The first paragraph is a description of Crescent Bay in the early morning mist, without any human characters present. Furthermore, it is rendered in the negative, not so much describing what is there as what is not:

> The sun was not yet risen, and the whole of Crescent Bay was hidden under a white sea-mist. [...] You could not see where they ended and the paddocks and bungalows began. The sandy road was gone and the paddocks and bungalows the other side of it; there were no white dunes covered with reddish grass beyond them; there was nothing to mark which was beach and where was the sea. (Ibid.)

Instead of the Bay, the object of the description, the readers see the mist: the narrator describes what is *not* available to the fictional "you" perceiving the scene. As readers learn about the limitedness of the perception of the imaginary witness to the scene, the passage gives way to the imagination. Julia van Gunsteren has observed how the distance of focalization in the passage distorts the perception depicted (Van Gunsteren, 1990, 135). However, by implying the existence of a nondistorted, correct perception that could be found behind the description, this choice of words risks an impression of overlooking the fictionality of the passage and the imaginary component that comes with it. To draw attention to the fictionality, following David Rodriguez's work on aerial descriptions, I would like to argue that the imprecise, or rather, indeterminate qualities are what is noteworthy in such literary description and the sense-making it invites.

Supplementing Roman Ingarden's and Wolfgang Iser's phenomenological approaches to reading with new materialism, Rodriguez reads literary descriptions of environments as "spaces of indeterminacy" and suggests that in them,

> the nonhuman form of environment [...] merges with the human intentionality that is the use of literary form, indeterminately affecting the outcome. From the perspective of the object—for example, a river valley—existing apart from the arrow of human intentionality, it can find itself articulated in the products of two types of intentionality, perceptual or imaginary. [...] Given a literary form, the actual environment finds its imaginary form articulated through its embeddedness—a reimplacement—in a new context.
>
> (Rodriguez 2019, 20–21)

The fictional text is a human artifact and a rendering of human perception, but it articulates nonhuman forms existing independently of this perspective, only not as facts of perception but as imaginary entities that become approachable for readers in a new, fictional context. This kind of approach is significant for my reading of Mansfield's perceptual techniques, because it avoids reducing the ontological shifts that occur as a result of the descriptions to human psychology and the distortions it causes in an individual's perception, but keeps the fictional and imaginary "thing-quality" of the literary work of art, as well as the nonhuman, indifferent and indeterminate materiality of the world it evokes in the foreground. This recognition of the recontextualizing work Mansfield's texts do has not been present in readings of it as impressionistic, though as I hope to show, both are in fact in agreement.

The end of the first paragraph of "At the Bay" explicitly evokes the imaginary in its employment of "as though" and "if": "It looked as though the sea had beaten up softly in the darkness, as though one immense wave had come rippling, rippling—how far? Perhaps if you had waked up in the middle of the night you might have seen a big fish flicking in at the window and gone again ..." (MCS, 205). The story gives its reader an impression of a particular material environment, but presents it with what becomes a double gesture: the material world escapes any totalizing description, but offers itself as an imaginary presence whose material characteristics create the affordances for the structure and expression of the passage, even when remaining unapproachable. As the description mimics perception, it suggests that perception too is affected by both the imagination and the material forms of the environment. The quoted passage is imaginary and fictional, but rests on the affordances of the environment: the capacity of the sea to expand to and swallow the beach, and of the mist to do the same as the residue of the contact between sea, land, and sky. With the humorous "as if" image of the fish flicking in at the window, the reader is invited to accept a more obvious blend of the perceived and the imagined; the imagination animates the environment like in the multiple cases of focalization by children discussed in the preceding chapters, but the grounds for the animation are already laid in the material properties of the environment itself.

The second paragraph of the story moves further in this direction, with the expressive, nonlinguistic sounds of the "sleepy" sea going "Ah-Aah!," water "gushing" and "splashing," a twig "snapping," and "then such silence that it seemed someone was listening" (ibid.). The passage draws attention to the narrator making these interpretations and the fictional observer by what seems to be an impersonal form of free indirect discourse. At the same time, it mimics sounds that are recognizable as produced by nonhuman elements of nature. In this case, the animation of the world is not imposed on the landscape but displayed as arising from its activity of gushing, splashing, stirring, shaking, and snapping. The transcriptions of the sounds are the work of a human mind, but they rely on the affordances of an environment, albeit a fictional one. The recognition of these sounds by the reader relies on their basic experiential background (Caracciolo 2014), their capacity to imagine, but also their capacity to recognize the referents of the transcriptions based on habitual use of such signifiers. Even this basis on use, however, does not mean that these signifiers are arbitrary, as they are also onomatopoetic, and thereby necessarily carry in them an expression of the environment in its nonhuman materiality. Here we might recall Stefan Herbrechter's post-humanist metaphor of haunting for the presence of nonhuman otherness within the humanist order, applied by Karoliina Lummaa to elements such as the sounds of birdsong in literary language (see Chapter 2; Herbrechter 2013, 86, 90; Lummaa, 2019, 43, 45). These ghosts appeal to the affective, embodied reader, and they may go unnoticed in a critical interpretation, but unavoidably haunt any reading of the text.

From the sea, air, rock, and plants, the description moves gradually toward the human, although it starts with nonhuman animals. In the next paragraph, a flock of sheep appears from "round the corner of Crescent Bay" (MCS, 206), shortly followed by a sheep-dog and finally the human figure of "the shepherd himself" (ibid.). Temporarily, this character becomes the focalizer of the scene, bringing the readers into the midst of the mist, which begins to dissolve as the sun rises. The shepherd witnesses the "leaping, glittering" sea, which becomes painful to look at with the sun; He smokes his pipe while the narration lingers on him, the sheep, and the dog, as they approach the summer colony and thereby the focus of the rest of the story. This, too, is approached indirectly, first through nonhuman elements. The "first inhabitant" that appears is the Burnells' cat Florrie, who is sitting on a gatepost and gets startled by the sheep-dog. The cat is given lines of speech that reproach the dog: "Ugh! What a coarse, revolting creature!" (207), while the narrator infers from the twitching of the dog's ear that it too has judgmental thoughts of the cat. Again there is an imaginary human observing, interpreting, and linguistically mimicking the animals' states of mind, but even this is based on their outward appearance as bodies in space, expressive as such, even though they are arguably readier for anthropomorphization than the glittering sea, for instance.

Instead of moving in a linear manner from the anthropomorphized animals to the end point of the descriptive prelude, and the starting point of the "actual" story with its human characters, the final paragraph of the first section of "At the Bay" follows the shepherd and animals a little further. In place of the Burnells, it introduces a multisensory collage of the smell of leaves and earth, the singing and skillful flight of birds, the repeated "baa's" of the sheep and the whistling of the shepherd; until they round the bend and disappear, "out of sight" of the imaginary observer. Until its conclusion, then, the first part maintains an imaginary focal point that is not an omniscient one. Things appear and disappear out of sight, which tempts the assumption that it is a fictional human observing the scene. It is not so much an "empty deictic center" in the sense discussed in Chapter 3, either, but a perspective vaguely from above. The assumption of the humanness of the observer who has a limited point of view and anthropomorphizing tendencies is part of the fictional framing of the story, but it is worth remembering that this very fictionality of the perspective makes it necessarily a "nonhuman" one: as Rodriguez (2019, 20–21) puts it, it is an imaginary construction afforded as much by the form of the environment as the form of the description. This way, the nonhuman haunts both the content of description, as in the onomatopoetic verbs and interjections, and its form, as in the focal structure.

Further, I would like to take the plentiful comparisons of Mansfield's work to the visual arts seriously and pay attention to the non-narrative, imagistic elements that the description brings to the fore. Angela Smith, for instance, illustratively associates the beginning of "At the Bay" to the sense of "expectation and immanence" in a Cézanne painting, which establishes a dynamic feel through the depiction of a still image (Smith 1999, 168). Sarah Sandley compares it to a "filmic pan shot" (Sandley 1994, 75), while Van Gunsteren sees it as an example the "imagistic patterns" (Van Gunsteren 1990, 171) Mansfield's stories use to introduce thematic elements in a condensed form—here one would be the fragmentariness of perception (see also New 1999, 74).

It is useful to follow Van Gunsteren's insight especially if we introduce another art form and interpret "thematic" as one would in music, from which Mansfield herself borrowed vocabulary, including the title "Prelude" (Kimber 2015, 16–17). A musical theme is a *formal* unit that becomes varied throughout the progression of the piece and carries its "meaning" onward. As in the case of a piece of music, I would argue that the "meanings" or "themes" of "At the Bay" are of a nonpropositional kind, and it is useful to look at them as predominantly affective patterns, which express a dynamic of silences and half-heard expressions, presences and absences, dramatic breaks, and an interplay of perceptive distance and emotional proximity. The diegetic order of the story first lays these schemas out in the environment. This strategy can be read as using environmental forms to express the thematic elements that belong to the human order, as in a projection of humanness onto the environment, but this does not seem to be the whole story. Rather, the way "At the Bay" lingers on the nonhuman tempts a reading in which the "human" thematics as well as affective structures are always already there, as forms with which we make sense of the world, of humans and of environmental forms. In fact, the beginning of the story asks us to take a prolonged look at the latter rather than the former. Read from an anti-anthropocentric point of view, a similar claim can be made about the entire story, even though its subsequent sections resume a more human-centered, yet fluctuating structure of focalization. Through a few more examples, I wish to show how this haunting presence of nonhuman impersonality, indeterminacy, and indifference is rehearsed throughout the story, and how maintaining this perspective can change how we understand the ways the story invites us to make sense of it.

The following section narrates Stanley Burnell's early morning swimming trip and his rivalry with the neighbor, Jonathan Trout. The comedy of the scene arises from the difference of perception between the two men, the first trying "to make a job of everything," even swimming, and the other one floating in romantic revelry (MCS, 209). I propose that even in this scene, whose "human comedy" forms a stark contrast to the obviously impressionistic beginning, it is the material, nonhuman environment that sustains the affective structure, which again is the basis for the emerging, interpretable meanings of the story—including the comedy. Stanley experiences the sea as a brisk participant, or even an opposing force in his morning sports routine, while Jonathan approaches it with a poetic greeting: "All hail, The Mighty One" (208). For Jonathan, the ocean is a thing of beauty and a confirmation for his determination to live "carelessly, recklessly, spending oneself" (209). This could be read to imply that the sea can mean whatever one wants it to mean—yet I suggest it would be an oversight to regard it as a blank canvas or a purely arbitrary signifier to be filled with meaning.

When we encounter the fictional ocean with the fictional characters, we encounter a set of imaginable material properties, which build the affective framework on which even the symbolism of the ocean rests. Following Gaston Bachelard's literary phenomenology (1942), water and the ocean in particular is an ambiguous space that lends itself to writers and swimmers alike to be imagined both as a soft and embracing presence and an adversary. Both meanings are due to the material characteristics of water, what ecological psychologists would call its affordances. Read like this, its symbolic functions are different for the two men because of their temperaments, but these temperaments become enacted in contact with the materiality of the water. It is the watery experience that frames the different perspectives that structure the section, taking the literary form of fluctuating focalization between the two men. Through their opposed perspectives, the story evokes an uninterrupted presence of the water's nonhuman being, a sort of *basso continuo* of its sounds and its affordances that in conjunction with the bodies of the swimmers sets the frames to how they move within and experience it.

This is apparent in the ending of the section, which suddenly presents the men as level with one another. Stanley gets out of the sea feeling angry and cheated out of the pleasure of his bath, while Jonathan exults in its embrace some more, but once out of the water he is shivering and feeling disappointed as well. With the wider perspective on the Crescent Bay of the earlier section potentially lingering in the reader's memory, the ending of the second section tempts contrasting the bodies of the two characters with the vastness of the sea, whose waves keep rolling in spite of their joys and disappointments, all the while also providing the necessary material conditions for the enactment of these affects. Vincent O'Sullivan comments on images in the posthumously published longer version of "Prelude," *The Aloe* (1930): "they are what *The Aloe* is about, and how it is told. They are not symbols nor mere illustrations, but images *as* narrative progression" (O'Sullivan 1982, xviii). The story is made of material images which never simply illustrate a point but rather constitute the affective progression which the experiential knowledge that the story creates rests on.

This reading of Mansfield's use of focalization and perspective adds a component that binds together what earlier research has rightly observed as its impersonal and impressionistic effects, and the recognition of the presence of the nonhuman throughout the story and its effect on the way we make sense of its affective, ironical, and comical tones. The middle of the story, section VII, echoes the descriptive structure of the beginning, once again beginning from afar and approaching the summer colony, from a general view of the beach spotted by sand-hoppers (again evoked onomatopoetically as a sound of "pit-pit-pit," MCS, 224), and even an imaginary scenery underwater, mingled with reflections, through the bungalows of the colony and another animal agent, the Trouts' dog Snooker, to Kezia and her grandmother having siesta. Similarly, the end of the long story returns to such widened perspective, after Beryl has had a disturbing nightly encounter with Harry Kember in the garden. It is unclear what happens next, but what the story does is to bring its readers' attention back to the environment as open to the senses as well as interpretations, and as indifferent to them. Blaming Beryl when she refuses his advances, Harry Kember asks "Then why in God's name did you come," at which point the narrator brusquely shifts the attention away from the scene by a gesture of silence:

Nobody answered him.

A Cloud, small, serene, floated across the moon. In that moment of darkness the sea sounded deep, troubled. Then the cloud sailed away, and the sound of the sea was a vague murmur, as though it waked out of a dark dream. All was still. (245)

In some editions, these lines in fact form their own, thirteenth section of the story. The ending is a highly ambiguous, as a very dramatic scene involving sexual violence is cut short by a return to an impressionistic description of the environment. This raises the question of what happens to the ethical implications the story if here, too, we see the narrative as foregrounding the indifference of the nonhuman, material world to human dramas. Should we see it as asking readers to be indifferent to sexual violence? Gerri Kimber reads the ending as an epiphanic moment in which Beryl sees the unattractiveness of Harry Kember. According to Kimber, the epiphany is enhanced by the "admonishment" of nature in the form of the garden described as "stern" (Kimber 2015, 24); she also interprets the murmuring sea as "speak[ing] for the troubled feminine psyche, eternal and mysterious" (ibid.). As in the earlier instances of sea symbolism, I would like to attempt a reversal of this logic of analysis: it is clear that the sea speaks, but what it does is tempt the readers' attention away from the psyche, even as such an archetypal construction that Kimber is referring to.

In this passage, the *performative*, nonpropositional meaning or "message" of the story seems clear: there is a question, which reflects the capacity of patriarchal power to shame a woman equally for acting and not acting on the basis of her sexuality, but there is no answer, except for the murmur of the sea, which the story posits, via the concrete shift of focus, as the indifferent alternative to oppressive norms and power-relations. Thereby the environment appears as an agent that helps to recontextualize the normative structures that are the focus of critique. We do not know what happens to Beryl, but what happens in the story is that the scene of her harassment and the conventional verbal interchange accompanying it are replaced by images of impersonal murmur followed by stillness. The story introduces an alternative schema in which the tacit habits and structures oppressing Beryl do not apply. The nature does not speak "for" the feminine psyche, but creates an alternative, imaginary space, which definitely could be called "eternal and mysterious," in which Beryl does not need speaking for, and the language that plays a part in oppressing her is replaced by "meaningless" environmental sounds. The return to the impersonal environment also recalls the beginning of the story and thereby creates a cyclic rather than a linear structure. The meaning of the story, as I read it, is indeed in the progression of material images and the affective response invited by them, and in the potential space to reimagine tacit, normative meanings thus created.

In "The Stranger" (1921), the life of John Hammond, a character not unlike Stanley Burnell, is thrown off the rails by a surprising encounter with death, a pattern already familiar from previously discussed stories. The beginning of the story, in the middle of its events unfolding, shares some characteristics with "At the Bay," as well as with the aesthetics of Rhys's *The Left Bank*. The point of view of the beginning, however, is not "within" the experience of the main character or focalizer of the rest of the story, but introduces a general, impersonal observer *en masse*:

It seemed to the little crowd on the wharf that she was never going to move again. There she lay, immense, motionless on the grey crinkled water, a loop of smoke above her, an immense flock of gulls screaming and diving after the galley droppings at the stern. You could just see little couples parading—little flies waking up and down the dish on the grey crinkled tablecloth. Other flies clustered and swarmed at the edge. Now there was a gleam of white on the lower deck—the cook's apron or the stewardess, perhaps. Now a tiny black spider raced up the ladder on to the bridge.

(MCS, 350)

In another formal choice that underscores the uncertainty of ontological categories, the narrator does not make clear what the "she" refers to, although the second sentence already is likely to lead the reader's mind to a ship. The focalizer of the first paragraph is positioned as one with the crowd on the wharf, to whom the human elements on board the ship seem like nonhuman insects. This time they are not *compared* to insects but presented directly as such, following the impressionistic paradigm of "rendering" described by Ford above. This recalls Rhys's use of dehumanizing descriptions that lead to a unified aesthetic effect in which human and nonhuman elements become part of a vivid, painterly scenery and appear as equally distant but recognizable things in the world. In "The Stranger," however, the point of view seems especially important for the contrasting perspective it provides to the human drama depicted in the rest of the story. The story has been described as "a psychological study that ultimately challenges the reader's assumptions, a bravura exercise in point of view writing, and a highly ambiguous examination not just of a psychology, but of a marriage" (Malcolm 2012, 224). I would like to add that it is precisely the ambiguity, realized on the level of description, and the experimentation with point of view that lead to an approach that indeed goes beyond psychology in its reexamination of marriage. In fact, "The Stranger" condenses the most important connections between focalization, description, and thematic sense-making that I have identified in a number of Mansfield's stories previously analyzed in this book, which is why its beginning and the relation of the beginning to the structural and thematic unfolding of the story merits some more scrutiny here.

The story features the technique of zooming Mansfield uses in "At the Bay," only on a smaller scale, as the main character is introduced in the second paragraph. Mr Hammond, who is waiting for the arrival of his wife, is first approached in a descriptive manner as though by someone observing animal behavior, and the narration explicitly recalls the shepherd theme of "At the Bay": "He seemed to be the leader of the little crowd on the wharf and at the same time to keep them together. He was something between the sheep-dog and the shepherd" (ibid.). Thus, in the space of two short paragraphs, the human characters have not only been compared to but also *seen as* animals, while the ship has been given quasi-human presence by the habitual feminine pronoun denoting it. Furthermore, the presence of the sea, especially when read with the other oceanic stories like "At the Bay" in mind, enhances the perspectival effect by the affective intensity its image encompasses, and the insignificance its perspective simultaneously lends to the human drama about to unfold. This drama recruits an array of everyday things we have already become familiar with as Mansfield's vehicles for displaying and reimagining social, gendered norms, such as the cigars John is handing over to people on the wharf, and the teacups that he is imagining his wife, Janey, holding on board the ship; his relief at her return seems to boil down to "no more going without his tea or pouring out his own" (352). The normative idyll is broken when he finds out that his wife's arrival from the ship has been delayed because a young man has died, and at the moment of death Janey has held him in her arms.

Researchers have noted parallels between "The Stranger" and James Joyce's "The Dead" (1914) (Robinson 1994, 5). Joyce's story ends with the quiet intrusion of another environmental element, the snow "falling faintly through the universe and faintly falling, like the descent of their last end, upon all the living and the dead" (Joyce 1994, 59). This explicit evocation of a cosmic scale in connotation with death also has a leveling effect in relation to the human story of a husband's jealousy for a long-dead young man. "The Stranger," on the other hand, ends with John Hammond's expression of the shattered normative security of his life, rendered in free indirect discourse: "They would never be alone together again" (MCS, 364). Structurally, then, Mansfield's story has moved from an expansive and non-anthropocentric, category-blending view to a tight focus "inside" the main focalizer, speaking, if indirectly, to the reader. On the other hand, the content of his words echoes the formal themes of the story: the events have forced him out of the privateness of his personal relationship that is based on a socially acceptable form of human ownership. The private sphere becomes permeated by the other, in the form of the young man who has died in Janey's arms; but beside this human other, the aesthetics of the story makes the privacy dwindle as a result of the presence of a whole impersonal world, again indifferent to the story John tells of his marriage.

In my reading, it is clear that the effect of John's final words is built throughout the story, not only in its ironical depiction of Mr Hammond's fussing and his patriarchal, traditional world that Janey's experience clearly exceeds. Death and the past spoil the couple's being alone together, but it is the mixed perception of the beginning of the story that has built the comical effect that puts the whole ideal of the dyad of a happily married heterosexual couple into question. Regardless of the contrast in the focal structures of the beginning and the end, I suggest that some of the openness of the beginning has actually extended its effect onto the ending, too. The rigid structure of the marriage, again condensed in images of teacups and pots, necessarily opens up to the messy, contingent, predominantly nonhuman world, full of unpredictable events that do not respect the boundaries of human bodies, not to mention ephemeral things like marriage.

In "The Stranger" and "At the Bay," Mansfield uses well-studied modernist means particular to the short story such as beginnings that avoid explaining the scene they are showing, open-endedness, the impressionistic rendering of a moment with the use of images, as well as the variation of structural and meaningful "themes" in the manner of a piece of classical music. What the stories result in is not so much the creation of one or several propositional meanings or messages, but a reconfiguring of what I have above called tacit meanings in the reader's mind. Further, I want to suggest that even though these aims may be achieved by the special formal characteristics of the stories, the method of reading I have employed here exposes something common to all literary works of art. They tap into our basic skills and habits of making sense of the world, and by shifting and recontextualizing them, ask us to reconsider how we see the world, be it for environmental forms, ontological categories of human and thing, or socio-cultural ones like husband and wife. The stories use both temporal and spatial shifts of scale to create an affective, aesthetic whole that is recognizable to anyone making sense of the world, but as a literary effect also becomes highlighted and thereby affords epiphanies, amusement, and potential shock: a reader has encountered the human players in the drama as insects and sheep moving about on a personified ship and a wharf, all framed by an indifferent ocean and the inevitable presence of death to which, as in "The Garden Party," things such as teacups and cigars matter very little. On the other hand, they matter a great deal: as we have seen, it is such small things, made strange and strangely meaningful by their recontextualization in the weave of a literary work of art, that create the affective whole of the narrative. This is a tension that the text asks us to live with, without resolving it to any totality of meaning either at the beginning or the end of the story. The final part of this chapter will look further into the indeterminacy of literary meaning achieved by different formal and thematic experiments in Djuna Barnes's stories, shifting our focus from aerial and distant descriptions to descriptions of detail.

Djuna Barnes's Detail and the Materiality of the Symbolic

During the discussions of Djuna Barnes's short stories so far, a number of things and characters have emerged as agents acting, interacting, or intra-acting in various assemblages. We have also learned that Barnes's fiction tends to include long descriptive sections dedicated to material detail. In some cases, the main affective content of a story comes across to the reader by means of description of assemblages and *tableaux*, which makes her work comparable to the visual arts similarly to Rhys's and Mansfield's stories. To complete the discussion of Barnes's work in this book, and the development of my approach to reading materiality in modernist short fiction, I set out to inspect this form of description and presentation of detail more closely. Barnes's characters share the thing-like presence of both Rhys's masses and Mansfield's "distorted" environments and bodies; however, the most characteristic way they appear is as parts of lists and floods of thingly detail.

Detail can be read as archaic and archival, in the vein of comparing the stories to museums or curiosity cabinets, filled with potentially useless information (Wilson 2011); another, opposite approach could be to read detail as symbolic and thereby central to the meaning of the story. What I want to suggest and what I hope my method of reading will demonstrate is that neither is quite the case in Barnes's short fiction. By construing a different reading, I wish to offer further tools to rethink how meaning is made in fiction, beyond the propositional and the symbolic alike. In the context of modernism and modernity, the notion of detail shares some of the theoretical ballast of Rhys's masses. As Naomi Schor (1987) has shown, attention to detail in art has been linked with triviality, femininity, decadence, and even crowds and riots. In classicist as well as high modernist theories of art, a good, useful detail is one which contains or produces *meaning* and stays within the confines of the hierarchy and perspective of the whole work (Ibid., 21, 42, 59). Detail, in these accounts, is often commensurate with material things. Willa Cather famously sketches a modern "Novel Démeublé" with an exclamatory expression of desire for literary change: "how wonderful it would be if we could throw all the furniture out of the window" (Cather 1922, 6).

Djuna Barnes has definitely not thrown all the furniture out of the window to create a new, modern form. We have seen how Barnes's work utilizes naturalist aesthetics and evokes intertextual connections to both decadence and naturalism, which Georg Lucáks describes as "realism whose details have gone bad" (Lukács 1971, 60; Schor 1987, 44). In the psychoanalytical framework, on the other hand, which Barnes's work is in a parodic relation to, a "good detail" can be characterized as one interpretable by the talking cure and thereby ultimately capable of producing meaning (Schor 1987, 68–75). In the Freudian unconscious, dreams and symptoms make overdetermined metaphors out of seemingly worthless fragments of the past. Walter Benjamin applies this idea to cultural history by turning his attention toward the material detail of 19th century Paris: "I needn't *say* anything. Merely show. I shall purloin no valuables, appropriate no ingenious formulations. But the rags, the refuse—these I will not inventory but allow, in the only way possible, to come into their own: by making use of them" (Benjamin 1999, 460, emphasis in the original). In the psychoanalytic and Benjaminian accounts, seemingly unimportant and excessive detail is given pride of place in the production of meaning, but the method of each is slightly different. Here I wish to view both psychoanalysis and decadence as intertextual elements to Barnes's stories rather than potential frameworks for interpretation. Barnes's work balances between tempting her readers to follow a path of symbolic interpretation, as if in relation to dream images, and cutting this path short, even parodying it, and instead using plentiful inventories of things as affective cues for tacit, bodily forms of sense-making.

To investigate this play of and on meaning, I will look closely at "Cassation" (1925)[5], a story in which the detail is especially conspicuous. Katya, the narrator of this story and the other "Little Girl" stories, tells the already familiar, silent narratee "Madame" about a phase of her life in Berlin. In a café, she meets a mysterious older lady named Gaya, who invites her to a house shared with a "declining" husband and a disabled child. In a seemingly mutual, yet silent understanding, Katya accepts the invitation and ends up staying a year. She compares this period to life in a convent and describes it as a happy, serene and rewarding coexistence of the two women, consisting of walks in the garden and philosophical discussions. The husband and child are seen and heard only occasionally. Their haunting presence, along with Gaya's display of signs of worry, leads Katya to think that "there was trouble in other parts of the house" (BCS, 384). After a year, the atmosphere and Gaya's behavior change. She asks Katya not to go out any more, to take care of her child and stay "forever" in the house, without leaving the child's bedroom; her discourse is more distracted than previously. Katya does not want to do this and leaves, in spite of proclaiming her love for Gaya. She returns once, to find the older woman lying in bed beside the child and making a buzzing noise. The end is marked a departure similar to many of Barnes's stories. "Go away," Gaya retorts; Katya goes and briefly concludes her narrative: "Things are like that, when one travels, *nicht wahr*, Madame?" (392).

The action of the narrative is constructed following an affective structure familiar from other stories, such as "Aller et Retour," "Spillway," and "Dusie": an arrival at a house, a conflict involving members of an actual or an allegorical family, and a departure. "Cassation" also shares many themes and motifs with other stories I have discussed: there is a slightly twisted Oedipal schema, which here involves a "declining" man, a child, a mother, and a woman-as-child; there is also a *sense* of psychological drama, realized ambiguously and theatrically by characters with unreadable minds. Even Katya, when telling the story, refrains from any psycho-narration, apart from her short description of her initial experience of living with Gaya in a defamiliarizing passive that points toward my reading in the previous chapter of the stories affectivity as a "state of things": "It was that I was happy" (387). She senses trouble as affectivity distributed "in the house"; she also asks Gaya, more specifically, "Why is it that you suffer so" (391), but Gaya seems to remain opaque to her.

Katya's description of the experience relies largely on material instead of psychological detail. These descriptions have a tendency to extend so that they stand out in the context of the whole story; they do so also because of the repetition of expressions and structures within and across stories. Katya describes the first bedroom she sees, the one with Valentine, the child, lying in the middle of a large bed:

> Everything was disorderly, and expensive and melancholy. Everything was massive and tall, or broad and wide. A chest of drawers rose above my head. The china stove was enormous and white, enameled in blue flowers. The bed was so high that you could only think of it as something that might be overcome. The walls were all bookshelves, and all the books were bound in red morocco, on the back of each, in gold, was stamped a coat of arms, intricate and oppressive. [...] (384–385)

A human element is introduced in the middle of the assemblage, in a manner recalling both Mansfield's and Rhys's indeterminate perception that crosses boundaries between human and animal, and Robin's presentation in *Nightwood* discussed in Chapter 3: "[...] it was not until some moments later that I saw a child, not more than three years old, a small child, lying in the center of the pillows, making a thin noise, like the buzzing of a fly, and I thought it was a fly" (385). The two women do not discuss the child. Katya leaves, only to come back later the same night. Gaya lets her in through a window to another bedroom and another description follows:

> It was a beautiful room, Madame, '*traurig*' as she said. Everything was important and old and gloomy. The curtains about the bed were red velvet, Italian you know, and fringed in gold bullion. The bed cover was a deep red velvet with the same gold fringe: on the floor, beside the bed, a stand on which was a tasselled red cushion, on the cushion a Bible in Italian, lying open. (386)

The two descriptions of bedrooms are variations of the same "theme" on the level of wording and rhythm: everything is disorderly, expensive, melancholy, massive and tall, broad and wide; everything is important, old, and gloomy. Image schemas of largeness and heaviness dominate the first room, while the second appeals to a sense of color and texture and evokes haptic affordances of surfaces. Both refer to luxurious materials in the colors of red and gold. The construction of the passages, beginning with "everything" and leading to detailed descriptions, creates a sense of excess even though the style of neither is particularly flamboyant: the adjectives used are matter-of-fact ones that denote color, material, and size. However, the very fact that there is *so much* of this description of material detail causes it to take on a sense of excess, that could be read as naturalist "detail gone bad." As the characters' motivations and actions remain opaque, readerly attention is directed toward existents instead of events.

One method of reading that this passage seems to call for is an "archaeological" instead of a symbolic one, exemplified by Elaine Freedgood's (2009) study of objects in Victorian literature. I wish to show that such an approach resonates with Barnes's fiction, but that it will benefit from an added attention to affective materialities in the manner developed throughout this book. Freedgood suggests that Victorian "showers" of things "often overwhelm us at least in part because we have learned to understand them as largely meaningless," and that they should be approached with an orientation toward the surface of the text *underneath* which we habitually expect meaning to reside (Freedgood 2006, 1). This resembles the Benjaminian "rag-picker" approach to detail when, in contrast with Victorian forms, the modernist gesture of showing the world of things and details as experienced, and the experiencing consciousness as embedded in the world, might invite readers to consider details as parts of the lived world, significant in themselves. Furthermore, in short stories, the constrictions of textual space suggest that the details of the material world that get to be mentioned *must be* significant. However, the challenges presented by Barnes's flood-like descriptions are also different from what could be expected of modernist, carefully selected, meaningful things. The way the text presents details and things may deny the meaning these readers are looking for, while affording other, more basic and embodied forms of sense-making. In "Cassation," the bedroom descriptions appear allegorical in that the things they present seem excessive as regards their possible "practical" uses in the story. They are formally related to the visual language of still lives and thereby also accompanied with an assumption of at least some allegorical content. However, the guidelines given by the text for readers to fill the gaps in meaning prove to be misleading. After providing a brief example of the allegorical lures of the story, I wish to map some of the adjacent domains of meaning that "haunt" "Cassation," namely Roman Catholic kitsch, decadence and psychoanalysis, and see how they open up for a reading that combines an archeological or "rag-picker" approach with the recognition of affective materiality.

Even though Katya compares herself to a nun, her stay in the house is framed by luxury rather than by the asceticism and abstinence associated with a convent. As a significant detail, the Bible in Italian that is lying open on the cushion on the stand in the second bedroom is a reference to the Christian faith and to Roman Catholicism. Katya uses ambiguous words to describe her experience: "a religion, Madame, that was empty of need, therefore it was not holy perhaps, and not as it should have been in its manner" (BCS, 387). She is not betrothed to Christ, as a nun would be; if she is someone's "bride," it is Gaya's, but their relation also resembles that of mother and daughter. On the other hand, Katya is supposed to act as a surrogate mother for the child, who in its other-worldliness associates with Christ, but with no resurrection or redemption to offer, quite the opposite: it seems to signify madness and emptiness, "vacancy" (391). Ludwig, the declining husband, is at best a parody of a paternal god figure, like the slightly extraneous Joseph, if we stay within the framework of the Holy Family. The Christian allegories seem to be challenged so much by the fluctuating and overlapping roles the characters play that any pattern of such explanation would seem too rigid and bound to leave out something essential.

The excess of material (be it concrete material things or other references) is presented *as if* it formed an essential part of the allegorical whole, but it never does: the "gloom" and "importance" of the room, the "intricate and oppressive" coats of arms on the back of books in red morocco, the war paintings and the general sense of mysticism, as well as the roles and dynamics of the characters alternating between nun, bride, mother, daughter, Christ and Mary, refuse to make a meaningful totality. The allegorical tableau refuses to be read, like the foreign Bible in the storyworld ("lying open at a page that I could not read," 387).There is simultaneously too much of "everything" and "nothing": references to "vacancy," "emptiness," and "nothing" are repeated in Gaya's speech. The reader seems to be led to the brink of allegorical explanation only to step back confused, with a general sense of affective movements and an ambience instead of an explanation. As Deborah Parsons (2003, 22) suggests about Barnes's early stories and plays, "Cassation" seems to be mocking everyone "reading for meaning."

The Bible in the story is primarily a thing, expressive in its material being, rather than a book whose contents could be read and understood by Katya. Similarly, the framework of Roman Catholicism is rather an expressive style than an explanation. The style of the room, with its red and gold colors and the velvet fabrics surrounding the *"religieuse"* and the bible, recalls Papal luxury, but it might as well be a royal abode or a luxurious brothel. In Barnes's use, Catholic iconography in general has a considerable amount of common ground with *kitsch*: repeatable, affordable, consumable reproductions of "beautiful" or "artistic" objects made of cheap materials (Calinescu 1987, 226–229). In "Cassation," kitsch is especially present in references to Valentine, the child. "It," which is the pronoun used for the child in the story discourse, lies as if hidden in plain sight, on the huge bed in the middle of the room, surrounded by the massive and ornamental furniture and the picture of a battle, like a baby angel in a baroque illustration. Katya formulates this association in a simile: "It was beautiful in the corrupt way of idiot children [...] like those dwarf angels on holy prints and valentines" (BCS, 388). Here the allegorical tendencies of the story appear on a formal, aesthetic level, as the child is presented in an impressive tableau, as an emblem, and compared to the pictorial motif of "dwarf angels" on a card that bears the child's name. Once again, the emblem remains ambiguous. Valentine is associated equally with Christ, the playful baby angels that might surround him in a picture, and romantic greeting cards.

The description of Valentine combines the lightness and newness of mass-produced kitsch objects and cards with the heavy, old, emblematic room. The kitsch objects are associated with another story from the same period, namely "Aller et Retour," in which the variety of objects Madame von Bartmann encounters in Marseilles includes arrangements of funeral wreaths with embossed tin images of the "bleeding heart" (part of Catholic iconography as a symbol for Christ's love for humanity) as well as lightly pornographical postcards ("showing women in the act of bathing; of happy mariners leaning above full-busted sirens with sly cogged eyes," 363). The effect achieved is a conceptual blend of the visual and haptic spheres. Instead of acting as an aid for allegorical meaning, the blend evokes fresh connections of meaning. Valentine, the postcards, and the embossed tin decorations create a tension and a connection between high and low, "important, old and gloomy," frivolous, cheap, and naughty. This is clearly a parodic and cheerfully blasphemous gesture whose dialogical tension appeals to both our sense of basic schemas and cultural contexts.

Decadence, like kitsch, is a phenomenon of modernity partly defined by an allowing relation to detail (Calinescu 1987, 161). Barnes's connections with decadence have been pointed out by earlier research (Taylor 2012, 1–3; Sherry 2014). Intertextually, both the qualities of the things in the passages of "Cassation" (antiquities, luxurious materials of velvet and leather, gold, and red) and their way of presentation recalls the lists of curiosities collected by Des Esseintes in J.K. Huysmans' *À Rebours* (1884), a staple work of decadence, and the repetition of a similar topos in Oscar Wilde's *Picture of Dorian Gray* (1890). Both novels can be cited as examples of the illumination of the detail at the expense of the whole: the flow of both narratives is interrupted by catalogues of things that go on for entire chapters. An ornamental, decadent style emphasizes the singularities of small units at the expense of *unity*, overall effect, which is why the detail in it tends to be seen as *excessive* (Schor 1987, 43; Calinescu 1987, 161; Bernheimer 2003, 18). The excess of things, however, depends on how "overall effect" is defined. I have pointed out how initially conflicting descriptions and their stray detail contribute to an overall *effect* as assemblages, even if they might not yield to an overall *interpretation*. The list-like passages in "Cassation," as in Huysmans and Wilde, may cause a reader to lose their way toward an expected turn or resolution of the plot, or to become highly interested in the different form of presentation. In any case, the aesthetics and materialities presented embed the whole narrative in a multisensory experience of luxurious things in their color, scent, taste, sound, and texture. Besides undergoing story-driven experiences solicited by these fictional things, a reader is also able to recognize and engage with the list form as a literary means of expression (Caracciolo 2014; Polvinen 2017).

The literary framing of the lists suggests the possible assertion of each thing as noteworthy in itself, even if they fail to conform to a totality of interpretation. Some object-oriented philosophers use the humorous term "Latour litanies" to denote such lists, common in the writings of their field, in which the objects or phenomena participating in an event are listed to highlight the equal importance of each of them (Bogost 2012, 38–39). In Barnes's case, especially, the detail is significant from the point of view of the affective potential of the work, as it has been included in the fictional assemblages on its pages and the phenomenon of reading. These cultural, intertextual associations built on embodied schemas are summoned in the sense-making process the reader is invited to take part in. Thus, departing from object-oriented ontology and thing theory, I view even the listed things as simultaneously independent beings and encompassed (and encompassing humans) in networks of affectivity and meaning, while neither affectivity nor meaning is to be seen as a human-dominated domain. Rather, the fictional lists of things help us to reimagine them as anti-anthropocentric, without resorting to a dual vision of the world in which things completely resist meaning and meaning thereby becomes exclusively human.

In addition to an intertextually vibrant style and subject matter, Barnes's short stories allude to decadence by way of concrete *decay*. In "Cassation," the "declining" husband suggests this interpretation. Material things decay also in "Aller et Retour": two chairs have broken during the mother's absence from the house, as Richter bashfully confesses. In "Spillway," the topos of material decay in the paternal house has a comical effect. Upon her arrival, Julie tells Paytor (who is still alive and well, in contrast to the other fathers and husbands, though apparently not for long) she is glad he has taken down the crystals she always hated, to which Paytor replies: "I didn't, the roof fell in—just after my last visit to you in December" (BCS, 270). The surprising introduction of a roof falling in adds to the high-strung drama of "Spillway" a touch of the slapstick comedy recurrent in Barnes's early work. This kind of comedy is not a customary part of decadent aesthetics, whereby readers face a stylistic blend that produces parodic effect. Barnes indeed approaches decadent literary style in a parodic tone that, in Linda Hutcheon's definition, shows reverence for the past text while making fun of a phenomenon or an ideology (Taylor 2014, 56–57; Hutcheon

1985, 35). In Barnes's stories, the gesture of blending heavy and solemn elements with light and comical ones permeates the levels of thematics, style, and fictional world building. All these contribute to the affective path of making sense of the work that the reader is invited to follow. Furthermore, if the stories are read as part of a collection, the tendency of recycling and repeating motifs and topoi between stories causes an associative, affective path to form throughout them. In this context, the references to literary decadence and material decay constitute an assemblage of their own, the cultural meanings supported by the material detail and vice versa.

The final frame of reference to be discussed in this survey of detail is Freudian psychoanalysis. In "Cassation," the unreal atmosphere, the ellipses in the events, the patterns of family combined with the overtones of seduction, as well as the "excess" of detail tempt readers to see detail as material for a symbolic interpretation of a dream or a symptom. However, while the cast of "Cassation" does not quite fit into an allegory of the Holy Family, the Oedipal family as a frame of explanation is not sufficient, either. The way the women take up agency and desire is in a parodic relationship to the Freudian framework, as we saw in the discussion of Barnes's fetishism in Chapter 2. The potential oedipal drama between Katya, Gaya, and other players is never acted out. In "Cassation," simple descriptions of slight movements remain most poignant: hands touching fabrics, taking off and putting on clothes, touching the pages of the bible, like an intimate ritual, or like a dream. The text offers no final dreamwork-like interpretation of the dreamlike excess of detail.

Except for outright allegorical tales such as fables, fiction is bound to host an interpretive excess: not all elements of a story fit into the overall picture, and a totalizing interpretation is seldom what any literary researcher would be looking for. In this sense, most narratives are "decadent" as to their details. A Freudian frame of reference could even incorporate any excess of detail and see it as a clue, a proof of over-determination. However, the "translation" of an array of objects into representations of genitalia or the maternal does not do justice to the aim of this study, namely the investigation of readers' affective and sensory engagement with the very materiality of things. This materiality, so clearly present in Barnesian detail, constitutes an excess that cannot be restored even to a Freudian interpretation. Rather, the Freudian framework is one more sphere of ideas that is stirred into the material-cultural assemblages of the stories and their combinations. Together with decadence and Catholically influenced kitsch, it participates in the interplay of high and low, heavy and light, realized through culturally defined concepts but also on the embodied schematic level.

This reading has shed light on the spheres of meaning, the "ideas" that the material detail evokes, while letting the things remain "literal," so as not to reduce them to any one framework of interpretation. However, considering the aims of this study, the fictional *materiality* of the things in these associations, as well as the embodied schemas that the associations themselves call forth, needs even more attention than an archaeological approach can offer. In what remains of this chapter, I want to ask some more questions about how materiality makes meaning in Barnes's stories. How does the very materiality of things, along with the materiality of words used to express ideas, affect the construction of symbols, allegories, and metaphors? In fact I suggest that, contrary to Freedgood's proposition, attention paid to allegory does not necessarily mean letting materiality slip away from the attention of the researcher (cf. Freedgood 2006, 2, 12).

Both passages from "Cassation" quoted at the beginning of this section are descriptions of a room (the bedroom where Valentine is sleeping, and the other one which Katya is invited to stay in) and the things contained in that room, a feature that serves to enact a schema of containment. The word "everything" is used at the beginning of both descriptive passages: "Everything was disorderly, and expensive and melancholy. Everything was massive and tall, or broad and wide"; "Everything was important and old and gloomy." Its repetition contributes to the sense of the room as a totality to be encountered at once. It is also noteworthy that in both passages the word "everything" is actually used in the concrete meaning of "all things." It refers to the physical reality of things that then collaborates in forming the ambience of the fictional room. The adjectives used to define "all things," however, are many and diverse: disorderly, expensive, melancholy, massive, tall, broad, wide; important, old, gloomy, deep. The characterizations of the room recall the culturally shared meanings discussed above, but they also directly involve the senses. The softness of the velvet of the curtains and the bed cover, the "red morocco" leather of book covers, the glitter of gold in fringes and tassels, all of which appeal to the reader's sensory imagination and contribute to the experientiality of the passage via Katya's focalization, are also involved in how we interpret cultural meanings evoked by the stylistic choices of the passages.

In my reading, the way these schemas are constructed has to do with our experience of inhabiting the spatial dimensions of the world: as Lakoff and Johnson (2003, 14) put it, "that we have bodies of the sort we have and that they function as they do in our physical environment." References to size are of interest here, as they rely on the bodily proportions of the narrator and invite an embodied engagement that draws on the reader's experiences of space. That a chest of drawers "rises" above one's head relies on a schema of verticality that is initially defined by the typically erect, bipedal posture of a human being and its sensorimotor affordances. The visual experience of a tall item is attained by raising our gaze along with it, while the thing itself actually does not rise;

recall here Vernon Lee's exemplification of aesthetic empathy with the sense of a mountain "rising" in the horizon (Chapter 4). The bed, on the other hand, is "so high that you could only think of it as something that might be overcome." These descriptions show both the typical human disposition and Katya's specific body in relation to the furniture. Therefore, the text not only follows schematic, conceptual metaphors but also harnesses them into artistic rewritings and re-contextualizations of tacit meanings: the bed is not trapped in one schematic meaning, as it appears to Katya both a threat and something to conquer, an adversary or an obstacle. As such it resembles Mansfield's ocean, with a multiplicity of meanings that all remain rooted in its material affordances.

The bed becomes a metaphorical locus of a sense of opposition and battle, and, typically for Barnes's work, this metaphor spills over the edges of one story. In "Cassation," the description of Valentine's room, before introducing the child, diverts into an ekphrastic sequence:

> A great painting hung over the bed; the painting and the bed ran together in encounter, the huge rumps of the stallions reined into the pillows. The generals, with foreign helmets and dripping swords, raging through rolling smoke and the bleeding ranks of the dying, seemed to be charging the bed, so large, so rumpled, so devastated. The sheets were trailing, the counterpane hung torn, and the feathers shivered along the floor, trembling in the slight wind from the open window.
>
> (BCS, 385)

There is no other explanation given to the state of the bed but the proximity with the battle depicted in the painting, whereby the two items together create a metonymical type of meaning. The bed is rumpled and the feathers from its depths "shiver" and "tremble" because of the wind that blows into the room from a window, but also as though both they and the bed were reacting to the doubly fictional representation of the tumult of battle in the painting. The subject matter of the picture, which also takes up a lot of space as a thing in the fictional space, "charges" from the canvas to the bed and to the room. In this sense, through Katya's description, the bed comes to embody simultaneously the opponent in a battle and the battleground. Like so many of the lived things I have studied here, it complements its role as the background of action (and here, a metaphor) by taking up space as an agent and an affectively interesting subject in its own right. It reminds us that we are reading a work of fiction, in which the bed and the painted horses are equally aesthetical and imaginary things "charging" at us.

The metaphor of the bed as a battleground appears in other stories as well, whereby it becomes something of a symbol within the closed system of Barnes's stories. For instance, the connotation comes across in "Aller et Retour," when Madame von Bartmann schools Richter in highly metaphorical terms:

> Horses hurry you away from danger; trains bring you back. Paintings give the heart a mortal pang—they hung over a man you loved and perhaps murdered in his bed. [...] Contemplation leads to prejudice; and beds are fields where babies fight a losing battle. Do you know all this? (370)

This passage becomes more meaningful when looked at in conjunction with other stories, especially "Cassation," and their private symbolism that draws on both common cultural meanings and embodied, metaphorical schemas. Horses, along with trains, are invited into the same schematic sphere with paintings, beds, battles, and babies, embodying (this time quite concretely) tumult and the power to charge and to resist. The metaphorical content in this passage is new and creative in its way of combining very different schemas: the association of battle and murder with the softness of beds and the innocence of babies, for instance. A reader of "Aller et Retour" might also be aware of the placement of these things together in "Cassation": the concrete position of the baby in the middle of the bed enforces the feeling of softness that clashes with the battle and the horses that surround it, as it were, charging from the painting into the description. Beds do not equal safety in this symbolic system, even though their softness and association with private space and sleep might do so in an embodied schematic understanding. Generally, the aesthetics employed by Barnes rest on the productive clash and occasional harmony of habitual conceptual metaphors and a private symbolism, which gives rise to new, poetic metaphors. Both systems rest partly on affective sense-making of materialities, partly on cultural meanings potentially shared by the authorial audience, but they create something new and unhabitual out of both.

The use of the motif of the child thing as a symbol in "Cassation" and "Aller et Retour" is affected by the material detail that it is surrounded by. A symbolic reading is certainly one that the framing of the child as a motif points toward. Valentine is a thing among things in various senses: it is referred to as "it"; it is human and has a name, but it does not move or speak, and even the name, Valentine, seems to be a symbolic gesture. In my reading, the child is a paradoxical symbol of the "non-symbolic," in the way it is shown to be untouched by language, making its own buzzing noise. There are also other ways in which Valentine as a symbol remains mute: the polysemy of the whole assemblage denies an exact reference to any outside symbolic system of the type "Valentine=Christ" (a special child, surrounded by Christian references, presented in an emblematic tableau with a parodic version of the holy family), or "Valentine= depression" (a condition beyond language in an "oppressive" maternal house, defined by "vacancy," stagnation, or "cassation"; cf. Kristeva 1989). In the spirit of Brown's thing theory, we can see Valentine as a thing that *resists* interpretation, evasive, and untouchable (Brown 2004, 4–5), yet I hope to have shown that this is not the only potential for agency that things have. I venture that Valentine actually does *mean*, not in spite of but because of "its" presentation as a thing, similarly to how the china stove, the painting, and the bed mean. First, the way the child is framed by the material detail already presents it to us as a *meaningful thing*, an object of interest toward which the narration of the story gravitates. Second, the description of the surrounding materialities evokes schemas of containment, bodily force, and heaviness, which are combined with cultural symbolical meanings around kitsch, decadence, and the allegorical families of both Christianity and psychoanalysis, leading further to new and creative metaphorical expressions of the bed as a battle scene, the house as a luxurious convent, the child as an angel beyond redemption. These together constitute a symbolic system within the collection, of which Valentine is part. In this chain of meaning, the material is essentially linked with the symbolic, not an alternative to it.

We have seen how making sense of "Cassation" can be driven by the affective, sensorimotor processes of imagining that a reader goes through while encountering the things-presented-as-significant in the story. This is not to say that the whole (the descriptive passage, the fictional space, or the story) and its parts (the material detail, particular words, and phrases) would make up a synecdochical or allegorical entity and thereby one coherent meaning, an ontologically separate thing available to be discovered by interpretation. If "Cassation" was to be read as detective fiction, the detail in it would present itself as clues, and Katya as the focalizer would appear as a sleuth figure. However, there is no temptation for detective work in the story. Katya's narrating voice does not encourage us to picture her as the reader's surrogate agent whose task is to find clues and make deductions, interpreting a mystery parallel to the task of the reader interpreting the short story (cf. Caracciolo 2012). She does not wonder about things that might be considered peculiar: Gaya's invitation, the decorations of the rooms and the battleground-bed, the child and the husband, or Gaya's subsequent demands and descent into a catatonic state. There is no narrative suspense related to the discovery of Valentine on the bed, or Gaya's psychological change; nor are they presented as moments of tragic culmination. Rather the opposite can be read in Katya's matter-of-fact statement at the end of the story: "Things are like that, when one travels, *nicht wahr*, Madame?" (BCS, 392).

The story is full of peculiar *things*, but what its narrator has to say about them is simply that they "are like that." The "*nicht wahr*" invites a savvy confirmation in the narratee and the reader, even though what has just been read is more likely to be strange than familiar. The reader thus becomes the recipient of a plea that denotes the ethos of the whole story in a gesture: a plea to accept "things as they are," even though they might go counter to the reader's tacit understanding of the world. Thus, readers are invited to form potentially new tacit meanings involving motherhood and sexuality but also being-in-the-world in general. Furthermore, rather than appealing to a reader's curiosity to find out what is *behind* the things (what the behavior of the women is a symptom of), Katya's narration, affirmed by the silent Madame, suggests: "This is *everything* there is."

An intratextual echo that supports this reading is found in "Aller et Retour," in Madame von Bartmann's instructional speech to her daughter:

> "Life," she said, "is filthy; it is also frightful. There is everything in it: murder, pain, beauty, disease—death. Do you know this?"
> The child answered, "Yes."
> "How do you know?"
> The child answered again, "I don't know."
> "You see!" Madame von Bartmann went on, "you know nothing. You must know everything, and *then* begin. You must have a great understanding, or accomplish a fall." [...]
> "Think everything, good, bad, indifferent; everything, and *do* everything, everything!"
>
> (370–371, emphasis in the original)

Madame von Bartmann is ready to be adopted as a guiding voice by a reader struggling to figure out how to make sense of "Aller et Retour" and experiencing similar difficulties with "Cassation." The relentless repetition of "everything" in both stories insists on the domain of excess and plenty that has been shown to characterize Barnes's writing: it portrays the abundance in both pleasure and pain that life offers, tragedy and comedy included. Solemn tones are paired with a crisp parody of Socratic dialogue: "Do you know this?"; "Yes"; "How do you know?"; "I don't know."

Both stories pair knowledge and "everything" with something like feminist liberation: the young women are invited out of the paternal house to see the world. The functions of the mother figures, however, are different. While Madame von Bartmann urges Richter to experience everything, pushing her out of the house, as it were, Gaya ultimately wants Katya to stay in and content herself with the pleasures of a solipsistic nothingness: "there are no swans, no flowers, no beasts, no boys—nothing, nothing at all, just as you like it. No mind, no thought, nothing whatsoever else. [...] no father, no mother no sisters, no brothers—only you, only you!" (391). However, Katya refuses and moves on, eventually to tell her story to Madame. Readers know nothing of the inclinations of this silent narratee, but they might, based on the intratextual links, imagine her as more like Madame von Bartmann, or one of Barnes's other Madames (see Chapter 2) than like Gaya: an accepting, expansive presence affirming Katya's "things are like that." In the unique symbolic system created by these stories, life equals everything: things, language, movement, pain, and pleasure. This life is also not exclusively human. The dominating mode of narration in "Cassation" is a gesture of showing everything performed by the narrator, but also ultimately by a virtual presence of an imaginary, embodied Djuna Barnes as the original mover of things, as I argue at length elsewhere (Oulanne 2017).

I hope my readings have shown that things are not foreign to meaning or interpretation, and that finding meaning in a thing does not have to equal imposing an interpretive framework on it or delving underneath its surface to find what is hidden. If the way we constantly interact with material things is crucial to our ways of making sense of the world, and the world that appears to us is always already colored by significance in the form of affordances and evaluative affectivity (Gibson 1979; Colombetti 2013), then there is no way that things would not "have meaning" for us, even if they also remain to some extent opaque in their materiality and independent agency. In the context of Barnes's fiction, this meaning is created as an interplay of references within and without the fictional world and between the stories, with intermingled evocations of the material and the cultural. When viewing the senses as part of sense-making, we might actually not always need to shed the study of symbols and metaphors to appreciate the materiality of things: on the contrary, that very materiality is necessarily at the core of sense-making on a metaphorical and symbolic level and can be studied alongside these processes. Again, this applies to modernist short stories, but can be taken as a cue to shift ways of reading any fiction that features human or nonhuman bodies in a world.

Therefore, even if the "take-home message" of "Cassation" seems to be "this is all there is, *nicht wahr*," a reading can never finish with a similar statement. Instead, I wish to end on a note that applies to all three writers discussed in this chapter and this book, derived from the typically Barnesian epigraph at the very beginning of the chapter: the material things in their stories mean "everything and nothing, much like all wisdom." By this I mean that the things are inescapably part of how we make sense of the stories, on basic as well as cultural and symbolic levels; at the same time, they are independent from us in their blend of imaginary and lived materiality. Rather than receding from meaning or resisting it, their materiality *exceeds* it, and refuses any total and final interpretation, whatever the means of reading. Fictional things given to us in a literary work of art bring with them both their intermingledness in human sense-making and their indifference to it, and as they are presented as part of an aesthetic whole, be it impressionistic, symbolist, or naturalist, they step out of their everyday usefulness—and while we make our way through the affective paths they create they quietly, almost unnoticeably ask us to reshuffle our repertoire for understanding the world.

Notes

1 Barnes 2010, 121.
2 This discussion can be traced back to Eve Kosofsky Sedgwick's critique of "paranoid," symptomatic mode of reading and the accompanying negativity of strong theory (1997), while the notion of "surface reading" was initiated by Best and Marcus (2009), who suggest paying attention to the materiality of the text under scrutiny with a descriptive attitude. See also Moretti 2013; Mitchell 2017.
3 In some basic definitions of enactivism, drawing from the Buddhist tradition, the connection between senses and sense is also explored as the mind is suggested to function like one of the senses, with thoughts as its "object" (Varela , Thompson, and Rosch 1991, 64).
4 This is a slightly misleading title for an otherwise useful concept, since these schemas do not (and Johnson does not claim they would) pertain exclusively to the sense of vision, and should not be conceived as "pictures in the head" with representational content (cf. Johnson 1987, 45).
5 Originally published as "A Little Girl Tells a Story to a Lady," revised version with the new title published in *Spillway* (1962).

Works Cited

Adorno, Theodor W. 1991. *The Culture Industry: Selected Essays on Mass Culture*. London: Routledge. DOI: 10.4324/9780203996065.

Bachelard, Gaston. 1942. *L'Eau et les rêves*. Paris: Librairie José Corti.

Barad, Karen. 2015. "On Touching: The Inhuman That Therefore I Am (V.1.1)." Forthcoming In *The Politics of Materiality*, edited by. Susanne Witzgall. Accessed May 25, 2017. https://planetarities.sites.ucsc.edu/wp-content/uploads/sites/400/2015/01/barad-on-touching.pdf.

Barnes, Djuna. 1996. *Collected Stories*. Los Angeles: Sun & Moon Press.

Barnes, Djuna. 1928/2010. *Ryder*. Champaign: Dalkey Archive Press.

Benjamin, Walter. 1999. *The Arcades Project*. Translated by Howard Eiland and Kevin McLaughlin. Cambridge, MA: Harvard University Press.

Bernheimer, Charles. 2003. *Decadent Subjects: The Idea of Decadence in Art, Literature, Philosophy, and Culture of the Fin de Siècle in Europe*. Baltimore, MD: Johns Hopkins University Press.

Best, Stephen and Sharon Marcus. 2009. "Surface Reading: An Introduction." *Representations* 108 (1): 1–21. DOI: 10.1525/rep.2009.108.1.1.

Bogost, Ian. 2012. *Alien Phenomenology, or What It's Like to Be a Thing*. Minneapolis: University of Minnesota Press. DOI: 10.5749/minnesota/9780816678976.001.0001.

Brown, Bill. 2004. "Thing Theory." In *Things*, edited by Bill Brown, 1–22. Chicago: University of Chicago Press.

Calinescu, Matei. 1987. *Five Faces of Modernity: Modernism, Avant-Garde, Decadence, Kitsch, Postmodernism*. Durham: Duke University Press.

Caracciolo, Marco. 2014. *The Experientiality of Narrative: An Enactivist Approach*. Berlin: DeGruyter. DOI: 0.1515/9783110365658.

Caracciolo, Marco. 2012. "J.M. Coetzee's Foe and the Embodiment of Meaning." *Journal of Modern Literature* 36 (1): 90–103.

Cather, Willa. 1922. "The Novel Démeublé." *The New Republic* 30: 5–6.

Cave, Terence. 2016. *Thinking with Literature: Towards a Cognitive Criticism*. Oxford: Oxford University Press. DOI: 10.1093/acprof:oso/9780198749417.001.0001.

Colombetti, Giovanna. 2013. *The Feeling Body. Affective Science Meets the Enactive Mind*. Cambridge, MA: MIT Press. DOI: 10.7551/mitpress/9780262019958.001.0001.

Deleuze, Gilles. 1969/1990. *The Logic of Sense*. Translated by Mark Lester. New York: Columbia University Press.

Di Paolo, Ezequiel A. 2014. "Foreword." In *Enactive Cognition at the Edge of Sense-Making: Making Sense of Non-Sense*, edited by Massimiliano Capuccio and Tom Froese, xi–xv. Basingstoke: Palgrave MacMillan.

Emery, Mary Lou. 2013. "Foreword." In *Rhys Matters: New Critical Perspectives*, edited by Mary Wilson and Kerry L. Johnson, xi–xiv. New York: Palgrave MacMillan. DOI: 10.1057/9781137320940.

Felski, Rita. 2015. *The Limits of Critique*. Chicago: University of Chicago Press. DOI: 10.7208/chicago/9780226294179.001.0001.

Ford, Ford Madox. 1935. "Techniques." Southern Review I (31): 39.

Ford, Ford Madox. 1927/1984. "Preface." In *The Left Bank & Other Stories*. Salem, NH: Ayer Company.

Frank, Joseph. 1991. *The Idea of Spatial Form*. New Bruswick: Rutgers University Press.

Freedgood, Elaine. 2006. *The Ideas in Things: Fugitive Meaning in Victorian Literature*. Chicago: University of Chicago Press. DOI: 10.7208/chicago/9780226261546.001.0001.

Froese, Tom, and Ezequiel A. Di Paolo. 2011. "The Enactive Approach: Theoretical Sketches from Cell to Society." *Pragmatics & Cognition* 19 (1): 1–36. DOI: 10.1075/pc.19.1.01fro.

Gardiner, Judith Kegan. 1989. *Rhys, Stead, Lessing, and the Politics of Empathy*. Bloomington: Indiana University Press.

Gibson, James J. 1979. "The Theory of Affordances." In *Perceiving, Acting, and Knowing: Toward an Ecological Psychology*, edited by Robert Shaw and John Bransdord, 127–43. Hillsdale, NJ: Lawrence Erlbaum Associates.

Van Gunsteren, Julia. 1990. *Katherine Mansfield and Literary Impressionism*. Amsterdam: Rodopi.

Harrington, Ellen Burton. 2007. "Introduction." In *Scribbling Women and the Short Story Form: Approaches by American and British Women Writers*, edited by Ellen Burton Harrington, 1–14. New York: Peter Lang Publishing.

Herbrechter, Stefan. 2013. *Posthumanism. A Critical Analysis*. London: Bloomsbury.

Hutcheon, Linda. 1985. *A Theory of Parody: The Teachings of Twentieth-century Art Forms*. Urbana & Chicago: University of Illinois Press.

Johnson, Erica L., and Patricia Moran. 2015. "Introduction: The Haunting of Jean Rhys." In *Jean Rhys: Twenty-First-Century Approaches*, edited by Erica L. Johnson and Patricia Moran, 1–17. Edinburgh: Edinburgh University Press.

Johnson, Mark. 1987. *The Body in the Mind: The Bodily Basis of Meaning, Imagination, and Reason*. Chicago: University of Chicago Press.

Johnson, Mark. 2008. *The Meaning of the Body: Aesthetics of Human Understanding*. Chicago: University of Chicago Press. DOI: 10.7208/chicago/ 9780226026992.001.0001.

Joyce, James. 1914/1994. "The Dead." In *James Joyce: The Dead. Case Studies in Contemporary Criticism*, edited by Daniel R. Schwartz, 21–59. Boston: Bedfort/St. Martin's.

Kimber, Gerri. 2015. *Katherine Mansfield and the Art of the Short Story*. Basingstoke: Palgrave Macmillan. DOI: 10.1057/9781137483881.

Kracauer, Siegfried. 1963/1995. *The Mass Ornament: Weimar Essays*. Translated by Thomas Y. Levin. Cambridge, MA: Harvard University Press.

Kristeva, Julia. 1987/1989. *The Black Sun: Depression and Melancholia*. Translated by Leon S. Roudiez. New York: Columbia University Press.

Lakoff, George, and Mark Johnson. 1980/2003. *Metaphors We Live By*. Chicago: University of Chicago Press. DOI: 10.7208/chicago/9780226470993.001.0001.

Lakoff, George, and Mark Turner. 1989. *More than Cool Reason: A Field Guide to Poetic Metaphor*. Chicago: University of Chicago Press. DOI: 10.7208/ chicago/9780226470986.001.0001.

Le Gallez, Paula. 1990. *The Rhys Woman*. London: Palgrave Macmillan. DOI: 10.1007/978-1-349-10677-6.

Levinas, Emmanuel. 1969. *Totality and Infinity*. Translated by Alphonso Lingis. Pittsburgh: Duquesne University Press.

Lukács, Georg. 1936/1971. "Narrate or Describe?" In *Writer and Critic and Other Essays*, edited and translated by Arthur D. Kahn, 110–148. New York: Grosset and Dunlap.

Lummaa, Karoliina. 2019. "Posthumanist Reading: Witnessing Ghosts, Summoning Nonhuman Powers." In *Reconfiguring Human, Nonhuman and Posthuman in Literature and Culture*, edited by Sanna Karkulehto et al, 41–56. London: Routledge. DOI: 10.4324/9780429243042-3.

Määttänen, Pentti. 2015. "Emotionally Charged Aesthetic Experience." In *Aesthetics and the Embodied Mind: Beyond Art Theory and the Cartesian Mind-Body Dichotomy*, edited by Alfonsina Scarinzi, 85–99 Dordrecht: Springer. DOI: 10.1007/978-94-017-9379-7_6.

Malcolm, David. 2012. "Katherine Mansfield: 'The Stranger.'" In *The British and Irish Short Story Handbook*, edited by David Malcolm, 224–227. Chichester: Wiley-Blackwell. DOI: 10.1002/9781444355239.

Mansfield, Katherine. 1973. *Collected Stories*. London: Book Club Associates.

Mitchell, Lee Clark. 2017. *Mere Reading: The Poetics of Wonder in Modern American Novels*. New York: Bloomsbury.

Moretti, Franco. 2013. *Distant Reading*. London: Verso.

New, William. 1999. *Reading Mansfield and Metaphors of Form*. Montreal: McGill–Queen's University Press.

O'Sullivan, Vincent, ed. 1982. *The Aloe: With Prelude*. Wellington: Port Nicolson.

Oulanne, Laura. 2017. "Writing Wounded: Reading Djuna Barnes's Writership as Affective Agency." In *Writing Emotions: Theoretical Concepts and Selected Case Studies in Literature*, edited by Ingeborg Jandl et al., 331–46. Bielefeld: Transcript. DOI: 10.2307/j.ctv1wxt3t.21.

Parsons, Deborah. 2003. *Djuna Barnes*. Tavistock: Northcote House.

Polvinen, Merja. 2017. "Cognitive Science and the Double Vision of Fiction." In *Cognitive Literary Science: Dialogues Between Literature and Cognition*, edited by Michael Burke and Emily T. Troscianko, 136–50. Oxford: Oxford University Press. DOI: 10.1093/acprof:oso/9780190496869.003.0008.

Rhys, Jean. 1927/1984. *The Left Bank & Other Stories*. Salem, NH: Ayer Company.

Rhys, Jean. 1979. *Smile Please: An Unfinished Autobiography*. London: André Deutsch.

Rhys, Jean. 1968/1972. *Tigers are Better-Looking*. London: Penguin Books.

Robinson, Roger. 1994. "Introduction." In *Katherine Mansfield: In from the Margin*, edited by Roger Robinson, 1–8. Baton Rouge: Louisiana State University Press.

Rodriguez, David. 2019. "Spaces of Indeterminacy: Aerial Description and Environmental Imagination in 20th Century American Fiction." Dissertation, Stony Brook University.

Rosenblatt, Louise. 1938/1995. *Literature as Exploration*. New York: MLA.

Sandley, Sarah. 1994. "The Middle of the Note: Katherine Mansfield's 'Glimpses'." *Katherine Mansfield: In from the Margin*, edited by Roger Robinson, 70–89. Baton Rouge: Louisiana State University Press.

Schor, Naomi. 1987. *Reading in Detail: Aesthetics and the Feminine*. London: Routledge. DOI: 10.4324/9780203944219.

Sedgwick, Eve Kosofsky. 1997. "Paranoid Reading and Reparative Reading: Or, You're So Paranoid, You Probably Think This Introduction is About You." In *Novel Gazing: Queer Readings in Fiction*, 1–37. Durham: Duke University Press. DOI: 10.1215/9780822382478.

Sherry, Vincent. 2014. *Modernism and the Reinvention of Decadence*. Cambridge: Cambridge University Press. DOI: 10.1017/CBO9781139941570.

Smith, Angela. 1999. *Katherine Mansfield and Virginia Woolf: A Public of Two*. Oxford: Clarendon Press. DOI: 10.1093/acprof:oso/9780198183983.001.0001.

Taylor, Julie. 2014. "'Grimly Sentimental': Pleasure, Trauma and Djuna Barnes's Ryder." In *The Sentimental Mode: Essays in Literature, Film and Television*, edited by Jennifer A. Williamson, Jennifer Larson, and Ashley Reed, 56–69. Jefferson, NC: McFarland & co.

Taylor, Julie. 2012. *Djuna Barnes and Affective Modernism*. Edinburgh: Edinburgh University Press.

Varela, Francisco J., Evan Thompson, and Eleanor Rosch. 1991. *The Embodied Mind: Cognitive Science and Human Experience*. Cambridge, MA: MIT Press. DOI: 10.7551/mitpress/6730.001.0001.

Wilson, Mary. 2011. "No Place Like Home: Nightwood's Unhoused Fictions." *Studies in the Novel* 43 (4): 428–48.

6 Conclusion: Reading Affective Materiality

The previous chapters have explored the world of nonhuman things and materiality in the short fiction of Djuna Barnes, Katherine Mansfield, and Jean Rhys. Things have been looked at as narrative devices that contribute to the experiential and affective structures and responses of stories, as fictional agents with a presence comparable to human characters, and players in various processes of interpretation and sensemaking from basic experiences of materiality to more complex forms of critical thinking and cultural contextualization. The "livedness" of the things has defined all these discussions. The fictional things in modernist stories are lively and agential in themselves, and indifferent to human norms and hierarchies, but instead of receding into their objecthood completely beyond the human, they are also intermingled with human experience of being—an experience is always lived with and through things.

In Chapter 2, which housed the first analyses, I showed how Jean Rhys's and Djuna Barnes's critical commentaries and feminist rewritings of gendered, social norms and hierarchies draw on experiences of material things, and drafted a way of reading that would be capable of bringing forth this connection. In relation to modernist topoi of animism, magic, and fetishism, this means complementing the attention to contemporary phenomena and their cultural meanings with a close, yet also surface-oriented reading of the lived materiality and power of things, realized through descriptive and focal strategies. Thereby, some new and affirmative tones emerged, as we noted how Rhys rewrites gothic motifs, contemporary attitudes to magic, and the surrealist obsession with the objectified female body, and how Barnes complicates the notion of fetishism as a male phenomenon based on female lack, and instead offers descriptions of abundance and power housed completely in the feminine.

In the third chapter, which experimented with more explicitly anti-anthropocentric conceptions of agency, we saw how Barnes overrides character psychology in abundant descriptions of material things, and thereby distributes agency among people and things and exposes the entangled qualities of bodies that we habitually perceive as separate things or objects. We also noted how the material things in Mansfield's stories form a chorus of alternative counter-narratives that complicate the rigid, gendered conceptualizations of what human life is supposed to look like, and that this presence seems to open up for a reading that takes seriously the nontotalizing and contingent perceptual experience rendered in the stories, especially in such sites of modernist enchantment as the party, and from the point of view of children. This extends into the equally enchanted realm of fiction, which read this way emerges as a potential space for the play of opposing meanings and ultimately for the reimagining of rigid norms and categories with which we may tend to view life.

These forms of agency are crucially of an affective kind, which the fourth chapter explored in detail. In it, I read Rhys's and Mansfield's moments of belonging, happiness, and empathy, which are at the same time ironical and touching, as built around material things. Thereby I showed how both in fact write against and recontextualize, with the help of the material world, the modern topoi of victimization and alienation that are often seen to color their work. This discussion also complicated the notions of empathy and sympathy, as we noted how nonhuman, material things in fact participate in the sharing of emotion. Looking at the form of Barnes's and Mansfield's short stories, I discussed how they are constructed around affective patterns of touching things and things that are incorporated into emotional experience. These things are what enables the experiential understanding of what something is like, the unique kind of knowledge afforded by literary fiction. All in all, like my interpretation of agency, the reading of affective materialities in the stories of Barnes, Mansfield, and Rhys brought to the fore the ways the texts invite the imaginative reconsideration of deeply rooted ontological categories of human and nonhuman, mind and matter.

Finally, I examined how material things contribute to the production of meanings in the stories from the appeal to basic embodied schemas to culturally informed, symbolic, and aesthetic interpretation and reflective, critical considerations of the ethical and political implications of the stories. I looked at the aesthetic whole formed by a collection of stories by Rhys, the relationship between the beginning, the middle, and the ending of two stories by Mansfield, and the way a single story by Barnes creates a private signifying system that relies on materiality. These readings led to a conviction that fictional things are never beyond meaning, even though they resist the imposition of human categories of significance. Rather, we cannot help but make sense of the world with the help of material things, which are unavoidably involved in our senses as well as our linguistic and schematic understanding.

What these experiments in reading have in common, methodologically, is that when encountering a material thing in the fictional world, they encourage taking a breathing pause before jumping to an interpretation—though this pause does not perhaps constitute a step back so much as a reaching toward. Instead of asking, what this particular thing signifies in the story, or alternatively passing by a descriptive passage dedicated to it, or even a simple mention of a thing in the middle of some active sequence of character action, it sometimes pays to take the time to ask different questions. What kind of sensory experience does the thing evoke—how does it feel? How does it invite me to engage with it, imaginatively, based on my lifelong experience of living with things? How are these effects accomplished with the means that a fictional narrative has available, such as varieties of description, narration, and focalization? And how do they relate to what is happening around the thing, and what the story seems to be inviting in terms of more critical interpretation and understanding: what new is built with the help of the thing, and in what way has something familiar shifted?

This is an approach to reading that draws from many existing sources, including phenomenological, anti-anthropocentric, and feminist thinking. Threrefore, I do not wish to parade it as an entirely new invention. Rather, my reading of modernist short fiction introduces a shift of focus arising from the combination of different forms of critical and embodied awareness. Barnes's, Mansfield's, and Rhys's texts have already been read carefully by many researchers, and the analyses in this book have built on this work. I hope that they have also contributed to the understanding of the writers' stories from a different, two-fold perspective, namely that of material things as affective agents and that of the specific narrative means of producing experientiality, on which the meanings teased out by various researchers often depend. Studying singular phenomena can create understanding of broader ones, be they related to fictional devices, cultural contexts, or real-world relations with things. The analysis of how an interaction between a dress and a character in Rhys's "Let Them Call It Jazz" can be conductive of kinesthetic and affective communication and empathy suggests a broadening of the scope of narrative empathy; the study of the abundance of things surrounding the child on the bed in Barnes's "Cassation" sheds light on the mutual constitution of the embodied, symbolic, aesthetic and cultural levels of sense-making involved in reading.

From the point of view of modernism studies, the readings suggest that such embodied, material thematics and means of presentation are quite central in the work of three writers stylistically and spatiotemporally quite near the heart of Anglophone modernism, even though too often marginalized. As regards specifically short fiction, my readings show short stories, sketches, and vignettes as forms of writing in which the lived materiality of the world is brought to the fore, while features such as plot, psychological character study and even symbolism appear as secondary. They display a phenomenological interest in the way they tap into human experience of being-in-the-world and making sense of it with and through material things, even in the absence of characters with a "readable" mind. Barnes's, Mansfield's, and Rhys's texts form a fruitful platform for experimentation with means of conveying and evoking glimpses of lived experience, a central concern in modernist fiction of the beginning of the 20th century, while also voicing critical concerns of the gendered order of things in the socio-cultural context as well as in theoretical frameworks such as psychoanalysis. Most importantly, the stories constitute potential spaces for reconfiguring and recontextualizing norms and categories, which is where anti-anthropocentric and feminist interests meet.

Specifically, I hope to have contributed to the study of Barnes's, Mansfield's, and Rhys's fiction by pointing out how affirmative and re-parative interpretations, which have more broadly arisen only recently in relation to their work, rely on basic embodied modes of sense-making, but are compatible with critical and ironic modes of reading. The stories of all three writers use fictional things to create literary affordances for slight shifts in the readers' understanding based on habitual, tacit meanings: possibilities to broaden their conceptions of subjectivity, empathy, gendered identity, and the family, for instance. Experientially, readers may undergo affective experiences of happiness induced by wearing nice clothes, moments of belonging built around a specific table setting, an inkling of the talismanic power evoked by the right kind of boots and a cape, or the pleasure involved in a collection of intricate things and their cataloguing, while appreciating the gendered problems of objectification related to fashion, the precarity of happiness as a so-ciocultural phenomenon, the multiple troubling implications of modern fetishism, and the individual symbolic potential of each item in a list.

Djuna Barnes, Katherine Mansfield, and Jean Rhys invite the readers of their short fiction to live through intense experiences and a variety of fic-tional settings with touching, inviting, repellent, oppressive, intriguing, rea-listic, and fantastic furnishings. Readers are dressed in flapper dresses and out-of-place hats, veiled and corseted, taken to lonely coffee tables, abundant salons, and swimming trips in the Crescent Bay. Simultaneously, they are provided with skillful organizations of words on a page, the experience of holding a book in their hands, materially rooted in their own bodies and life-worlds, and capable of reflecting on what they read. The fictional world, the real world being of the reader, and even the reading consciousness have something in common: the way the material and the cultural, the human and the nonhuman, the symbolic and the embodied are mutually constituted and permeated by one another.

Index

4E-approaches to cognition 7, 85, 115, 122–3, 134
Abbott, H. P. 104
affect: definitions of 85; as potential 53, 57, 153; as narrative dynamic 63, 90, 100–16, 140–2; as social orientation 87, 94; negative 75, 86; positive 86–94
affirmative reading 30, 64, 75, 127, 168
affordances 2, 8, 9, 130, 138, 141, 160
Agamben, G. 65
agency: of nonhuman things 49–80, 99; new materialist definitions of 52–4, 134; in assemblages 53, 57, 59
Ahmed, S. 87, 91, 129
Alaimo, S. 56–7
alienation 86–7, 89, 91–4
allegory 150–8 see also symbolism
animals 43, 58–9, 128–9, 139, 144, 157
animation 71, 75, 77–9, 138 see also anthropomorphism, personification
animism 23, 66; and technology 26 see also magic, spiritualism, supernatural
anthropocentrism 32, 66, 97, 115, 134
anthropomorphism 31–2, 61, 71, 96–7, 139–40 see also animation, personification
Apter, E. 38
Aragon, L.: Le Paysan de Paris 11
archaeology: as method of reading 150–5
Atget, E. 33, 35, 125
assemblages 53–5, 57, 59, 67, 84, 97, 99, 110, 113–15, 147, 152–3 see also affect; agency

Bachelard, G. 141
Barad, K. 5, 52, 134–5
Barnes, D.: "Aller et Retour" 44–5, 101, 105–8, 152–3, 157, 159; "A Boy Asks a Question" 58–60; "Cassation" 148–60, 167; "Dusie" 39–40, 44, 51–5; "Finale" 55–7, 64; "The Grande Malade" 40–1; "The Hatmaker," 44; "A Night Among the Horses" 41–3; Nightwood 38–9, 57–8, 104n10; "Spillway" 101–8, 153
Benjamin, W. 10, 147–8
Bennett, J. 5, 24, 52–4, 65, 97
Boscagli, M. 38, 93
Braidotti, R. 6, 65, 75
Breton, A.: Nadja 11
Brown, B. 4, 89, 158 see also thing theory

Caracciolo, M. 57, 94, 96
Cather, W.: "The Novel Démeublé" 147
Cave, T. 108, 122
children: as focalizers 61, 66–70, 75–6
cognitive literary studies 7–9, 85, 91
cognitivism 103
Colombetti, G. 113
commodification see objectification
commodities 10–11
consumerism 10

decadence 152–4
dehumanization see objectification
Deleuze, G. 56, 65, 122
description 38–9, 51–2, 56, 109–11, 115, 124, 137–40, 142, 144, 158
detail 51, 71, 147–61
Di Paolo, E. 122–3

embodiment: and critical reading 25, 29, 63, 87, 92–4, 108, 135; in phenomenology 94, 99; in reading 8–9, 36, 38, 43, 35, 85, 98, 100–1, 121–3, 155 *see also* experientiality
empathy 31, 94, 97–9, 133–4; definitions of 94–5, 97; for nonhuman things 95–100, 134, 167; in aesthetic experience 95, 155; modernist critiques of 95, 98–9
empty deictic center 55
environment: descriptions of 43, 109–10, 129, 137–8; natural and artificial 73–4, 77, 92, 106–7
epiphany: in short fiction 14, 62, 78, 96, 143; and anti-epiphany 62–3, 70, 73, 80, 98–9
epistemology 115–16
ethics 32, 37, 66, 75, 128, 133, 146
experientiality 28, 43, 56–7, 80, 94, 105, 113, 139, 167; definitions of 8–9; and knowledge 30, 65, 80, 100–1, 108, 135

Felski, R. 121, 123, 135
feminism 3, 6, 25, 32, 45, 77, 159, 167–8 *see also* gender
fetish *See* fetishism
fetishism: as dismemberment 39–40; feminist rewritings of 31, 36, 38, 40, 44–5; definitions of 23, 38, 41; of the female body 31, 33, 38–9; of the male body 42; talismanic 38 *see also* Freud, S.; Marx, K., psychoanalysis
Fludernik, M. 7
Ford, F. M. 124, 136
Freedgood, E. 150, 155
Freud, S. 11, 24, 32, 37, 147, 154 *see also* fetishism; psychoanalysis

gender 29–30, 33, 37–9, 43–4, 64, 66, 70, 73–5, 77, 79, 87–8, 92–3, 134, 143, 145, 168 *see also* feminism
Gardiner, J. K. 127
Gibbs, A. 97
Gibson, J. 7, 127
Gilman, G.P.: "The Yellow Wallpaper" 76
gothic 28, 78

haunting 25, 27, 36, 139

Heidegger, M. 4, 89
Herbrechter, S. 25, 139
Herman, D. 11, 85, 110, 111, 115
Hoffmann, E.T.A.: "Der Sandmann" 32
Hutto, D. 100–1
Huysmans, J. K.: *À rebours* 152

image schema 127–8, 149
impersonality 66, 70–1, 74–5, 80, 136
impressionism 133, 136, 142–3, 161
incorporation: of things in affective experience 113–14, 132
intra-action 52, 114
irony 28–30, 36, 61, 62, 70–1, 79, 87, 99
Iser, W. 30, 89

Johnson, M. 121–2, 155
Joyce, J. 11, 26, 93, 145; "The Dead" 145; *Ulysses* 11, 93

Keen, S. 94
Kimber, G. 143
kitsch 151–2
Kukkonen, K. 9, 85

Lakoff, G. 121–2, 155
Latour, B. 4
Lee, V. 95, 156
Levinas, E. 134
life: philosophical definitions of 65–6, 70, 74; as narrative form 79
lists 44, 51, 73, 152, 168
Lucáks, G. 147
Lummaa, K. 25, 37, 139

masses: aesthetics of 124–36; in modernity 124, 134
McHale, B. 115–16
magic: as modernist topos 23–45, 61; occult practices of 23
Mansfield, K.: "All Serene" 88–90; *The Aloe* 142; "At the Bay" 87–8, 137–43, 146; "The Doll's House" 69–70, 79; "The Garden Party" 61–6, 98, 146; "Her First Ball" 70–5; "Miss Brill" 98; "Prelude" 75–9, 137; "The Stranger" 143–6; "Sun and Moon" 66–8, 79; "Taking the Veil" 108–10; "The Voyage" 111–15

Marx, K. 5, 10, 23, 76
Masson, A. 33–4
Merleau-Ponty, M. 7, 84, 94
metaphor: and materiality 29, 157–8;
  conceptual 29, 103, 121–2, 132
  see also symbolism
Mossé, S. 33n6
music 140

new materialisms: 38, 65, 85, 137;
  definition of 5

objectification 25, 33, 42, 61, 64, 68,
  71–4, 79, 92–4, 125, 134–5, 168
ontology 29–30, 37–8, 45, 64–9,
  71–3, 114–16
O'Sullivan, V. 142

Palmer, A. 103
Parsons, D. 104
parties: as a modernist topos 61–2, 68
perception 67–8, 71, 73–7, 115,
  137–8, 144
personification 31, 71, 133 *see also*
  animation, anthropomorphism
phenomenology 2, 7, 52, 66, 94, 96,
  113–15, 141, 167
Poe, E. A. 14
Polvinen, M. 9, 29
posthumanism 6, 30, 65, 139
psychoanalysis 11, 23–4, 37, 147–8,
  154, 168

Rhys, J.: "At the Villa d'Or" 26–7, 91,
  94, 131–2; "From a French Prison"
  128–9; *Good Morning, Midnight*
  33, 36, 93n4; "The Grey Day" 129;
  "La Grosse Fifi" 92–3; "Illusion"
  30–1, 96–7, 132; "In a Café"
  130–1; interviews 86; "In the
  Luxemburg Gardens" 133; *The Left
  Bank* 124–36; "Let Them Call It
  Jazz" 95–7, 167; "The Mannequin"
  32–7, 124–6; "Mixing Cocktails"
  131–2; "A Night" 90–1, 94; "On
  Not Shooting Sitting Birds" 31;
  Smile Please 132; "A Spiritualist"
  27–30; "Tea with an Artist" 90, 94;
  "Till September Petronella" 132;
  Vienne 126–8
Rochat, P. 94
Rodriguez, D. 115, 137–8, 140

Roman Catholicism 151–2
Rosenblatt, L. 9, 122

Sand, G. 40
scale 115–16
Schor, N. 40, 147
Sedgwick, E.K. 84–5, 121n2
sense-making: and materiality 121–61,
  167; definitions of 122–3
sensory experience 43, 58–9, 99, 102,
  108, 111, 138–9, 153, 167 *see also*
  touch
short fiction: definitions of 14;
  aesthetics of 14, 62, 66, 100, 111,
  146; detail in 150; spatial form of
  14, 126, 143
spiritualism 23, 26
Stevens, W. 11
supernatural 27–8
surrealism 11; exhibition of 1938
  33–6: magical thinking in 23;
  mannequin motif in 32–3
symbolism: modernist movement 6,
  11; material basis of 29, 45, 88,
  113, 141, 155–161; alternative
  readings of 70, 72–3, 147–61
  see also metaphor, allegory
sympathy *see* empathy

tableaux 100, 108, 151
Taylor, J. 51, 100, 103
thing-power 24–5, 29, 38, 45, 67
thing theory 4, 158
things: boats 111, 144; books 90, 109,
  149, 151, 155; boots 40–2, 44;
  bottles 131–2; cane 43; clothes 1, 8,
  30–1, 63, 67–8, 71–2, 93–6, 98,
  101, 105–7, 112, 125, 133; cabs 71;
  corsets 44; decorative objects 52–3,
  67, 72, 76, 149; dolls 38–39, 42,
  69–70; food 58–59, 62–63, 67;
  furniture 52–4, 58, 66, 69, 75, 149,
  151, 155–6; hats 43, 62–4, 66–7,
  76, 111; jewelry 105; key 106;
  mannequin dolls 32–7; paintings
  52–3, 58–9, 156; plants 58–9, 62–3,
  66–7, 76, 129; record player 27;
  scarf 55; tableware 88–90, 145;
  teapots 88–90; toiletries 91–2;
  tombstone 27–30; toys 69–70;
  umbrella 111–14; whip 42
touch 6, 84–5, 101–3, 105–7, 111–12

trans-corporeality 56–7, 114
transitional object 112
typification 36, 104, 124–7, 135

unreadability 104

Van Gunsteren, J. 136–7, 140

Walpole, H.: *The Castle of Otranto* 28
Wilde, O.: *The Picture of Dorian Gray* 152
Winnicott, D. W. 112
Woolf, V. 26; *To the Lighthouse* 11

Zahavi, D. 94

For Product Safety Concerns and Information please contact our EU
representative GPSR@taylorandfrancis.com
Taylor & Francis Verlag GmbH, Kaufingerstraße 24, 80331 München, Germany